BARNETT'S MANUAL VOLUME 3: HANDLEBARS, SEATS, SHIFT SYSTEMS, BRAKES, and SUSPENSIONS

ANALYSIS AND PROCEDURES FOR BICYCLE MECHANICS

FOURTH EDITION

by John Barnett,
founder of Barnett Bicycle Institute

Illustration, Design, Layout, and Typesetting
by John Barnett

VELOPRESS • BOULDER, COLORADO

Barnett's Manual Volume 3: Handlebars, Seats, Shift Systems, Brakes, and Suspension
  Analysis and Procedures for Bicycle Mechanics
Copyright © 2000 by John Barnett

Volume 3
International Standard Book Number: 1-884737-88-9

Volumes 1 – 4 (set)
International Standard Book Number: 1-884737-85-4

Library of Congress Cataloging in Publication Data applied for.

Printed in the USA

Distributed in the Unites States and Canada by Publishers Group West.

VeloPress
1830 N. 55th Street
Boulder, Colorado 80301-2700 USA
303/440-0601; fax 303/444-6788; e-mail velopress@7dogs.com

To purchase additional copies of this book or other VeloPress books, call
800/234-8356 or visit us on the Web at www.velogear.com.

Cover design by Rebecca Finkel, F+P Graphics
Designed by John Barnett

GUIDE TO VOLUMES

Volume 3 of Barnett's Manual covers a variety of topics, including handlebars, seats, shift systems, brake systems, and suspension systems. The seats and handlebar chapters cover installation of seats, seat posts, stems, and handlebars. The shifting-systems chapters cover installation and service of shift-control mechanisms, cable systems, rear derailleurs and front derailleurs. The chapters on brakes cover installation and service of brake levers for all styles of bikes, installation and service of brake cable systems, installation and service of sidepull, dual-pivot, cantilever and transverse-wire brakes (V-brakes). In addition, the brake chapters cover installation and service of hydraulic rim brakes and disc brakes. The suspension chapter covers service of a wide variety of recent and current suspension forks and rear shocks.

In most cases, when performing a procedure covered in this volume, there is no need to reach for the other volumes. There, of course, are a few unavoidable exceptions. For example, in this volume in the directions for adjusting a brake, a reference is made to use a procedure in chapter 12 (Volume 1) for adjusting the hub bearing (to prepare for brake adjustment).

The contents below provides an exact list of what is covered in this volume, chapter-by-chapter, and a general idea of what is covered in each of the other volumes.

REGISTER NOW! •

To register your ownership of this edition of Barnett's Manual, simply fill in your address in the place provided on a copy of this page, then mail to: BBI, 2755 Ore Mill Dr. #14, Colorado Springs, CO, 80904

BUT WHY REGISTER?

To receive complimentary samples of a useful BBI product*
To receive notices of updates and corrections to this edition
To be eligible to purchase replacements for damaged or lost pages
(at a nominal cost)

Your name:_____

Shop name (if any): _____

Address:_____
City:_____ State:_____
Zip:_____

REGISTER NOW (or you'll probably forget)!

* **Useful BBI product:** Several sheets of the bearing calibration stickers that are recommended in this book for quick and precise adjustment of bottom brackets, headsets, and hubs.

28 – HANDLEBARS, STEMS, AND HANDLEBAR EXTENSIONS

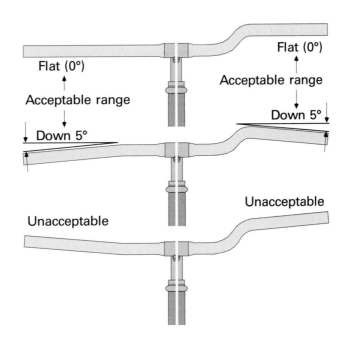

Flat (0°)

Acceptable range

↓ Down 5°

Flat (0°)

Acceptable range

Down 5° ↓

Unacceptable

Unacceptable

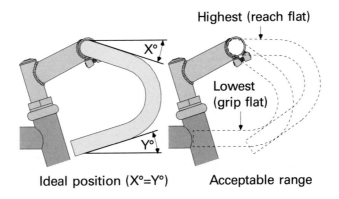

Highest (reach flat)

X°

Lowest (grip flat)

Y°

Ideal position (X°=Y°)   Acceptable range

28 – HANDLEBARS, STEMS, AND HANDLEBAR EXTENSIONS

28 – HANDLEBARS, STEMS, AND HANDLEBAR EXTENSIONS

ABOUT THIS CHAPTER

This chapter is about stems, handlebars, handlebar extensions and clip-ons, and handlebar coverings. With regard to stems, it covers removing stems from the bike, fitting stems to the bike, installing and aligning the stem, and problems with stems. With regard to handlebars, it covers removing handlebars from the stem, fitting handlebars to the stem, installing and aligning the handlebars, and problems with handlebars. With regard to handlebar extensions and clip-ons installation, alignment and security are covered. Each of these subjects simultaneously addresses road and off-road varieties. With regard to handlebar coverings, there are instructions for installing and removing off-road handlebar grips and road-bike handlebar tape.

Supplemental information about BMX/Freestyle bars and stems and upright (touring and cruiser) styles is also included. There are no specific procedures included for these types.

One type of stem is not covered in this chapter. Bikes with a threaded fork column have a headset that threads onto the fork column and a stem inserts inside the fork column. Bikes with a threadless fork column have a headset that slides onto the fork column, and a stem that clamps onto the fork column where it extends above the headset. Because the stem in this system functions as a lock for the headset adjustment, it is covered in the **HEADSET** chapter in the section on threadless headsets (page 11-21).

GENERAL INFORMATION

TERMINOLOGY

Handlebar: The tube that is gripped in the hands, and to which the brake levers and shift levers are usually mounted.

Bar: Short for *handlebar*.

Drop bar: The traditional road-bike handlebar that goes out from the stem, hooks forward, than curves down and back (the drop).

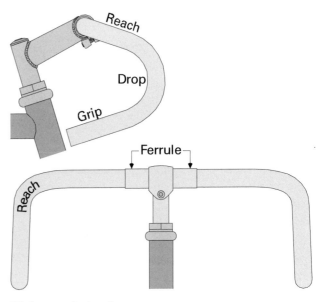

28.1 *Parts of a drop bar.*

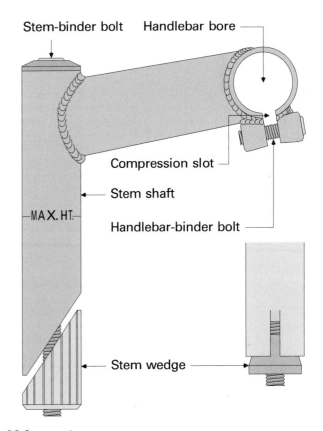

28.2 *Parts of a stem*

Bar center: The usually bulged or sleeve-reinforced center of the handlebar.

Handlebar ferrule: A reinforcing sleeve on a handlebar where the bar goes through the stem.

Stem: The component that connects the handlebar to the fork. It has also been called a "gooseneck," or "neck."

Stem shaft: The vertical shaft of the stem that inserts in the fork.

Stem rise: The vertical height of the stem.

Stem extension: The horizontal length of the stem.

Handlebar bore: The hole through the stem that the handlebar goes into.

Handlebar-binder bolt: The bolt that compresses the handlebar bore to secure the handlebar in the stem.

Compression slot: The slot in the handlebar bore that is compressed when the handlebar-binder bolt is tightened, causing the inside of the handlebar bore to compress on the handlebar. There is also a compression slot in the fork column bore of some stems that are used in threadless headsets (see page 11-21).

Stem-binder bolt: The vertical bolt that goes through the stem shaft that is used to secure the stem in the fork.

Stem wedge: The wedge piece below the stem shaft that secures the stem in the fork column when the stem bolt draws the wedge up. The wedge is usually a cylinder with a sloped end that slides across a corresponding slope on the bottom of the stem shaft. As the sloped wedge is drawn up, it displaces the bottom of the stem shaft laterally, causing it to bind against the inside of the fork column. Occasionally the wedge is a conical shape that slides up into a conical hole in the bottom of the stem, causing the split stem shaft to expand. (See figure 28.2, page 28-1.)

Handlebar extension: The forward extension that can be mounted on the outward end of an off-road handlebar.

Handlebar clip-on: A forward extension of the handlebar that can be mounted to a drop bar to enable the rider to ride in a more aerodynamic position.

Handlebar grips: The rubber or plastic sheaths that cover the end of an off-road bar where the bar is grasped. Also called "grips."

PREREQUISITES

In certain instances, it is necessary to disconnect the brake-control wires and/or the shift-control wires in order to remove and replace a handlebar or stem. If this is the case, it will be necessary to adjust the derailleurs and/or brakes.

If changing stem length or bar size, it is possible that all the control cables will need to be re-sized. Once again, it will be necessary to adjust derailleurs and/or brakes.

INDICATIONS

The primary reasons to change the bar or stem is to upgrade quality or change the way the customer fits the bike. Bent MTB bars are somewhat common, as well. A stem would be also taken out to service the headset or replace a fork.

Maintenance cycles

Although stems and bars do not have moving parts, maintenance is very important. The stem runs the risk of becoming a permanent installation if the bike is exposed to a wet or humid environment, or if the customer rides a lot indoors and sweats on the stem. At least once every six months (and as often as monthly if conditions dictate it), the stem should be removed from the bike and the stem shaft, head of the stem bolt, stem-bolt threads, and stem wedge should be liberally greased. Bars need monthly inspections for fatigue bends and fatigue cracks. Handlebars should also be closely inspected for bends and cracks after every crash.

Symptoms indicating bars should be replaced

Handlebars need to replaced when they crack. Bent handlebars are bars in the process of cracking, so all bent handlebars should be replaced immediately. Regular inspections of handlebars for cracks is very important. The most likely place for a crack to appear is on top of the bar and just outward of the stem. Other places to check for cracks on off-road bars is on either side of the brake-lever clamp and just inward of any handlebar-extension clamp.

Inspect for bent handlebars after any crash. With someone holding the bike straight up and the front wheel straight, crouch down in front of the bike and look straight at the handlebars. If the two sides are not symmetrical then the bars are bent.

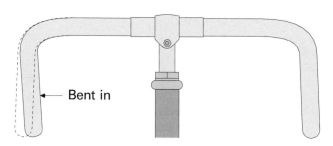

28.3 Crash-bent bars.

Bars bend from fatigue as well as from crashing. This is particularly true of extra-light-weight off-road bars. When bars bend from fatigue, they will appear symmetrical, but when viewed from in front it will be apparent that they begin to drop down immediately from the point that they come out of the stem. When drop bars bend from fatigue, they exhibit this same symptom, and the drops move closer together, as well. For example, a drop bar that originally measured 40cm from center of one bar end to center of the other bar end might measure as little as 36cm.

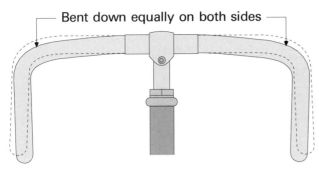

28.4 Fatigue-bent drop bars

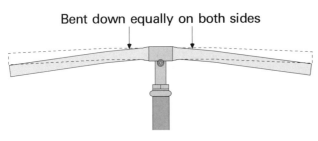

28.5 Fatigue-bent MTB bars.

Symptoms indicating bars should be secured

Handlebars can exhibit two symptoms when they are loose and need to be secured. They may make creaking sounds or they may slip.

Creaking sounds can be caused by other things, but nothing is more important than loose handlebars so always treat this symptom as reason to check the bar security.

Slipping can be sudden and dramatic, in which case there will be no wondering whether the bars need to be secured, or it can be gradual and subtle. On road bikes with drop bars, it might be noticed that the brake levers seem lower, or that when riding on the drops it feels different. When installing bars, it is a good idea to note the angle of the bottom portion of the bar, and inspect after the first few rides to see if it remains the same. It is normal for the bottom of a drop bar to point down to the back or be flat. Anytime the bottom of the drop bar is pointing up to the back, check if the handlebars are loose.

Off-road bars experience less leverage than drop bars, unless they have bar extensions or have a forward bend. Once again, note the angle of any built-in or bolt-on forward extension when the bar or extension is first installed. Check this angle after a few rides to see if it has changed. If both bolt-on extensions change the same amount, then the bar is probably slipping. If one changes more than the other, then either the bar or the extension(s) could be slipping.

Symptoms indicating stem should be replaced

Stems can bend in a crash or may bend or crack from fatigue. If they bend from a crash, the bars may also be bent and the damage to the stem may not become obvious until after replacing the bent bar. If the bars are in good condition but one side is lower than the other, then the stem is bent. Stems that bend from fatigue are rare, but what happens in these cases is that the stem shaft makes a forward bend where it comes out of the headset. Stems that crack from fatigue will have cracks in numerous locations. The cracks may appear around the handlebar-binder bolt, where the extension joins the handlebar clamp, where the stem shaft and forward extension join, or in the stem shaft in the portion below the top of the headset.

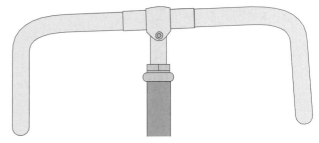

28.6 If these bars are straight, then the stem is bent from a crash.

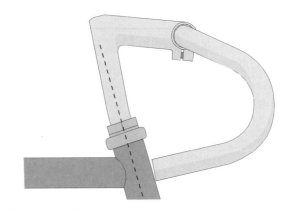

28.7 This stem is bent forward from fatigue.

Symptoms indicating stem should be secured

The symptom indicating that the stem is loose could be creaking or slipping. Creaking is more likely. Creaking can be caused by other things, so if securing the stem does not solve the problem be sure to check handlebar security. Creaking can also be caused by the fit of headset pressed races to the head tube and by a looseness between the bar center ferrule and the bar. A loose stem will slip by rotating, not by sliding down. Rotation that happens when a crash occurs does not indicate that the stem is too loose. In fact, it is desirable that the stem rotate to prevent damage to the bars. A stem that rotates when riding is one that is too loose.

Headset overhaul and replacement

Stem removal is required for headset overhaul or replacement.

Fork replacement

Stem removal is required for fork replacement.

TOOL CHOICES

There are no special tools required for stem and bar service. There is one optional type of tool, used for cleaning out a fork after removing a stuck stem. This is either a Flex-hone BC27 (1" fork columns), BC29 (1–1/8" fork columns), or BC35 (1–1/4" fork columns). These tools are installed on a drill and spin at high speed inside the fork column to clean out rust.

TIME AND DIFFICULTY

Removing and installing a *stem and bar set* is a job of little difficulty that takes 2–4 minutes. If the stem is corroded in place, it can become a job of high difficulty.

Replacing a *stem* is a job of little difficulty in itself, but to the extent that it requires disconnection of brake or derailleur cables, it can become a job of moderate to high difficulty.

Replacing a *handlebar* is a job of little difficulty in itself, taking only 5–10 minutes, but to the extent that it requires disconnection of brake or derailleur cables, it can become a job of moderate to high difficulty. If the stem is corroded in place and must be removed to access the bars, it can become a job of high difficulty.

COMPLICATIONS

Wedge will not go down after loosening stem-binder bolt

It is normal to have to strike the top of the handlebar-binder bolt after loosening, to get the wedge to drop. When this does not work, it means that the wedge is badly corroded in place. See step #6, page 28-6.

Stem will not remove once wedge has dropped

It is natural to assume that this is caused by corrosion, but it could be as simple as binding caused by an off-center hole in a headset locknut. Try loosening the locknut before preparing to work on a corroded stem.

Stem will not install even if it is the correct size

This could be caused by corrosion, in which case the inside of the fork should be honed. It could also be caused by an under-sized or off-center headset-locknut hole. Check the installation with the locknut loosened or removed.

Handlebars slip when properly torqued

This is caused by poor bar-to-stem fit, or contamination on the mating surfaces. The complication comes when it occurs during a assembly of a bicycle that came with a fully assembled and taped bar set, which must be stripped on one half to clean the mating surfaces or measure to check fit.

Extensions slip when properly torqued

Handlebar extensions are prone to slipping due to contamination on the mating surfaces, poor fit, or painted or anodized mating surfaces. Check fit, clean mating surfaces, and sand mating surfaces to expose raw aluminum.

Control cables end up too short after installing wider bars or a longer stem

This one should be caught before the job is ever started. Nothing can be done but install new cables and adjust any brakes or derailleurs affected.

Cables will not allow stem to lift far enough to remove from fork

Sometimes a cable will interfere with removal of a stem. Cables routed under the handlebar tape to a front sidepull brake often cause this problem. It is usually easiest to remove the caliper from the fork. It all other cases, try to operate the mechanism in a way that will cause the inner wire to slacken and then slip a housing end out of any split housing stop.

ABOUT THE REST OF THIS CHAPTER

The rest of this chapter is in six sections. The first is *STEM REMOVAL, REPLACEMENT, AND INSTALLATION*. It is followed by *HANDLEBAR REMOVAL, REPLACEMENT, AND INSTALLATION*. This is followed by *INSTALLING HANDLEBAR CLIP-ONS AND EXTENSIONS* . Next there is a brief section on *HANDLEBAR-COVERING REMOVAL AND INSTALLATION*. Following this is a section, *OTHER BAR SYSTEMS*, regarding BMX and upright (touring and cruiser) systems. The last part is *HANDLEBAR AND STEM TROUBLESHOOTING*. Depending on what operation is being done, use any section by itself, or it may be best to include parts (or all) of various sections to complete the task.

STEM REMOVAL, REPLACEMENT, AND INSTALLATION

STEM REMOVAL

When removing the stem from the fork, any derailleur- and/or brake-control cables can interfere with being able to pull the stem out of the fork column. Furthermore, any of these cables are more prone to damage if left attached to the bar set and they end up supporting the weight of the bar set. How these control cables can be disengaged is highly variable depending on the type of equipment. The following are guidelines that will apply often, but not always.

Mountain-bike brake levers: Usually brake cables can be released from the brake levers and reconnected in a way that will not require any adjustment. Unhook the lead-beaded end of the straddle wire from one of the caliper arms. On the brake lever, line up the slots in the cable adjusting barrel, adjusting barrel locknut, and bottom of the body of the lever. Pull the housing and end cap straight out the end of the adjusting-barrel socket and then swing the inner wire down through all the lined-up slots. If necessary, compress the lever to the grip and then slip the head of the inner wire out the back face (usually) of the lever.

Cables to front cantilever brakes when the cable is routed through the stem: Unhook the lead-beaded end of the straddle wire from one of the caliper arms. The straddle wire may be connected to the primary brake wire by a roughly triangular device called a cable carrier. If this is the case, the straddle wire is usually resting in an open cradle in the back of the cable carrier. By deflecting the loose end of the primary wire, the straddle wire can be lifted out of the cradle. If the cable carrier is a circular disc and there is no open cradle, then unhooking the wire from the cable carrier will require full re-adjustment of the brake. It would be easier to just unmount the caliper arm (that still has the cable attached to it) from the frame by loosening the bolt that goes through the caliper arm and into the fork. Be familiar with mounting cantilever arms before deciding to remove one.

Non-aero' road-bike brake levers: If the brake cables are free loops of housing that come down into the top of the brake levers on drop bars, they can usually be released from the brake levers in a way that re-adjustment will not be required. Release any quick-release mechanisms on both brakes. Remove both wheels from the bike. Using a third-hand tool, squeeze a caliper so that the brake pads meet. Squeeze the brake lever in just enough so that the point that the cable head hooks into the anchor (inside the lever) can seen. If there is a slot in the anchor, then push enough slack cable into the lever so that the cable head drops below the anchor, push the cable out the slot in the anchor, then pull the cable out of the lever and lever body.

Aero' road-bike brake levers: Only the front cable can be freed without requiring re-adjustment of the brake. In many cases, this will be all that is needed to get the stem out of the fork column or to replace the stem. Simply unbolt the brake caliper from the fork. There will be a 10mm hex nut or 5mm Allen nut on the back of the fork crown for this purpose. The only brake adjustment needed will be centering the pad clearance.

Mountain-bike shift levers: All cables are attached to the shift levers in a way that the cable cannot be released from the lever without having to adjust the cable after re-installation. However, it is sometimes possible to release the lever from the handlebar without having to re-adjust the cables/derailleurs. If the shift-control mechanism is a separate unit from the brake lever and has a thin steel strap that wraps around the handlebar, then a binding bolt can be removed and the strap can be spread to allow removal of the entire lever unit from the handlebar. If the lever is a separate unit and has a thick cast aluminum body that wraps around the lever, it may be possible to remove the shifting unit from the mounting body. Look for a 5mm or 6mm Allen bolt on the backside from the lever face.

drops. If the bottom grip of the bar is parallel to the ground, it favors riding primarily in the drops, and handicaps access to the brake levers when riding on the tops of the bars. Usually the best position is a compromise between these extremes, with the top extensions of the bars sloping slightly down toward the brake levers, and the grips sloping slightly down toward the back of the bike. This position is recommended if setting up new bikes, without a customer preference indicated. For the ideal neutral position, the angle of the reach should equal the angle of the grip.

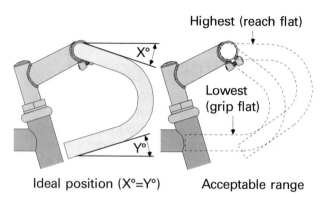

28.14 Acceptable range of drop handlebar rotations.

23. [ ] Rotate bar to desired position.
24. Transfer measurement in step 18 to here (_____mm) and torque handlebar-binder bolts to one of following torque ranges depending on handlebar-binder-bolt-thread diameter:
    [ ] Torque bolts w/ thread diameter ≤6mm to 120–145in-lbs (20–24lbs@6" or 30–36lbs@4").
    [ ] Torque bolts w/ thread diameter >6mm to 205–240in-lbs (34–40lbs@6" or 51–60lbs@4").
25. [ ] Install control levers per **SHIFT-CONTROL MECHANISMS** (page 30-10 or 30-15) and/or **BRAKE LEVERS** (page 34-6) chapter instructions.
26. If *Need to test fit* option is checked in step 16, perform following security test:
    [ ] With bike on floor, stand facing bike and straddle front wheel.
    [ ] Grasp brake-lever bodies in similar fashion to when riding with weight supported at brake levers, and support full weight on brake levers until feet lift off floor.
    [ ] Check if bar position has changed.
    [ ] If bars slip and handlebar-binder bolts are not torqued to maximum recommendation, add torque and test again.
    [ ] If bars slip at maximum torque, fit is bad. Change bar or stem to improve fit.
27. [ ] Attach control cables to derailleur and/or brake levers and adjust derailleurs and/or brakes as per instructions in derailleur and/or brake chapters.

OFF-ROAD-HANDLEBAR INSTALLATION

28. [ ] Remove handlebar-binder bolt(s) from stem.
29. [ ] Use caliper to measure diameter of handlebar-binder-bolt thread and record here: _____ mm.
30. [ ] Grease threads and under head of handlebar-binder bolt(s).

NOTE: If positioning and securing already-installed off-road bars, skip to step 33.

31. [ ] Use alcohol or acetone to clean inside of handlebar bore in stem and center section of handlebar.
32. [ ] Insert handlebar into stem & center bar in stem.
33. [ ] Install and gently snug handlebar-binder bolt(s).

The rotation of the handlebars is strictly a matter of personal preference, but it is likely that the customer has simply been living with whatever position the shop set them up at. If the customer would like to try the bars in a different position, consider these guidelines. If the grips of the bars slope up to the outside, it tends to put the elbows in an inflexible position, which reduces comfort and control. If the grips are flat or slope down to the outside no more than five° (about 3/4" drop over the length of the grip), the elbows are relaxed. If the grips slope down too much, then the hand will tend to slip off the end of the grip. Somewhere between flat and 5° down is recommended if setting up new bikes, without a customer preference indicated.

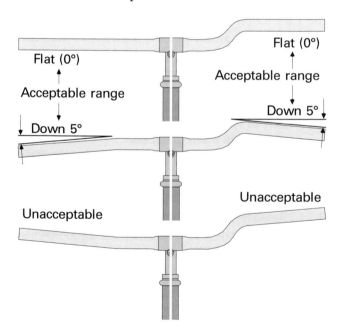

28.15 Acceptable range of MTB-bar rotation.

34. [ ] Rotate bar to desired position.

35. Transfer measurement in step 29 to here
(_____mm) and torque handlebar-binder bolts
to one of following torque ranges depending
on handlebar-binder-bolt thread diameter:
[ ] Torque bolts w/ thread diameter ≤6mm to
120–145in-lbs (20–24lbs@6" or 30–36lbs@4").
[ ] Torque bolts w/ thread diameter >6mm to
205–240in-lbs (34–40lbs@6" or 51–60lbs@4").
36. [ ] Install control levers per **SHIFT-CONTROL
MECHANISMS** (page 30-3 or 30-8) and/or
BRAKE LEVERS (page 34-5) chapter instructions.
37. If *Need to test fit* option is checked in step 16,
perform following security test if handlebar
extensions are being used:
[ ] With bike on floor, stand facing bike and
straddle front wheel.
[ ] Grasp handlebar extensions and support full
weight on extensions until feet lift off floor.
[ ] Check if bar position has changed, or if
handlebar extensions have slipped.
[ ] If bars slip and handlebar-binder bolts are
not torqued to maximum recommendation,
add torque and test again.
[ ] If bars slip at maximum torque, fit is bad.
Change bar or stem.
38. [ ] Attach control cables to derailleur and/or
brake levers and adjust derailleurs and/or
brakes as per instructions in derailleur and/or
brake chapters.

INSTALLING HANDLEBAR CLIP-ONS AND EXTENSIONS

DROP-BAR CLIP-ONS

NOTE: Skip to step 8 if installing extensions on an off-road bike.

Aerodynamic clip-on extensions for drop handlebars may be great for improved perfomance or comfort riding, but mechanically they are a nightmare. Manufacturers make the clamps for clip-on bars in two configurations, V-block and radius clamp. The V-block system has the advantage of fitting any diameter handlebar, but slips easily and damages bars easily if tightened enough to avoid slippage. The radius-clamp type is a more secure grip, but only if it matches the diameter of the bar closely. Either type is adequate to secure if the rider *always* rides in the intended fashion with the bulk of load on the elbow pads. In an emergency, or with poor riding habits, the load may end up at the outer end of the clip-on, which is when the clamps may slip. Even if the clamps do not slip,

the handlebar may be subjected to more rotational load than the stem clamp is designed to withstand, resulting in the bars slipping in the stem.

To reduce problems with clip-ons, follow these several rules: 1) recommend that the customer always use them as they are intended and do not rest weight out at the end of the clip-ons; 2) always clamp them directly to the bar, and not on top on any handlebar covering; 3) always clean the mating surfaces of the clamps and the bar thoroughly, including removing epoxy, paint, or anodized finishes with emery cloth; 4) lubricate bolts properly and follow torque recommendations closely; 5) inspect bars for fatigue cracks regularly where clip-on clamps engage bars.

1. [ ] Remove handlebar tape or handlebar covering
from portion of the bar where clamp secures.
2. [ ] Remove anodization finishes, paints, or epoxy coats from inside of clamp and outside
of bar where clamps engage.
3. [ ] Clean mating surfaces with alcohol/acetone.
4. [ ] Remove clamp bolts, measure thread diameter, and record here: _____mm.
5. [ ] Thoroughly grease bolt threads and under
bolt heads.
6. [ ] Mount clip-ons, install bolts, and gently
secure.
7. [ ] Position clip-ons at desired angle.

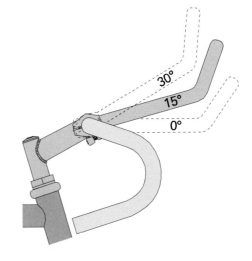

28.16 Normal range of clip-on positions.

8. Torque bolts to following torque ranges depending on thread diameter:
[ ] ≤5mm, torque to 50in-lbs (8lbs@6" or
12.5lbs@4").
[ ] 5.1–6mm, torque to 120–145in-lbs
(20–24lbs@6" or 30–36lbs@4").
[ ] 7–8mm, torque to 155–205in-lbs
(26–34lbs@6" or 39–51lbs@4").

OFF-ROAD-HANDLEBAR EXTENSIONS

Off-road-handlebar extensions may be great for improved perfomance or comfort riding, but mechanically they are a nightmare. Manufacturers make the clamps for clip-on bars in two configurations, external and internal clamping. The external system has the advantage of fitting any handlebar equally well, but the clamp is bulkier and requires that the grips and controls be moved inward. The internal-clamp type doesn't require moving grips and controls, and the clamp is less bulky, but will be secure only if it matches the inside diameter of the bar closely (there are no standards for inside bar-diameter). Provided that an internal-clamp extension is a good fit, either clamp type will adequately secure the extension, if the rider *always* rides in the intended fashion, which is using extensions when climbing or high-speed cruising on smooth terrain. In an emergency, or with poor riding habits, the load may end up on the extensions when the customer hits a bump, which is when the clamps may slip. Even if the clamps do not slip, the handlebar may be subjected to more rotational load than the stem clamp is designed to withstand, resulting in the bars slipping in the stem.

Extra-light-weight bars create another problem. The external extension clamp can crush the bar due to the thin wall. Inserts are made to reinforce the bar. The insert should match the bar I.D. closely and be at least as wide as the extension clamp.

To reduce problems with handlebar extensions, follow these several rules: 1) recommend that the customer always use them as they are intended and do not rest weight on them when traveling on rough terrain; 2) always clean the mating surfaces of the clamps and the bar thoroughly, including removing epoxy, paint, or anodized finishes with emery cloth; 3) lubricate bolts properly and follow torque recommendations closely; 4) inspect bars for fatigue cracks regularly where clamps engage bars.

1. [ ] If installing external-clamp handlebar extension, move controls and grips inward enough to provide room for full engagement of clamp to bar.
2. [ ] Rremove paint, epoxy coats, or anodization finishes from inside of clamps and outside of bar where clamps will engage.
3. [ ] Clean mating surfaces with alcohol/acetone.
4. [ ] Thoroughly grease bolt threads and under bolt heads.

5. [ ] Mount extensions, install bolts, and gently secure.
6. [ ] Position extensions at desired angle.

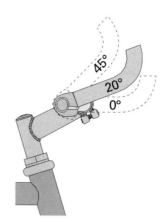

28.17 Normal range of extension positions.

7. [ ] Torque bolts to 120–145in-lbs (20–24lbs@6" or 30–36lbs@4").

HANDLEBAR-COVERING REMOVAL AND INSTALLATION

OFF-ROAD GRIPS

Steps #1–5 are 100% reliable and safe. Filling the bars with compressed air to remove grips works in some cases, but not if grips are torn on the end or made of certain foams. Cutting the grips off with a sharp knife always works if the grips will not be re-used, but the following procedure has no risk of self-injury.

Removal

1. [ ] Insert long skinny screwdriver between grip and bar to create gap between grip and bar.
2. [ ] Spray or drip water between grip and bar then remove screwdriver.
3. [ ] Insert screwdriver between grip and bar at a 180° opposite original insertion.
4. [ ] Spray or drip water between grip and bar then remove screwdriver.
5. [ ] Twist grip back and forth to spread water around, then pull grip off.

Installation

1. [ ] Clean bar of any contamination with alcohol.
2. [ ] Spray inside of grip with hair spray and slip grip onto handlebar quickly.
3. [ ] Allow several hours for hair spray to set before riding, check grip security before riding.

DROP-BAR TAPING

1. [ ] Remove old tape unless fatter bar diameter is preferred.
2. [ ] Roll back rubber cover on brake lever to expose base of brake-lever body.
3. [ ] Unless provided, cut 3" piece from end of tape and cover brake-lever mounting strap, so that both ends of piece will end up under rubber cover when rubber cover is down.

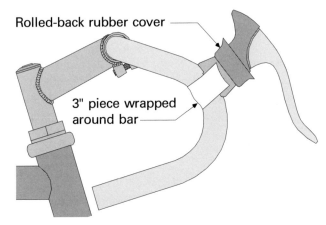

28.18 Put a 3" piece of tape over the brake lever mounting strap.

4. Check fit of handlebar plug or cap to end of bar and check one of following options:
   [ ] No handlebar plug will be used, handlebar-end shifters are mounted in bars, first wrap of tape will start flush with end of bar.
   [ ] Handlebar plug is snug fit to bar, first wrap of tape will start flush with end of bar.
   [ ] Handlebar plug is loose in bar, first wrap of tape needs to overlap end of bar by 10–15mm.
5. [ ] Start tape at bottom of bar, with end of tape on top of bar and pointing in, with edge of tape flush to or overlapping bar as determined in step 4.

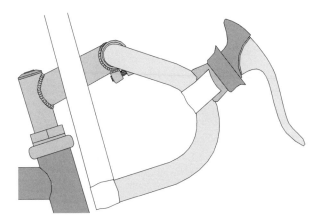

28.19 Start with a full wrap with no advance.

6. [ ] Complete one wrap of tape without advancing it so that end of tape is hidden by wrap.

7. [ ] Pulling with a gentle-to-firm pressure, continue wrapping around bar, advancing tape with each wrap so that each wrap overlaps the last by about 1/3 the tape width until first bend of bar is reached.

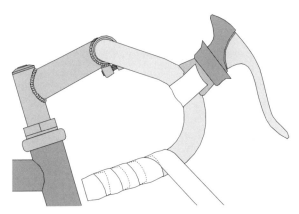

28.20 Overlap each wrap by 1/3 the width of the tape.

8. [ ] Continue advancing up bend of bar, maintaining 1/4 – 1/3 of tape width overlap *at outside of bar bend.*

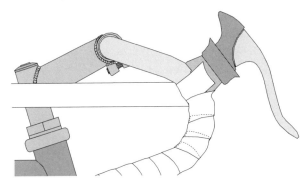

28.21 Overlap each wrap by 1/4 – 1/3 the width of the tape on the outside of the bend of the bar.

9. [ ] Adjust amount each wrap overlaps last wrap so that when tape reaches bottom of brake lever, it overlaps bottom edge of lever body by 1/8" to 1/4".
10. [ ] After overlapping bottom of brake lever, advance next wrap enough to end up above brake lever at completion of wrap, and overlap top of brake lever body by 1/8" to 1/4".

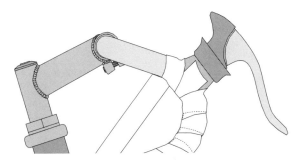

28.22 Wrap around the brake lever like this.

11. [ ] Continue wrapping around upper bend of bar, maintaining 1/4 – 1/3 of tape overlap at outside bend of bar.

12. [ ] Finish wrapping with tape-edge flush to edge of fat center section of bar, then cut tape so end is on bottom side of bar.

13. [ ] Use colored friction tape or tape supplied with handlebar tape to cover last wrap, leaving end on bottom side of bar.

14. [ ] If using friction tape, use soldering iron or hot knife blade to weld end of friction tape to overlap.

15. [ ] Tuck any excess tape into bottom end of bar and install handlebar-end plugs (if any).

OTHER BAR SYSTEMS

BMX/FREESTYLE

BMX handlebar positions

BMX and freestyle handlebars should be positioned with the rise of the bar ranging from 10° forward from straight up to 30° back. The normal position when setting up new bikes is with the rise of the bars pointing straight up.

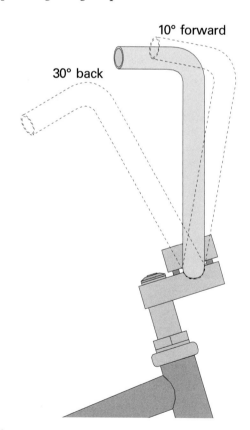

28.23 Position BMX/freestyle bars in this range.

Securing BMX/freestyle stems

BMX/freestyle stems should be torqued in the fork to 170in-lbs (28lbs@6" or 42lbs@4").

Most BMX and freestyle bikes have a stem with four handlebar-binder bolts. The handlebar is sandwiched between two blocks of metal. When the binder bolts are secured, these two blocks need to remain parallel to avoid bending the bolts (see figure 28.24, below). In addition, the bolts should be tightened in a specific sequence to avoid effectively loosening one bolt while tightening another. Basically, this means always crossing over the handlebar to get to the next bolt. See figure 28.25 (below) for a tightening pattern. The bolts should be tightened in several stages, to a final torque of 240in-lbs (40lbs@6" or 60lbs@4").

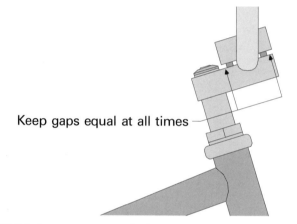

Keep gaps equal at all times

28.24 Keep an even gap at the front and back of the bar clamp at all times.

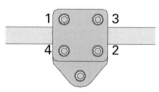

28.25 Tighten the four bolts in this pattern.

UPRIGHT BARS

See figure 28.26 for the acceptable range of handle-bar positions.

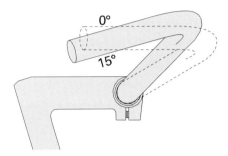

28.26 *This the range of acceptable positions for upright bars.*

HANDLEBAR AND STEM TROUBLESHOOTING

Cause	Solution
SYMPTOM: *Wedge will not drop when tapping the stem-binder bolt with a ballpeen hammer.*	
Wedge is rusted in place.	Unthread handlebar-binder bolt, remove stem without wedge, drive wedge out with punch.
SYMPTOM: *Stem will not remove after the wedge has dropped.*	
Off-center hole in locknut is cutting into stem shaft.	Loosen headset locknut before removing stem.
Stem is corroded in place.	See procedure for removing difficult stems (page 28-6, steps 6 and 7).
SYMPTOM: *After loosening handlebar-binder bolt, bars will not slip easily through stem.*	
Handlebar bore had to be spread for installation, so in relaxed state it is still exerting pressure.	Insert something in compression slot to expand handlebar bore.
SYMPTOM: *Stem jams in bend of drop bar when installing or removing the stem from the bars.*	
Stem with wide bar clamp for MTB-type bars is being used on drop bars.	Do not use this combination if installing. Spread compression slot as much as necessary if removing the bars from the stem.
SYMPTOM: *Bar center is difficult to fit in stem.*	
Bar center is wrong dimension for handlebar bore in stem.	Measure both diameters. The bar should be no more than .2mm larger than the handlebar bore I.D. in the stem.
Stem is good fit, but handlebar-bore diameter is slightly collapsed or undersized.	Expand compression slot in stem after verifying stem and bar are compatible.
SYMPTOM: *Stem is difficult to install in fork column.*	
Stem is over-sized for fork column.	Measure stem O.D. and fork column I.D. Stem cannot be larger than fork column by any amount.
Headset-locknut seal is displaced.	Check seal and insert correctly if displaced.
Headset locknut has off-center hole.	Loosen locknut and install stem to test. Replace locknut to fix.
Corrosion in fork column or on stem shaft.	Clean stem shaft with emery cloth and hone inside of fork column.

(Continued next page)

HANDLEBAR AND STEM TROUBLESHOOTING (continued)

Cause	Solution
SYMPTOM: *Stem will not secure.*	
Stem was installed with stem-binder bolt too loose, and slope-style wedge has rotated 180° out of position.	Remove stem and install with stem-binder bolt no looser than necessary to get stem into fork column.
Stem-binder-bolt head, stem-binder-bolt threads, and wedge surface are not greased.	Grease all appropriate points.
SYMPTOM: *Handlebars slip when properly torqued.*	
Handlebar-binder bolt(s) need grease on threads and under head.	Grease handlebar-binder bolt.
Bars are undersized to handlebar bore in stem.	Measure both and make sure bar diameter is not more than .2mm less than bore diameter.
Bar center has collapsed or is worn out from previous slipping.	Remove bars and check condition of mating surface to stem.
Mating surfaces are contaminated.	Remove bars from stem and clean mating surfaces with alcohol or acetone.
Reinforcing sleeve has separated from handlebar.	Check if bar center sleeve is staying stationary when bar slips. If so, replace handlebar.
SYMPTOM: *After installing new handlebars, one side is lower than the other.*	
Stem was bent in a crash.	Replace stem.
SYMPTOM: *Handlebar extension or clip-on will not secure when bolts properly torqued.*	
Bolt heads and threads not greased.	Grease bolts.
Mating surfaces are contaminated.	Remove and clean mating surfaces.
Mating surfaces coated with paint or annodization.	Clean to raw aluminum with emery cloth.
Internal extension clamp, or radiused clip-on clamp diameter is wrong diameter for bar.	Change bar, or clip-on, or extension, for better fitting item.
SYMPTOM: *Handlebar-binder bolt breaks when torqued.*	
Torque was excessive for bolt diameter.	Check thread diameter and use appropriate torque.
If torque was correct, bar diameter is too small for stem, causing bolt to bend before bar is secured.	Check fit and replace one item to improve fit.
SYMPTOM: *Stem-binder bolt breaks when torqued.*	
Torque for steel bolts is being used on aluminum bolt.	Check material and use correct torque.
SYMPTOM: *Handlebars creak when riding.*	
Handlebar-binder bolt is loose.	Check torque.
Stem-binder bolt is loose.	Check torque.
Stem shaft is creaking inside fork column due to lack of grease.	Remove and grease stem shaft.
Headset is creaking.	Check headset for marginally-loose pressed races and loose headset locknut.
Reinforcement sleeve is creaking.	Can only be identified by eliminating all other choices. Try dripping penetrating Loctite into end of sleeve. If this fails, live with noise or replace handlebar.

29 – SEATS AND SEATPOSTS

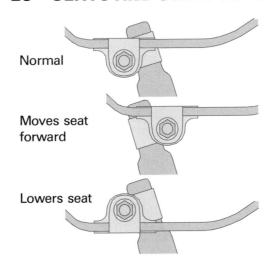

Normal

Moves seat forward

Lowers seat

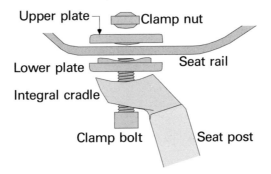

Upper plate — Clamp nut

Lower plate

Seat rail

Integral cradle

Clamp bolt

Seat post

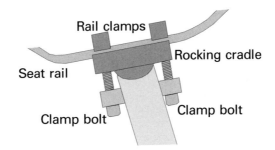

Rail clamps

Rocking cradle

Seat rail

Clamp bolt

Clamp bolt

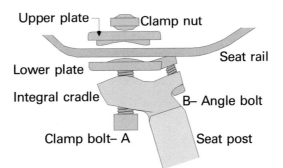

Upper plate — Clamp nut

Seat rail

Lower plate

Integral cradle

B— Angle bolt

Clamp bolt— A

Seat post

29 – SEATS AND SEATPOSTS

29 – SEATS AND SEATPOSTS

ABOUT THIS CHAPTER

This chapter is about removing and installing seats and seatposts.

GENERAL INFORMATION

TERMINOLOGY

Seat: The platform on which the rider sits. It may also be called a "saddle."

Seatpost: The shaft that the seat is mounted too that inserts into the seat tube of the frame.

Seat clamp: The mechanism that clamps the seat to the seatpost.

Integral seat clamp: A seat clamp that is built into the seatpost.

Non-integral seat clamp: A seat clamp that is separate from the seatpost.

Seat rails or **rails:** The rods or wires that are underneath the seat to which the seat clamp attaches.

Seatpost binder: The mechanism that secures the seatpost to the frame.

Seat lug: The portion of the frame where the seatpost inserts.

Compression slot: The slot in the seat lug that is compressed by the seatpost binder to secure the seatpost.

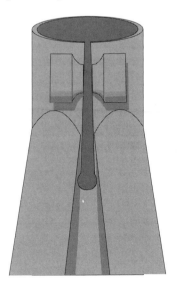

29.1 *The compression slot in the back of the seat tube.*

PREREQUISITES

There are no prerequisites for removing and installing seatposts and seats.

INDICATIONS

Seatposts

There are three reasons seatposts need to removed and installed; 1) because they are bent; 2) because they are undersized and will not secure; 3) or because they are being upgraded.

Seatposts can corrode and stick inside the seat tube so it is good preventive maintenance to remove them and grease them periodically.

Seats

Seats need to be removed and installed for the following reasons: 1) because the seatpost is being changed; 2) the seat rails are bent; 3) the seat is torn or worn out; 4) or because the seat is being upgraded.

TOOL CHOICES

There are no special tools required for servicing seatposts and seats, but Odyssey MS-200 sizing rods are extremely convenient for determining the correct seatpost size.

TIME AND DIFFICULTY RATING

Seatpost removal is a 1 minute job of little difficulty, unless it is stuck.

Seat removal and installation is a 1–3minute job of little difficulty.

COMPLICATIONS

Difficult seatpost removal

Seatposts can easily get stuck in the frame. They may even get permanently stuck. There is a section of this chapter about dealing with stuck seatposts.

Sizing seatposts

Because the seat lug may be deformed, it can be difficult to determine the correct size of seatpost. Because the hole may not be round, measuring with a caliper can give misinformation.

30 – SHIFT-CONTROL MECHANISMS

30 – SHIFT-CONTROL MECHANISMS

ABOUT THIS CHAPTER

This chapter is about shift levers and twist-grip shifters. There are separate chapters about the setup of control cables that attach to the shift-control mechanisms (**DERAILLEUR-CABLE SYSTEMS**, page 31-1), but this chapter includes information about installing the inner wire into the shift-control mechanism. There is a separate **REAR DERAILLEURS** chapter (page 32-1) and **FRONT DERAILLEURS** chapter (page 33-1).

GENERAL INFORMATION

TERMINOLOGY

Shift-control mechanism: A lever or twist grip that the rider uses to control the derailleur operations.

Shift lever: A lever that is rotated about a pivot to move the inner wire that operates the derailleur.

Shifter drum: A cylinder that the cable wraps around when the shifter is rotated.

Twist grip: A cylinder that is part of the hand grip on the handlebar that is rotated around the handlebar to move the inner wire that operates the derailleur.

Grip Shift: See *twist grip*.

Down-tube levers: Shift-control mechanisms that are mounted on the down tube of the frame.

Stem shifters: Shift-control mechanisms that are mounted on the vertical shaft of the stem.

Bar-end shifters: Shift-control mechanisms that are mounted in the ends of drop-style handlebars.

Bar cons: See *bar-end shifters*.

Top-mount shifters: Shift-control mechanisms that are mounted on top of MTB-style handlebars.

Thumb shifters: See *top mount shifters*.

Below-bar shifters: Shift-control mechanisms that are mounted so that they are reached by using the thumb below the bar on MTB-style handlebars.

Integral shift/brake levers: Shift-control mechanisms found on road bikes with which the shift levers are integrated into the brake levers.

Inner wire: The wire portions of the shift-control cable.

Housing: The outer sheath of the shift-control cable.

Shift-control cable: The inner wire and housing that work as a unit to transfer a change at the shift-control mechanism to the derailleur.

Adjusting barrel: A hollow bolt that the inner wire passes through, with a socket head that the housing inserts into. The adjusting barrel is screwed in and out of the shift-control mechanism to adjust the relative length of the inner wire.

Indexed (shifting): A shifting system in which the shift-control mechanism stops at prescribed increments, rather than anywhere within a prescribed range. When an indexed shift-control mechanism is moved to one of the prescribed positions, the shift is completed automatically.

Friction (shifting): A shifting system in which the shift-control mechanism moves to an infinite number of positions within a prescribed range. The shift-control mechanism is moved to wherever the operator chooses to complete the shift. It is not automatic.

Front derailleur: The mechanism that moves the chain between gear choices on the crankset.

Rear derailleur: The mechanism that moves the chain between gear choices on the rear hub.

PREREQUISITES

If installing a new shift-control mechanism or replacing an existing one, cable installation and derailleur indexing adjustment will be required. There are no other prerequisites.

INDICATIONS

Maintenance

Most of the time, the only maintenance needed by a shift-control mechanism is lubrication. Sometimes they need partial disassembling and cleaning.

Derailleur replacement

Derailleurs and shift-control mechanisms must be compatible. Sometimes changing a derailleur means that a new shift-control mechanism is needed.

Rear cogset replacement

Sometimes a cogset will be changed to have more gears. The derailleur may be able to handle the increase, but an indexing shift-control mechanism is almost always set for a specific number of gears.

Symptoms indicating need for cleaning

Any shifting system is complex, and a symptom may be caused by any of several parts of the system. An indexing lever in need of cleaning will create a symptom of the indexing adjustment being too tight and too loose at the same time. This can also be caused by control-cable problems, dirty or worn-out chain or derailleur, or compatibility problems with the shift-control mechanism, derailleur, chain, and cogset.

Symptoms indicating need for replacement

The symptom indicating need for replacement is the same as the symptom indicating need for cleaning, except when all the other causes have been eliminated and cleaning has been done, the symptom persists.

Indexing shift-control mechanisms have delicate internal parts that sometimes break. The symptom will be either a lever that will not move, or it moves but the control cable cannot. The same symptom can also be caused by the inner wire being installed wrong. If the inner wire is in correctly, the shift-control mechanism needs to be replaced.

TOOL CHOICES

Installing and removing a shift-control mechanism requires no special tools. As a consequence of installing a shift-control mechanism, a derailleur will need adjustment, but any special tools for this are covered in the **REAR DERAILLEURS** chapter (page 32-5) and **FRONT DERAILLEURS** chapter (page 33-3).

Shimano STI levers (road-bike shift levers that are integrated into the brake levers) require a couple of special tools called the TL-ST01 and TL-ST02 for disassembling the lever.

TIME AND DIFFICULTY

In most cases, installing a shift-control mechanism is a 2–5 minute job of little difficulty. Adjustment of the derailleur is additional. If installing bar-end shifters, taping the bars is additional. If changing between a lever system that is integrated with the brake levers and one that is not, brake-lever installation and brake adjustment would take additional time. For the time and difficulty rating of all these additional factors, see the chapters that pertain to them.

COMPLICATIONS

Compatibility with derailleur

Shift-control mechanisms must be compatible with the derailleurs they are used with. An indexing shifter moves a fixed amount of cable for each click of the control. This amount of cable motion must be the correct amount to move the derailleur precisely from one gear to the next.

Any table of compatibility is doomed to becoming outdated rapidly. Manufacturer's technical support and literature will always be a better source of information. As a general guideline, different brands of shifters and derailleurs can rarely be matched (except Grip Shift brand, which are made specifically for other brands of derailleurs). Even models within a brand may be incompatible; for example, Shimano Dura-Ace components can't be mixed with other Shimano components.

When in doubt, it is possible to test for whether two components are compatible. In the **REAR DERAILLEURS** chapter is a section called **FUNCTIONAL RANGE OF ADJUSTMENT** (page 32-21) that describes a test that measures shifting performance. If mismatched equipment performs well in this test, it is compatible.

Compatibility with inner wire

Shape and size of the inner-wire head is important. Some modern shifters have plastic sockets that the inner-wire head seats in. If it is not a good fit, it can jam in place and be very difficult to ever get out. Before using a wire, insert its head backwards into the shifter socket and make sure it slips all the way in and out easily.

Inner-wire diameter is important with indexing shifters. The amount of cable pulled with each click of the shifter is a function of the diameter of the cylinder (shifter drum) that the cable is wrapping around and the inner-wire diameter. Until 1995, all indexing levers used a 1.2mm inner wire except Shimano Dura-Ace (1.6mm). Shimano switched to a 1.1mm wire in 1995, and back to 1.2mm in 1996.

Integration with brake levers

Certain shifters on MTBs share a mount with the brake lever. The configuration of the mount is specific to the model of shifter. When one of these older shifters needs replacement, it is possible that the brake levers and shifters will both need replacement.

Symptom caused by multiple items

When indexing shift performance is poor, the nature of the symptom will not necessarily point to one specific cause. A shifter, cable, derailleur, chain, or rear cogset could all cause the same symptom.

Patience to investigate all the possible causes of the symptom is required to narrow it down to, or to exclude, the shifter as the cause.

ABOUT THE REST OF THIS CHAPTER

The rest of this chapter is divided into seven sections for each type of shift-control mechanism. Each section is divided into an installation sub-section and a service sub-section. Some sections are divided further, when different brands or models within a category require different procedures. The seven sections are:

BELOW-BAR SHIFTERS
TOP-MOUNT SHIFTERS
TWIST-GRIP SHIFTERS
INTEGRAL SHIFT/BRAKE LEVERS
DOWN-TUBE LEVERS
BAR-END SHIFTERS
STEM SHIFTERS

BELOW-BAR SHIFTERS

Types

Many below-bar shifters are integrated with the brake lever. They can be removed from the brake lever for cleaning or replacement, but to install and align them, the brake lever must be installed and aligned.

Another type of below-bar shifter is not integrated with the brake lever. This type needs to be positioned relative to the brake lever after correctly positioning the brake lever.

Terminology

Up-shift lever: The lever that is pushed to move the derailleur from a smaller diameter gear (fewer teeth) to a larger diameter gear (more teeth).

Release lever: The lever that is pushed to release the derailleur to a smaller diameter gear (fewer teeth) from a larger diameter gear (more teeth).

Shifter pod: The complete shift-control mechanism that is part of an integrated shift/brake lever.

Pod-mounting plate: The flat plate that is part of the brake-lever body.

Brake-lever binder bolt: The bolt that secures the brake-lever clamp to the handlebar.

Pod-mounting bolt: The bolt that secures the shifter pod to the pod-mounting plate.

INSTALLATION
Integrated shift/brake levers
1. [ ] Remove grip if necessary.
2. [ ] Slide shift/brake lever over end of bar.
3. [ ] Install grip to final position.
4. [ ] Slide shift/brake lever outward until clamp is against inside edge of grip.
5. [ ] Remove and lubricate brake-lever binder bolt.
6. [ ] Install brake-lever binder bolt and gently snug.
7. [ ] With bike in on-ground position, use dial protractor to rotate lever so that brake lever body is 45° from horizontal.

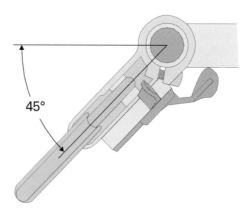

30.1 Rotate the brake lever 45° down from horizontal.

8. [ ] Tighten brake-lever binder bolt to: 35–50in-lbs (9–12lbs@4").

Non-integrated below-bar shifters
1. [ ] Remove binder bolt from shifter-mounting strap or clamp.
2. [ ] Lubricate binder-bolt threads.
3. [ ] Install shifter, brake lever, then grip onto handlebar. Correctly position brake lever (adjacent to grip and rotated down 45° from flat), then secure brake lever.
4. [ ] Install shifter binder bolt and gently snug.
5. [ ] Slide shifter outward against brake lever, until release lever is just far enough outward to not touch brake lever when shifter is operated.
6. [ ] Rotate shifter so that shifters will operate in a plane 45° down from horizontal.

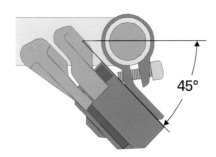

30.2 Rotate the shifter 45° down from horizontal.

8. [ ] Tighten shifter-clamp binder bolt to: 25-30in-lbs (6-8lbs@4").

SunTour X-Press shifters

The correct rotational alignment for these shifters is 60° down from horizontal (starting with shifters at horizontal *in front* of handlebars).

INNER-WIRE INSTALLATION

Shimano Rapidfire and Rapidfire Plus inner-wire installation

Shimano Rapidfire levers (both levers pushed with the thumb) have a cover plate retained by a Phillips screw that has to be removed to access the inside of the shifter for inner-wire installation. Some Rapidfire Plus levers have a plug in the access hole for the inner wire. Rapidfire SL levers (described after the next heading), have a completely different cable-installation process.

Shimano Rapidfire and Rapidfire Plus (release lever operated by index finger) shifters need to be fully released in order to correctly install the inner wire. The wire can be installed without fully releasing the shifter, but the lever will not operate correctly.

1. [ ] Remove access cover plate if any.
2. [ ] Operate release lever at least 7 times to insure lever is fully released.

Earlier Shimano levers were difficult to install inner wires in, because once the inner wire was installed through the hole in the shifter drum it would not pass easily through the adjusting barrel. Sometimes it is necessary to remove the adjusting barrel from the shifter to complete the inner-wire installation.

3. [ ] Insert end of wire through access hole into inner-wire head socket and out adjusting barrel.
4. [ ] Pull inner wire through until head seats into socket in the shifter drum.
5. [ ] Pulling firmly on inner wire, push up-shift lever and then release lever to make sure wire moves to and away from shifter as levers are operated. (If not, inner wire is in wrong and should be removed.)

Shimano Rapidfire SL inner-wire installation

Shimano Rapidfire SL shift mechanisms are distinguished in appearance by the fact that there is a slot in the derailleur-cable adjusting barrel for quick-releasing the cable out of the shift mechanism. On less expensive models, there is a cover that swings out of place to expose the anchor for the inner-wire head. More expensive models have a similar cover, but instead of

swinging out of place, two tiny Phillips screws hold it in place. In both cases, the cover is accessed from the back face of the lever unit, just below the handlebar; where the inner-wire slot ends in the mount for the adjusting barrel, the cover begins. Underneath the cover is a pivoting cable anchor, just like the one in the brake lever that the brake inner wire attaches to.

1. [ ] Press release lever 7 times to make sure shift mechanism is in fully-released condition.
2. [ ] Remove cable-anchor cover by pivoting it up towards handlebar, or by removing small Phillips screws and lifting cover off lever (depending on model).
3. [ ] Line up slot in adjusting barrel with slot in adjusting-barrel mount.
4. [ ] Swing cable anchor up towards handlebar.
5. [ ] Hook inner-wire head into cable anchor.
6. [ ] Swing inner wire into slot in adjusting-barrel mount and into slot in adjusting barrel.
7. [ ] Rotate adjusting barrel 1/2 turn so inner wire will not accidentally come out.
8. [ ] Replace cable-anchor access cover.

SunTour X-Press inner-wire installation

1. [ ] Unscrew shifter cover screw at center of shifter cover and remove cover.
2. [ ] Feed inner wire out adjusting barrel.
3. [ ] Hook inner-wire head into socket in shifter plate inside shifter.
4. [ ] Replace shifter cover.

SERVICE

Shifter pods can be replaced or cleaned, but they are never disassembled to replace individual parts because the individual parts are not sold.

Shimano shifter-pod replacement

Shifter pods are attached one of three ways at this time. First, a little orientation. The front of the shift/brake-control unit is the side that can be seen when standing in front of the bike and facing it. The back face is the side that would face toward the rider's knees. Some models have the shifter pod mounted on a plate that is visible from the front. There is a bolt head in the center of the shifter pod on the back face of the assembly. These will be called **exposed-plate models** (see figure 30.3, page 30-5). Some models have the shifter pod mounted on a plate that is enclosed between the shifter pod and the gear-indicator unit. There is a bolt head in the center of the shifter pod on the back face of the assembly. These will be called **enclosed-plate models** (see figure 30.4, page 30-5). Shimano Rapidfire SL models have an exposed plate, but there is no bolt head in the center of the shifter pod (see figure 30.5, below, right). Rapidfire SL levers can also be identified by the unique fact that they have a slot in the derailleur-cable adjusting barrel that is used for moving the inner wire in and out of the adjusting barrel. This last type will be called Rapidfire SL models.

Exposed-plate models: To remove the shifter, loosen the bolt that is visible on the front face of the mounting plate. Note the rotational orientation of the shifter because it may have multiple mounting positions. When the bolt is fully removed, the shifter pod will pull off the back side of the plate. When reinstalling, make sure that the positioning pegs go into the desired positioning holes in the mounting plate. Use Loctite #222 on the mounting-bolt threads and torque the bolt(s) to 25in-lbs (6lbs@4").

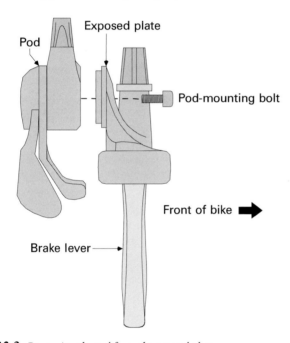

30.3 Removing the pod from the exposed plate.

Enclosed-plate models: The shifter-pod mounting bolt goes through the center of the pod and is accessed from the back face of the pod. It is often secured with a heavy-duty Loctite and may be difficult to break loose. The bolt is threaded into a sleeve nut with a flatted flange that is hidden behind the gear-indicator unit. The flatted flange tends to pop out of its recess and just spin, so pull out on the shifter pod firmly while loosening *or* tightening the mounting bolt. If the sleeve nut spins uncontrollably, it will be necessary to remove the gear-indicator unit. When installing the pod, make sure the lever is fully released so that the post on the colorful plastic plate that activates the gear indicator goes in the hole that is sup-

posed to engage it. Use Loctite #222 on the mounting-bolt threads and torque to 25in-lbs (6lbs@4"). On some models, the pod cannot be removed unless the gear-indicator unit is also removed. This includes STX and Alivio Models with "MC" in the model number, which are visually distinguished by having an enclosed mounting plate and an under-the-bar indicator unit.

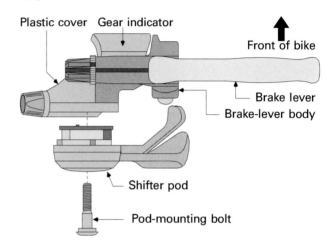

30.4 Removing the pod from an enclosed-plate unit.

Rapidfire SL models: Remove the gear indicator and the derailleur inner wire first. The shifter pod on these models is held in place by three Phillips screws. All the screws are on the back face of the pod. One is close to the derailleur-cable adjusting barrel. Another is just clockwise of the release lever. The third one is just counterclockwise of the release lever. One of the screws near the release lever will be hidden by the up-shift lever. When these three screws are removed, the shifter pod pulls easily of its mount. (See figure 30.5, below.)

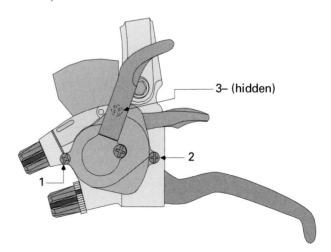

30.5 To remove the pod from a Rapidfire SL model, remove screws 1, 2, and 3.

Shimano Rapidfire and Rapidfire Plus gear-indicator-unit replacement

The following information covers gear-indicator removal and replacement for earlier Shimano Rapidfire and Rapidfire Plus models. There is another section following this one for Rapidfire SL models (distinguished by slot in derailleur-cable adjusting barrel). There are several ways that the gear indicator is mounted to the shift/brake control. When the pod is mounted to an *exposed-plate model*, the indicator unit comes off with the pod. These will be called **integrated type** (figure 30.6). Other types on *enclosed-plate models* may be over-the-bar or under-the-bar indicator units. All of these are not integrated with the shifter pod and come off separately. The under-the-bar type will be called **non-integrated under-the-bar type** (figure 30.7). The over-the-bar types come in *three* variations at the time of this writing! These will be called **hidden-screw over-the-bar type** (figure 30.8), **visible-screw over-the-bar type** (figure 30.9), and **Rapidfire SL type** (described under separate heading).

Integrated type: This is found on 700CX and 400CX models. After removing the pod from the mount, unthread two Phillips screws on the back side of the pod that are just below the indicator window. The indicator unit cover will lift off of the pod. The indicator itself is a thin sliding plastic strip that cannot be removed correctly without fully disassembling the pod unit, which *should not be done.* If the strip is damaged and jamming, it can be ripped out with a pair of pliers after removing the cover.

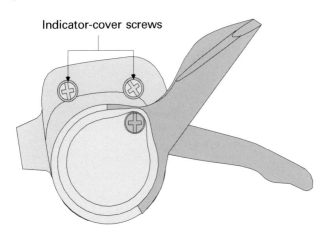

Indicator-cover screws

30.6 Shifting pod with an integrated gear indicator.

Non-integrated under-the-bar type: Remove two Phillips screws that are on the backside of the pod and just outside the perimeter of the pod cover, which rotates when the up-shift lever is operated. Remove the brake-lever reach-adjustment screw.

On the front side of the indicator unit, remove the Phillips screw that is adjacent to the brake-cable adjusting-barrel locknut. Lift off the indicator-unit cover. The orange indicator arm (spring loaded, be careful) just lifts out of the cover plate. When reinstalling the indicator arm, the spring must be set up to force the arm fully counterclockwise. The plastic actuator lifts out of the shifter-pod mounting plate to expose the flanged sleeve nut that the pod-mounting bolt screws into. When reinstalling, the pod unit needs to be shifted to the fully-released condition so that the long pin on the actuator will line up properly with the hole it inserts in.

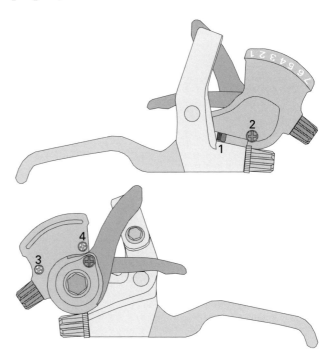

30.7 To remove an indicator unit from a non-integrated under-the-bar type, remove screws 1, 2, 3, and 4.

Hidden-screw over-the-bar type: When this type is on the handlebar, no screws can be seen in the indicator unit when viewed from the front. The whole shift/brake control must be removed from the handlebar to remove the indicator. Once the whole assembly is off the bar, one screw will become visible that was hidden by the handlebar. The other screw is on the back face of the casting just below the bottom of the shifter pod. Remove both these screws. *Do not remove the two screws in the indicator unit that are close to the window!* Remove the brake-cable adjusting barrel. On the front face of the control unit, the brake-lever reach-adjustment screw must be removed so that the indicator unit can be lifted off. Pull on the indicator unit to remove it from the lever body.

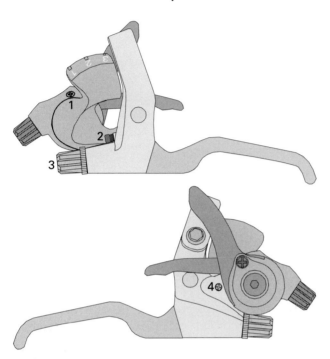

30.8 *To remove the indicator unit from a hidden-screw over-the-bar type, remove screws 1 and 2, adjusting barrel (3) and screw 4.*

Visible-screw over-the-bar type: This type can be removed without removing the whole shift/brake control unit from the lever. Viewed from the front, small screws at the base of the indicator-unit tower and close to the brake-cable adjusting barrel will be seen. Remove these with a #0 Phillips screwdriver, and the indicator unit lifts right off. *Do not disassemble the unit!* The plastic actuator lifts up, and the mount cover snaps off.

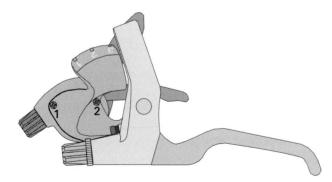

30.9 *To remove the indicator unit from a visible-screw over-the-bar type, remove screws 1 and 2.*

Shimano Rapidfire SL gear-indicator-unit removal and installation

Rapidfire SL models are distinguished by a slot in the derailleur-cable adjusting barrel. The gear indicator is on the front face of the plate on which the shifter pod mounts. Removing two small Phillips screws enables the gear-indicator unit to be lifted off the mounting plate. An asymmetrical hexagonal plastic stud in the back face of the gear indicator engages an asymmetrical hexagonal socket that is in a hole in the mounting plate; if the shifter pod is in the fully-released mode when installing the gear indicator unit, the asymmetrical stud and socket will line up automatically. When installing the gear-indicator unit, the brake-lever reach-adjusting bolt may need to be removed in order to line the gear-indicator unit up properly.

Shimano shifter-pod cleaning and lubrication

Before replacing a shifter pod that is not functioning, consider cleaning and re-lubing it. To clean it, the pod must be removed from the mount and the cover must be removed from the pod. On pods with *integrated indicators*, the indicator cover should also be removed.

The technique for removing pod covers is different for different models. On *exposed-mount* types only, there may be a single large Phillips screw at the center of the pod cover on the back side. Some *exposed mount* types have an additional small Phillips screw at the perimeter of the pod cover that must also be removed. Some *exposed mount* types have only a small Phillips screw at the perimeter of the pod cover. All *enclosed mount* types have only a small Phillips screw at the perimeter of the pod cover.

The Rapidfire SL models have a small Phillips screw at the base of the up-shift lever that must be removed in order to remove the pod cover.

After removing the pod and cover(s), soak the pod in solvent. After it has soaked, agitate it in the solvent and repeatedly operate the levers while it is submerged. Blow it dry *thoroughly* and generously lube it with a heavy-weight spray lube.

TOP-MOUNT SHIFTERS

INSTALLATION

Top-mount shifters are installed inward of the brake levers. The shifter is above and in front of the handlebar.

The end of the lever extends to the grip, and if the lever is positioned too far outward the lever can interfere with use of the grip. Some models have cast clamps and must be slid on the bar from the end before installing the brake lever or grip. Some models have strap clamps that can be spread open and slipped over the bar while the brake lever and grip are in place.

1. [ ] **With brake lever and grip in final positions, mount shifter loosely, inward of brake lever.**
2. [ ] **Lubricate mounting-bolt threads and snug bolt gently so that shifter can easily be moved, but will stay in place by itself.**
3. [ ] **Operate shift lever so that lever is parallel to handlebar.**
4. [ ] **Move lever unit laterally so that end of lever is even with *and not overlapping* inward end of grip.**
5. [ ] **Rotate lever unit around handlebar until lever swings in a plane that is parallel to ground.**

Lever rotation is acceptable in a range from parallel to the ground, to rotated 45° forward. A position of 25–30° forward is recommended.

6. [ ] **Rotate lever forward to desired angle (25–30° recommended).**
7. [ ] **Secure mounting bolt to 20–25in-lbs (5–6lbs@4").**

INNER-WIRE INSTALLATION

When installing the inner wire, thread it fully through the socket on the shifter drum so that the head ends up in the socket, *then* put the end of the wire through the housing stop or adjusting barrel and draw the wire fully through. Putting the wire partially through the hole in the shifter drum and then through the housing stop, before pulling the wire all the way through the hole in the shifter drum, will result is the inner wire developing a corkscrew bend.

SERVICE

Look for a shifter-mounting bolt on the bottom side to remove the shifter from the mount. If there is a screw in the shifter cover, remove it. Soak and agitate the shifter in solvent, then blow dry and lubricate thoroughly. There is no point to disassembling the mechanism because there are no parts available.

TWIST-GRIP SHIFTERS

GRIP SHIFT

Models

The following instructions are suitable for models SRT 100/150, SRT 400i/300i/200i, SRT 500R, Quickshift, MRX-100, and SRT 400/600/800/900 (X-ray). These models were current in 1995 at the time of this writing. Models after this time may be similar or completely different.

Installation

1. [ ] **Loosen brake lever.**
2. [ ] **Slide Grip Shift shifting unit onto handlebar.**

The washer installed in the next step is very important because it keeps the shifter from binding against the grip.

3. [ ] **Slide 7/8" thin plastic washer onto handlebar.**
4. [ ] **Install grip fully onto handlebar.**
5. [ ] **Slide Grip Shift shifter outward so that it is against inward end of grip.**
6. [ ] **Secure brake lever at final rotational and lateral positions.**

For securing the Grip Shift to the handlebar, there is either a binder bolt or set screw with an Allen head. Either is located at the inward end of the unit, at a location that will be toward the back side and bottom, when the unit is on the handlebar with the adjusting barrel positioned just below the brake lever.

7. [ ] **Remove and lube mounting-binder bolt or set screw.**

Depending on the set-up of the frame and handlebars, the conventional positioning of the adjusting barrels below the brake levers might create an awkward cable routing. If this is the case, do not hesitate to try positioning the Grip Shift adjusting barrels above the brake-lever bodies.

8. [ ] **Rotate Grip Shift shifter until its adjusting barrel is just below brake-lever body, then install and gently secure binder-bolt/set-screw.**
9. [ ] **Operate brake lever to make sure Grip Shift does not interfere with operation and reposition shifter as necessary.**
10. [ ] **Secure set screw (2.5mm Allen) to 20in-lbs (7lbs@3"), or binder bolt (3mm Allen) to 17in-lbs (6lbs@3").**

Detaching cable

1. [ ] **Rotate shifter forward to fully release inner wire and disconnect inner wire from derailleur.**

Cover-plate removal

Most Grip Shift mechanisms have a cover plate that must be removed for dissassembly, but some do not.

If the inner wire is exposed in a groove around the bend at the base of the adjusting barrel, there is no cover plate.

If there is no exposed wire, look for a Phillips screw in the outward face of the base that goes out to the adjusting barrel (see figure 30.1). When the screw is removed, the plate comes right off.

If there is no exposed wire or Phillips screw, look for a shallow slot that just fits a 3/16" screwdriver blade on the inward face of the base that goes out to the adjusting barrel (figure 30.11). Insert a screwdriver in this slot and twist or pry to pop the cover plate off.

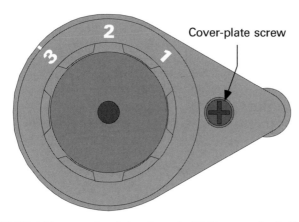

Cover-plate screw

30.10 *This outward-end view shows the Phillips screw that holds on the cover plate on some models.*

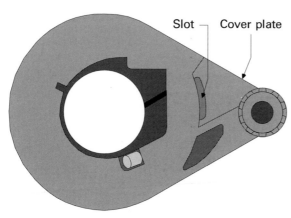

Slot   Cover plate

30.11 *This inward-end view shows the slot used to pry off the cover plate on some models.*

2. [ ] Remove cover plate on base that goes out to adjusting barrel.

Removing twist unit and cable

3. [ ] Remove the grip and washer just outward of shifter.

If a cover plate was removed, the twist unit will pull out of the housing effortlessly. If the model had no cover plate, it must be rotated fully back (pulling the cable as far as possible) before pulling it off with some effort.

4. [ ] **Pull twist unit out of housing. Models with no cover plate must be rotated *fully* back before pulling.**
5. [ ] **Push inner wire into adjusting barrel until end is through and out of adjusting barrel.**

Some shifters have the inner-wire head inserted in a socket that is in the inward face of the shifter housing. Some shifters have the inner-wire head inserted in the large cylinder surface of the twist unit.

6. [ ] **Push inner wire out of twist unit or out of shifter housing.**

Cleaning and lubrication

7. [ ] **Parts should only be cleaned with a mild soap. Solvents may degrade plastic parts.**
8. [ ] **Lubricate shifter-housing barrel, spring, spring cavity, cable groove on way to adjusting barrel, and détentes in twist unit with Grip Shift Jonnisnot grease or petroleum jelly *only*.**

NOTE: If inner-wire head is in twist unit, skip to step 12.

Inserting inner wire in shifter with wire-head socket in shifter housing

NOTE: If wire is already installed, skip to step 14.

9. [ ] **Feed wire end into socket on inward face of shifter housing and seat head fully.**
10. [ ] **Wrap wire one time around shifter-housing barrel and then into adjusting barrel, pulling so that loop ends up slightly smaller than diameter of enclosure.**
11. [ ] **Slide shifter onto barrel of housing and place loop of housing up feed ramp and into groove around inward end of twist unit, then go to step 14.**

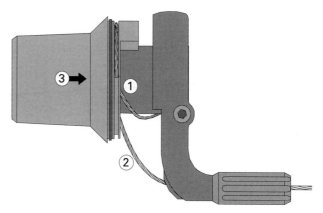

30.12 *To install the inner wire: 1) wrap the wire once around the shifter-housing barrel, 2) feed the wire onto the ramp and into the groove around the twist unit, 3) then push the twist unit into the shifter housing.*

Inserting inner wire in shifter with wire-head socket in twist unit

12. [ ] Insert wire into socket in twist unit, and seat head fully.
13. [ ] Slide twist unit onto barrel of shifter housing, and insert wire through adjusting barrel.

Assembling shifter

14. [ ] Line up twist unit so that any part of gear-indicator range on twist unit lines up with gear-indicator mark on shifter housing.
15. [ ] Pull firmly on inner wire while pressing in twist unit with firm pressure. Rotate twist unit back-and-forth to get spring to line up with détente, until parts seat together fully.
16. [ ] Install cover plate, if any.
17. [ ] Pull on inner wire while operating twist unit back-and-forth to check that cable moves and twist unit clicks in détentes.

SACHS POWER GRIP AND POWER GRIP PRO

Installation

1. [ ] Install brake lever on handlebar loosely.
2. [ ] Slide shifter onto handlebar and leave loose.
3. [ ] If shifter has separate grip, slide both 7/8" I.D. washers onto handlebar and install stationary grip fully on, then slide shifter out gently against washers.
4. [ ] If shifter includes full grip, slide shifter fully on bar.
5. [ ] Position and secure brake lever.
6. [ ] Rotate shifter until adjusting barrel is just below brake-lever body.
7. [ ] Secure shifter bolts on bottom side of housing to 35in-lbs (12lbs@3").

Inner-wire replacement and service

Before performing the following procedure, confirm that the model being dealt with is one this procedure covers. The most current models do not require any disassembly for wire removal. Simply detach the inner wire from the derailleur and attempt to push it out of the shifter.

If this works, do not use the following procedure for inner-wire replacement.

1. [ ] Leave shifter on handlebar during disassembly.
2. [ ] Shift to release all cable tension and detach inner wire from derailleur and remove all cable housings.
3. [ ] *Pull* cable-adjusting barrel out of shift-mechanism cover.
4. [ ] Remove both bolts in bottom of shift-mechanism cover.

5. [ ] While holding bottom cover up against handlebar, pull cover off top of shift mechanism.
6. [ ] Pull lock button up out of back side of lower cover.
7. [ ] Pull J-ring off of top of inward end of twister.
8. [ ] Pull inner-wire guide out of front side of lower cover.
9. [ ] Drop lower cover off of handlebar and slide cover off end of inner wire.
10. [ ] If cleaning parts, remove grip and twister from handlebar.
11. [ ] Clean all parts, if desired.
12. [ ] Grease inside of twister & both sides of J-ring.
13. [ ] Install twister and grip on bar, if previously removed.
14. [ ] Insert inner wire into hole on twister.
15. [ ] Insert inner wire into back side of adjusting-barrel hole in lower cover.
16. [ ] Slide lower cover up inner wire and put lower cover on bottom side of handlebar so that lip on inner edge engages groove in bottom side of twister.
17. [ ] Holding lower cover up against bottom of handlebar, place lock button in back face of lower cover with tab going down into cover.
18. [ ] Place J-ring over inward end of twister so that pawl on inside surface of J-ring engages top-most détente in twister.
19. [ ] Rotating twister and deflecting end of J-ring as necessary, seat end of J-ring in slot in lower cover.
20. [ ] Install inner-wire guide in lower cover so that small end goes in back side of adjusting barrel hole and top end catches under shoulder on twister where inner wire first appears.
21. [ ] Place upper cover over mechanism.
22. [ ] Insert bolts in lower cover and gently snug.
23. [ ] Slide adjusting-barrel assembly over cable and insert nut on adjusting barrel into hole in lower cover.
24. [ ] Position and secure shifter as described in previous section, *Installation*.

INTEGRAL SHIFT/BRAKE LEVERS

INSTALLATION

1. [ ] Pull out on rubber cover on outward side of shift/brake lever to reveal head of lever-mounting bolt and loosen bolt until almost out of nut in mounting strap.

2. [ ] Lubricate threads of nut in mounting strap.
3. [ ] Slide lever onto bottom of handlebar. If lever is correct for this side of bike, housing stop will point inward.
4. [ ] Snug mounting bolt so that lever can just be moved up and down.
5. [ ] Move lever up or down so that bottom tip of lever is .5" above or below line extended forward from bottom of bar.
6. [ ] Rotate lever so that it points straight forward.
7. [ ] Secure lever-mounting bolt to 70–85in-lbs (17–21lbs@4").

SHIMANO STI SERVICE

Terminology

Shifter unit: The entire lever assembly that pulls back to the handlebar to operate the brake, or pushes to the center of the bike to operate the gears.

Brake/shift lever: The primary lever, that is pulled back for braking and pushed inward to pull the derailleur inner wire.

Release lever: The secondary lever that is pushed inward to release the derailleur inner wire.

Housing-stop/front-cover: The cover in front of the head of the brake/shift lever. The housing-stop portion is the protrusion that points inward that has a socket in it for the cable housing to insert in.

Lever-pivot stud: A small axle that the shifter unit pivots on when pulling the brake/shift lever backward to operate the brake.

Brake-lever housing: The stationary body of the lever that attaches to the handlebar.

Chrome adapter: A large piece of chromed metal that connects the shifter unit to the brake-lever housing.

Shifter-unit removal

1. [ ] While pedaling, operate release lever until chain reaches last gear, then detach inner wire from derailleur.
2. [ ] Remove cable housings and pull inner wire from all guides on frame.
3. [ ] Compress brake lever to handlebar to reveal cable head in socket in outward side of head of brake/shift lever.
4. [ ] Push inner wire into housing stop on inward side of lever and pull inner-wire head out outward side.
5. [ ] Remove entire brake lever from handlebar.
6. [ ] Loosen brake-lever-stud fixing screw using 2mm Allen key, one complete turn.

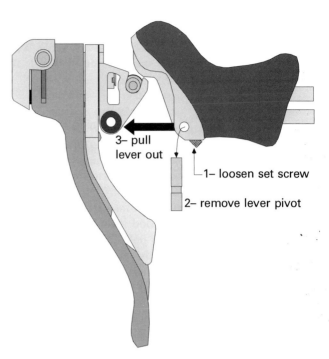

3– pull lever out

1– loosen set screw

2– remove lever pivot

30.13 *To remove the shifter unit: 1) loosen the set screw, 2) push out the lever pivot, 3) then pull the shifter unit out of the lever body.*

7. [ ] Operate brake lever to relieve pressure from brake-lever return spring and push brake-lever pivot stud inward using 4mm Allen or similar tool. (Note orientation of stud. Recessed portion of stud is on end to inward side of lever.)
8. [ ] Carefully remove lever assembly from lever housing. (Watch for lever bushings and lever-return spring that may fall out.)

Dura-Ace models: lever-unit service

See figure 30.14 (page 30-12) for an illustration of steps #1–5.

NOTE: Perform shifter-unit removal before this procedure.

1. [ ] Gently pry cable-anchor pivot upward using small tipped screwdriver. (Note orientation of bushings and place on bundle.)
2. [ ] Remove retaining nut at back of shift lever by turning TL-ST01 with 5mm Allen wrench. (Hold tool square to nut and apply force toward nut while turning counterclockwise.)
3. [ ] Remove lock washer that was behind nut.
4. [ ] Remove chrome adapter and plastic dust cover together from lever assembly. (Note the spring is engaged on dust cover. Leave spring on cover.)
5. [ ] Remove small metal washer from splined stud.
6. [ ] Noting engagement of release lever to release plate, remove release plate from splined stud.

8. [ ] Tip release lever to disengage from spring, then rotate release lever approximately 90° to pull it out of brake-lever body.
9. [ ] Lift up toothed ring and pull partially out of brake-lever body until long end of spring clears spring hole in brake-lever body.
10. [ ] Rotate toothed ring approximately 180° and tip to pull out of lever body.

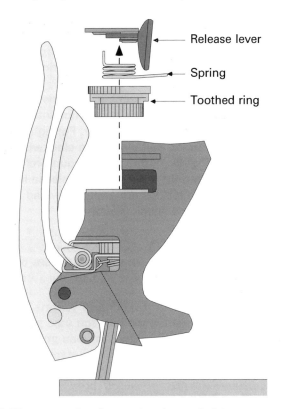

30.17 Remove release lever, spring, then toothed ring.

11. [ ] Note any washers under toothed ring and remove.
12. [ ] Lift prong on coil spring and gently pull spring out of toothed ring.
13. [ ] Use needle-nose pliers to remove two odd-shaped (indexing) springs down inside lever body that were exposed by removal of toothed ring.

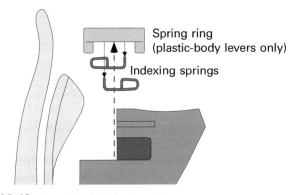

30.18 Removing the indexing springs.

14. [ ] Use small screwdriver or seal pick to gently encourage ring (in which indexing springs were mounted) out of lever body.
15. [ ] Further disassembly is possible, but not usually required. Cleaning of unit possible while still assembled. (To disassemble further, remove brake lever to better access internal parts. Remove snap ring from back of body to fully disassemble.)
16. [ ] Using care not to displace any internal parts, clean parts using mild solvents.
17. [ ] Carefully dry with compressed air.

Assembling the shift mechanism

1. [ ] Grease new indexing springs, grease inside indexing-spring mounting ring, as well as ring seat in lever body.
2. [ ] With flatter side of indexing-spring mounting ring facing down, install indexing springs into small holes so that curve of springs matches curve of mounting ring.
3. [ ] Install indexing-spring mounting ring into body, seating it on two studs.
5. [ ] Front levers have a split washer under toothed ring. Grease washer, and place on top of spring-mounting ring. (Align split with hole in lever body for release-lever spring.)
6. [ ] Grease outside and inside of toothed ring. Grease the return spring.
7. [ ] Place release-lever spring into toothed ring so that long end of spring sticks out of slot in toothed ring.
8. [ ] Aluminum body levers only, align toothed ring so that vertical-spring end enters big slot in lever body first, then slide toothed ring into lever body.
9. [ ] Rotate toothed ring so that horizontal end of spring points at spring hole in lever body.
10. [ ] Use tip of small screwdriver to deflect horizontal end of spring to line up with hole, then push toothed ring in all the way. (Indexing spring can displace below toothed ring and interfere. If this is difficult, removed toothed ring and make sure indexing spring is against wall of mounting ring.)
11. [ ] Rotate toothed ring so that flats in hole line up with flats on stud below, then drop toothed ring onto stud below.
18. [ ] With recess in release-lever disc facing up and end of lever pointing toward brake lever, insert release lever over toothed ring and engage release-lever spring into hole in release lever.

As an alternative to the previous step, put the release lever in place *without* engaging the spring, with the big hole in the disc lined up with the hole in the toothed ring, and the release lever positioned where it stops against the lever body. Modify a very small slotted screwdriver by putting a notch in its tip and use this to guide the vertical end of the spring into the small hole in the disc of the release lever.

19. [ ] **Pivot release lever around end of spring until hole in release lever is centered over hole in toothed ring. (Expect this to be awkward since the spring will provide resistance.)**
20. [ ] **Reinstall any shims on retaining bolt. Apply Loctite 242 to threads of bolts.**
21. [ ] **Maintaining upward pressure on the end of the release lever to keep the spring down in the toothed ring, install and secure retaining bolt to 50in-lbs (17lbs@3"). Right-hand lever secures by turning bolt counterclockwise. Left-hand lever hand secures clockwise.**

DOWN-TUBE LEVERS

INSTALLATION

Clamp-mounted shifters

Clamp-mounted shifters have a strap that wraps around the down tube, with a binder bolt that pulls the ends of the strap together, located on the bottom side of the down tube. There is usually a small tab brazed to the top side or bottom side of the down tube that locates the shifters. The strap should be up the tube from the tab, but touching it. In case there is no tab, locate the shifters so that the ends of the levers come within 1–1.5" of the back side of the head tube. Secure the binder bolt to 24–30in-lbs (8–10lbs@3").

Braze-on mounted shifters

Braze-on mounted shifters mount to brazed-on fittings mounted on both sides of the down tube. They sometimes have a unitized construction and go on all at once, and they sometimes are several parts that are placed on the braze-on one at a time.

If they are a single unit, simply slip them onto the braze-on and tighten the screw or bolt that goes through the center of the lever drum. The screw threads should be treated with Loctite 222, and the torque should be 10–15in-lbs (3–5lbs@3").

If they are friction (non-indexing) levers, they will usually consist of several parts. The first part is usually a plate that fixes to the large square at the base of the braze-on. This plate usually has a stop that stops the forward motion of the lever. If the plate is on wrong, the lever will not stop parallel to the down tube when pushed all

the way forward. The next part is usually a thick washer with a round hole in the middle. This is followed by the lever itself. After the lever is another washer that usually has a flatted hole that engages the flats on the end of the braze-on. A cover plate typically follows this, and the last part is the mounting/tension screw that holds everything on and adjusts the amount of friction. This screw should be oiled, not treated with Loctite.

If the lever has too much friction and will not operate smoothly without loosening the tension screw to the point that it will not resist the derailleur return spring, try lubricating both faces of the lever where it is sandwiched between the washers.

SERVICE

If the lever comes off as a unit, then the only service is to soak it in solvent, dry with compressed air, and inject oil. If this does not solve the problem, the lever must be replaced.

Levers that come off in parts when the central screw is undone can be cleaned thoroughly, dried, then lubricated and installed. In rare cases, the washers that sandwich the lever can be replaced (if worn out).

BAR-END SHIFTERS

REMOVAL

The shift mechanism usually must be removed from the mount to access a bolt that secures the mount inside the handlebar. Turn the bolt *clockwise* to loosen the mount. If the bolt will not turn clockwise without stripping the Allen socket, turn the mount counterclockwise.

INSTALLATION

The shift unit must be removed from the mount to install the mount in the end of the handlebar. When installing, be sure to grease the mounting-bolt threads *and* the inside and outside surfaces of the expander that fits inside the handlebar. Align so that shifter will point straight down and torque bolt (counterclockwise) to 50in-lbs (12lbs@3").

SERVICE

Bar-end shifters usually have a unitized construction. The only service is to soak in solvent, dry, and oil. If problems continue, replace the shifters.

STEM SHIFTERS

INSTALLATION

Stem shifters are installed on the vertical shaft of the stem. They should be mounted as close to the headset locknut as possible, unless this position causes the cable housings to deflect awkwardly around the headset. Lubricate bolt threads and torque bolt to 50in-lbs (12lbs@3").

SERVICE

Stem shifters can be disassembled, cleaned and oiled. There are no individual parts available, so nonfunctional levers should be replaced as a unit.

SHIFT-CONTROL-MECHANISM TROUBLESHOOTING

Cause	Solution
SPECIAL NOTE: *All shifting problems can easily be caused by other parts of the drive train. Always check derailleur, shifter, cable, chain, and gear compatibility before assuming the problem is with the shift-control mechanism. Check for cable-friction problems, derailleur wear, and chain wear, also.*	
SYMPTOM: *Shimano Rapidfire lever will not operate.*	
Inner wire was installed when lever was not fully released.	Remove inner wire and install when lever is fully released. Remove pod cover if necessary.
Internal mechanisms are dirty.	Remove pod and pod cover, soak in solvent, dry, and oil.
Parts have failed internally.	Replace pod after checking for first two causes.
SYMPTOM: *Grip Shift does not allow derailleur to align with cog after completing shift.*	
Inside of Grip Shift needs lubrication.	Disassemble Grip Shift, clean, and lubricate.
Grip Shift is worn out internally.	After eliminating other possible causes, replace shifter.
SYMPTOM: *Shimano rear derailleur operated by Grip Shift will not shift to outermost cog without hesitation when derailleur adjustments, shifter lubrication, and cable setup are all good.*	
Some models of Shimano derailleurs had too light a return spring to pull the cable through the Grip Shift even when everything was set up correctly.	An additional spring can be installed on the derailleur (see page 32-??), or a Grip Shift Bassworm can be added to the cable system.
SYMPTOM: *Shimano STI integrated shift/brake levers on road bike will not stay in a gear after shifting inward.*	
Internal part in shifter has failed.	Contact Shimano for warranty.
SYMPTOM: *Friction-type shift lever will not hold its position after completing the shift.*	
Tension/mounting screw needs to be tightened.	Tighten tension/mounting screw.
SYMPTOM: *Friction-type shift lever is sticky at loosest tension setting that will hold against derailleur return spring.*	
Friction washers need lubrication.	Drip oil in crevasses on both faces of lever drum, or disassemble shifter and lubricate faces directly.

Cause	*Solution*
SYMPTOM: *Friction-type shift lever will not hold its position after completing the shift, no matter how much the tension screw is tightened.*	
Friction washers that sandwich lever are worn out.	Replace washers, if parts available.
Slick-plastic friction washers that do not need lubrication have been oiled.	Disassemble lever, clean washers with alcohol, and re-install.
Tension/mounting screw is not screwing fully into braze-on because of interference in hole.	Put washers under head of tension/mounting screw.
SYMPTOM: *Braze-on-mounted down-tube friction lever keeps loosening up after proper friction tension has been achieved.*	
Flats in hole in outer friction washer are a loose fit to flats on braze-on stud.	Replace outer friction washer.
If washer is fresh, braze-on flats are under-sized or worn.	Deform washer to create tighter fit, or find shim stock to jam between washer and braze-on flats.
SYMPTOM: *Mounting screw will not start threading into braze-on when installing down-tube shifter on braze-on.*	
5 × .8mm mounting screw is being installed in braze-on with more rare 4.5mm thread type.	Replace screw with correct size, or install shifter that comes with correct screw.
Threads in braze-on are damaged.	Chase thread with correct tap (usually 5 × .8mm)
SYMPTOM: *Campagnolo/Sachs integrated brake/shift levers are difficult to operate when pressing on the release lever.*	
Levers are new and need to break in.	Make sure lever is clean and lubricated, and if so, allow adequate time for break-in.
Levers are dirty internally.	Disassemble, clean, and lubricate.

End view   Sheath cut away

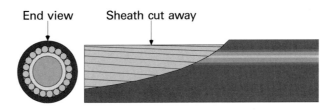

End view   Sheath cut away

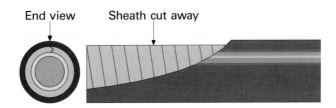

31 – DERAILLEUR-CABLE SYSTEMS

31 – DERAILLEUR-CABLE SYSTEMS

ABOUT THIS CHAPTER

This chapter is about setting up and servicing the cables that operate the derailleurs. It covers selection of the inner wire and housing, and the sizing and preparation of the housings. Attaching the inner wire to the shifter is covered in the **SHIFT-CONTROL MECHANISMS** chapter (page 30-1). Attaching the inner wires to the derailleurs and adjusting the tension on the inner wires is covered in the **REAR DERAILLEURS** (page 32-1) and **FRONT DERAILLEURS** (page 33-1) chapters.

GENERAL INFORMATION

TERMINOLOGY

Indexing-compatible: This term signifies that a component is suitable for use with an indexing derailleur system. Most modern derailleurs are indexing. This means that the shifter moves in distinct increments. When the shifter is moved from one position to the next, it is supposed to be just the right amount to move the derailleur from one gear to the next. The thickness of an inner wire determines how much inner wire will move as it wraps around the shifter drum. The friction and compression in the cable system have to be low and consistent for the indexing to work.

Cable: The term cable will be used to refer to the complete cable system, including the inner wire, housings, and fittings. The term *cable* is often used to refer to the inner wire as well. To avoid confusion, this book will always use *cable* to describe the whole system, and *inner wire* to describe the wire portion of the cable system.

Housing: The outer sheath that covers part of the inner wire. It is used to guide the inner wire around bends and to connect two points that move in relation to each other.

Compressionless housing: This housing type has stiff wires embedded in it, running along the housing length, that reduce compression. To identify this housing, look at the cut end. Many wire-ends will be seen.

Housing liner: A plastic sheath inside the housing that is used to reduce friction. These days, it is almost always fixed permanently in place.

Wound housing: This type of housing, more typically used on brakes, consists of a single coil wound from one end of the housing to the other. It is usually covered in a plastic sheath and usually has a liner inside. To identify it, look at the cut end. It will look like the end of a coil spring. If not sure after looking at the end, strip off the plastic sheath for a few millimeters at the end. Whether it is a single coil (wound), or multi-strand (compressionless), will become completely clear. Wound housing is not considered suitable for use on indexing derailleur systems.

Ferrule: The cap that fits on the end of the housing to improve fit to the housing stop.

Inner wire: The wire that is attached to the shifter, passes through housing on the way to the derailleur, and attaches to the derailleur. At times, it may just be called the *wire*.

Drawn wire: A type of inner wire that has been drawn through a die to change its shape. The process flattens the individual strands of the inner wire so that the surface of the inner wire is smoother.

Inner-wire head: The drum- or disc-shaped bead at the end of the inner wire. It fits in a socket in the shifter.

Housing stop: The socket-like fitting on the frame, shifter, or derailleur that is the point where the housing stops and the inner wire continues.

Adjusting barrel: An adjustable housing-stop that is threaded into the derailleur and/or shifter. An adjusting barrel is a screw with a socket on the end that the housing fits into. There is a small hole all the way through that the inner wire passes through.

Cable guide: An *inner-wire guide*, but the conventional term will be used here to avoid confusion. It is usually a plate of plastic with a groove or tunnel that guides a bare inner wire around a bend, such as the bottom of the bottom-bracket shell.

PREREQUISITES

Whenever cables are serviced or installed, derailleur adjustments must be done.

HOUSINGS

Housing for derailleur systems may be the compressionless variety, or the wound variety.

Compressionless housing

Compressionless housings are required for indexing systems, but are optional for friction systems. However, they improve performance of a friction system. Housing is compatible with a particular inner wire as long as the wire inserts comfortably into the housing. In 1995, Shimano made compressionless housing that was specifically for use with a 1.1mm inner wire. The 1.2mm wires are a tight fit in this housing. To use a 1.2mm inner wire on a bike with this housing, just replace the housing. All compressionless housing has a plastic liner inside.

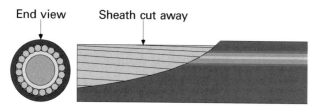

31.3 Compressionless housing.

Wound housing

Wound housings have a metal strip that is wound like a coil spring. These coils compress under load, which translates into lost motion at the shifter. Lost motion occurs when the shifter moves, but the derailleur does not respond. Most wound housing has a plastic liner inside to reduce friction, but some cheap varieties are exposed metal inside. The ones without a liner are not recommended for use with any derailleur system, indexing or friction.

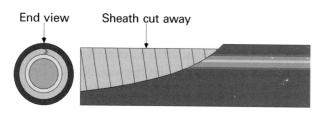

31.4 Wound housing.

The Shimano Dura-Ace indexing down-tube levers that use a 1.5mm inner wire require high-quality wound and lined housing for the loop at the rear derailleur.

SIZING HOUSING LOOPS

MTB-SHIFTER LOOPS

Normal routing

In normal routing, the loop from the right shifter goes by the right side of the head-tube/stem to a housing stop on the right side of the frame, and then the inner wire stays on the right side of the bike all the way to the rear derailleur. The left side is the same, except everything is on the left. On bikes with narrow handlebars (and particularly if the stem is short also) the normal routing may cause the housing to have a dramatic double-bend on its way from the shifter to the housing stop on the frame. If this is the case, consider crisscrossed routing.

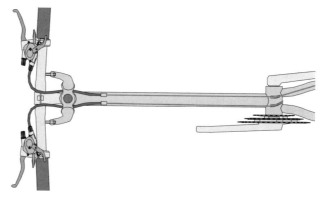

31.5 Normal routing, but crisscross routing would be more suitable on this bike.

Crisscrossed routing

Crisscrossed routing is used only when normal routing is a problem. Crisscrossed routing cannot be used on all frames, even when the normal routing is a problem. Any time using crisscrossed routing causes an inner wire to drag on a frame tube on its way from the housing stop to the cable guide, it is unacceptable.

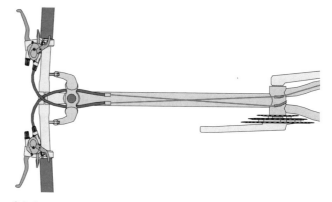

31.6 Crisscrossed routing.

Crisscrossed routing is done by routing the housing loop from the right shifter around the *left* side of the head-tube/stem to the housing stop on the *left* side of the frame. The inner wire is then routed back to the right side of the cable guide at the bottom-bracket shell. The left side is the reverse. The inner wires end up crossing each other between the top of the down tube and the bottom-bracket shell.

Sizing procedure

1. [ ] Slide piece of housing onto inner wire that comes out of shift-control mechanism.
2. [ ] Route housing to the housing stop on frame that will be used, making sure that loop does not have to deflect around any existing brake cables.
3. [ ] Rotate handlebars to limit (180° max.) to side that is opposite housing stop on frame that loop is being routed to.
4. [ ] Pull housing as it will go past the housing stop on the frame (without damaging housing), making sure housing remains inserted in housing stop on shift-control mechanism.

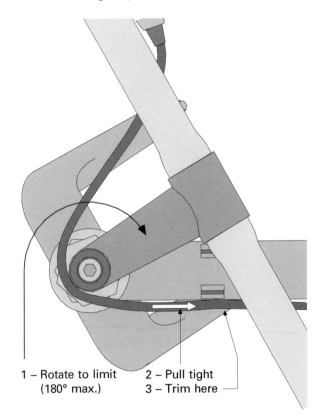

1 – Rotate to limit   2 – Pull tight
    (180° max.)   3 – Trim here

31.7 Sizing the housing loop from a bar-mounted shift control mechanism.

5. [ ] Mark housing at point that is even with closed end of housing stop on frame.
6. [ ] Remove housing from inner wire and cut housing at mark.

INTEGRAL SHIFT/BRAKE-LEVER LOOPS

Normal routing

In normal routing, the loop from the right shifter goes by the right side of the head-tube/stem to a housing stop on the right side of the frame, and then the inner wire stays on the right side of the bike all the way to the rear derailleur. The left side is the same, except everything is on the left.

Sizing procedure

1. [ ] Slide piece of housing onto inner wire that comes out of shift-control mechanism.
2. [ ] Route housing to housing stop on frame that will be used, making sure that loop does not have to deflect around any existing brake cables.
3. [ ] Rotate handlebars to limit (90° max.) to side that is opposite housing stop on frame that loop is being routed to.
4. [ ] Pull housing as it will go past the housing stop on the frame (without damaging housing), making sure housing remains inserted in housing stop on shift-control mechanism.

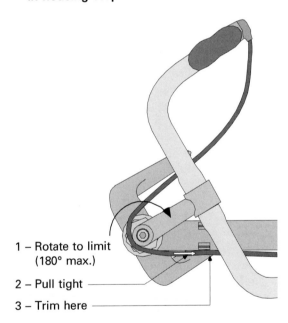

1 – Rotate to limit
    (180° max.)

2 – Pull tight

3 – Trim here

31.8 Sizing the housing loop from an integral shift/brake lever.

5. [ ] Mark housing at point that is even with closed end of housing stop on frame.
6. [ ] Remove housing from inner wire and cut housing at mark.

BAR-END-CONTROL LOOPS

Housing loops from bar-end controls on drop-style handlebars are run under the handlebar tape where the housing leaves the shifter. The housing comes out of the handlebar tape where the curve of the bar starts up toward the brake lever.

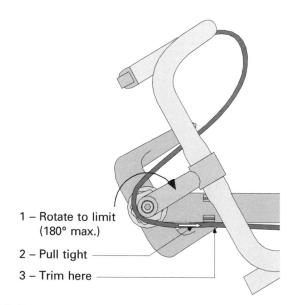

1 – Rotate to limit (180° max.)

2 – Pull tight

3 – Trim here

31.10 Sizing the housing loop from the handlebar to the frame.

6. [ ] Mark housing at point that is even with closed end of housing stop on frame.
7. [ ] Remove housing from inner wire and cut housing at mark.

STEM-SHIFTER LOOPS

1. [ ] Slide piece of housing onto inner wire that comes out of shift-control mechanism.
2. [ ] Route housing to the housing stop on the frame that will be used, making sure that loop does not have to deflect around any existing brake cables.
3. [ ] Rotate handlebars to limit (180° max.) to side that is opposite housing stop on frame that loop is being routed to.
4. [ ] Pull housing as it will go past the housing stop on the frame (without damaging housing), making sure housing remains inserted in housing stop on shift-control mechanism.
5. [ ] Mark housing at point that is even with closed end of housing stop on frame.
6. [ ] Remove housing from inner wire and cut housing at mark.

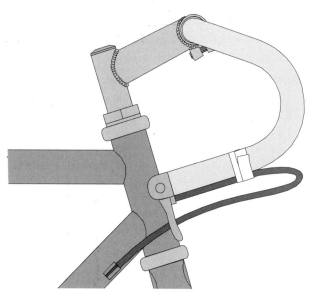

31.9 Routing of the housing loop from a bar-end control.

1. [ ] Slide piece of housing onto inner wire that comes out of shift-control mechanism.
2. [ ] Temporarily retain housing to handlebar only to point bar begins to curve upward, with adhesive tape or ties.
3. [ ] Route housing to housing stop on frame that will be used, making sure that loop does not have to deflect around any existing brake cables.
4. [ ] Rotate handlebars to limit (180° max.) to side that is opposite housing stop on frame that loop is being routed to.
5. [ ] Pull housing as it will go past the housing stop on the frame (without damaging housing), making sure housing remains inserted in housing stop on shift-control mechanism and does not pull out of tape or tie on handlebar.

REAR-DERAILLEUR LOOP

Sizing the cable-housing loop for the rear derailleur is a somewhat subjective process. Consistantly factories set this loop up too short, resulting in frequent kinking of the housing or housing ferrule where it comes out of the adjusting barrel. This factory setup leads to mechanics getting used to seeing *too short* as normal. Consequently, when setting the loop length up by the following rules, it is likely to look too long to an experienced mechanic.

The key to setting the length of the loop to the rear derailleur is to just focus on the entry of the housing into the cable-adjusting barrel. As the housing loop gets longer and shorter, the end of the housing in the adjusting barrel will twist up and down, and not come straight out of the adjusting barrel. When it is not twisted up or down, the length is correct.

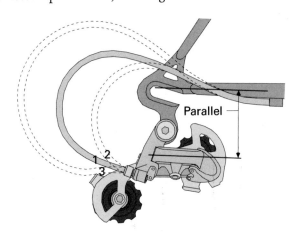

31.11 *Sizing the housing loop at the rear derailleur.*

1. [ ] **Install inner wire into housing piece, but do not route inner wire through housing stop on frame.**
2. [ ] **Install a ferrule on one end of housing piece, then insert that end into cable-adjusting barrel, with inner wire going into adjusting barrel, as well.**
3. [ ] **Hold other end of housing piece adjacent to housing stop on frame.**
4. [ ] **Position derailleur so parallelogram body is roughly parallel to line from axle to center of bottom bracket, or pointing *slightly* down.**
5. [ ] **Move housing back and forth at housing stop at frame and stop at point housing ferrule in adjusting barrel is not twisted up or down in adjusting-barrel socket.**
6. [ ] **Mark housing at point that is even with closed end of housing stop on frame.**
7. [ ] **Remove housing from inner wire and cut housing at mark.**

FRONT-DERAILLEUR LOOP

Most front derailleurs do not have housing going to the front derailleur. When they do, try to make the loop a simple curve without any abrupt bends or double bends at the points the housing enters a housing stop.

PREPARATION AND INSTALLATION OF THE CABLE SYSTEM

HOUSING-END FINISH

Compressionless housing

Compressionless housing should be cut with an *enclosing* style of cable cutter, such as the Shimano TL-CT10. Careful alignment and stabilization of the tool and housing will insure a relatively square cut. If cutting the housing makes it out-of-round, a gentle squeeze between the handles of the tool or pliers will make it round again.

The inner liner often gets closed when the housing is cut. A push pin or similar sharp object can be used to open up the liner again.

Unlike wound housing, *compressionless housing should never be filed or ground flat on the end!*

Wound housing

Wound housing is used much more on brake systems than it is on derailleurs. Discussion of the proper finishing of wound housings is covered in the ***BRAKE CABLE SYSTEMS*** chapter (page 35-9).

INSTALLING FERRULES

It is critical to use ferrules *anytime they will fit*. Fit a ferrule onto the housing and check if the ferrule will install into the housing stop or adjusting barrel. If it fits without jamming, it must be used.

Ferrules for compressionless housing

There are ferrules made for wound housing that will fit onto compressionless housing, but are not suitable. Compressionless-housing ferrules are specially reinforced at the closed end to resist corruption from the ends of the wires that are part of the compressionless housing. If the wrong ferrule is used, the housing wires will force themselves though the hole in the ferrule where the inner wire comes out. Pre-sized pieces of compressionless housing come with appropriate ferrules installed. Most packages of bulk compressionless-housing come with a supply of suitable ferrules. When purchasing separate ferrules that are suitable for use with compressionless housing, they are more likely to be described as fitting *Shimano SIS housing* than as fitting compressionless housing. In any case, to identify a compressionless-housing-compatible ferrule, look at the hole at the end where the inner wire comes out. If the material is obviously more than .5mm thick, the ferrule is compressionless-housing compatible.

Reusing ferrules

Factory ferrules that are on compressionless housing can be reused when installing new housing if there are no new compatible ferrules available.

1. [ ] Put old housing in vise about 1/2" from end of jaws, with end of ferrule sticking up above vise about 3/4".
2. [ ] Gently grasp housing with needle-nose pliers just below ferrule.
3. [ ] Lever pliers down against vise to lift ferrule off end of housing.
4. [ ] Place ferrule(s) on new housing.
5. [ ] Insert old derailleur inner wire through a ferrule until inner-wire head is against ferrule.
6. [ ] Use cable fourth-hand tool to draw inner wire through housing, simultaneously pressing both ferrules onto housing.

Crimping ferrules onto housing

Ferrules come from the factory crimped onto the housing so that they won't get lost in transit. Once a cable is installed on a bike, there is no advantage to having the ferrules crimped on. Crimping is a waste of time, and it complicates reusing ferrules. Crimping on ferrules is not recommended.

LUBRICATION

Any housing used for derailleur systems should be lined with a plastic sheath. Performance will always be improved by dripping or spraying oil into the housing before installing the cable system. Oil will reduce the friction caused by dirt that gets into the housing, and will reduce the tendency for the inner wire to rust. Grease should not be used because it can congeal when it gets cold or old, which will lower the performance of the cable system.

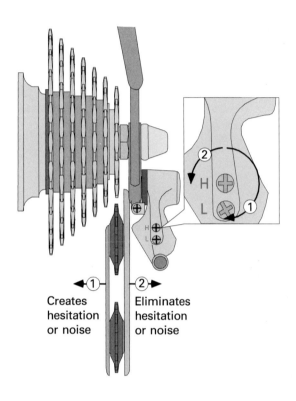

Creates
hesitation
or noise

Eliminates
hesitation
or noise

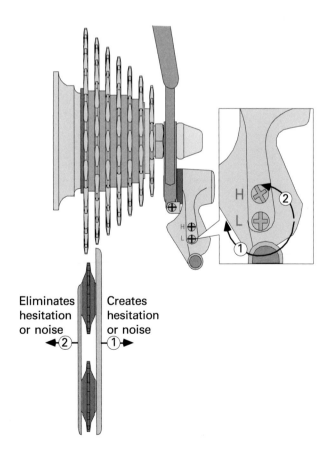

Eliminates
hesitation
or noise

Creates
hesitation
or noise

32 – REAR DERAILLEURS

32 – REAR DERAILLEURS

ABOUT THIS CHAPTER

This chapter is about installing, adjusting, and servicing rear derailleurs. The procedures for installation and adjustment make references to installing the wheel, chain, shift-control mechanism, and cable. These items are fully covered separately in preceding chapters. This chapter also covers repair of derailleur-hanger threads.

The procedure assumes that the front derailleur is installed. The front derailleur need not be precisely adjusted, but must be capable of moving the chain to the innermost and outermost chainrings. It may seem like a good idea to install and adjust the front derailleur first, because of this. However, the front-derailleur procedure requires that the rear derailleur be able to shift the chain to the innermost and outermost positions, as well. Whichever is done first, to complete one derailleur adjustment it may be necessary to do some preliminary work on the other derailleur, as well.

There is some confusing and contradictory terminology used in regard to derailleurs, so be sure to become acquainted with the following terminology section to become clear on the terms used in *this* book.

GENERAL INFORMATION

TERMINOLOGY

High gear: With regard to rear derailleurs, high gear typically means the rear cog with the fewest number of teeth. It is called high gear because it results in the highest number when calculating gear ratios. It is confusing because the cog with the greatest number of teeth sticks up higher, and more teeth may seem to some to be "higher." For this reason, this book will always use the more wordy alternative, *outermost gear*, or a letter code that is described in the following section **NAMING COGS AND GEAR COMBINATIONS** (page 32-3).

Top gear: Same as *high gear*.

First gear (or first position): Called *first gear* because it is the first one counted when counting cogs on the freewheel/freehub, this term is avoided because the innermost cog provides the lowest gear ratio, which might also be called *first gear*.

Outermost gear: The cog on the rear wheel that has the fewest teeth and is closest to the dropout. This term will be used instead of *high gear*, *top gear*, or *first gear*, or a letter code (described in the following section **NAMING COGS AND GEAR COMBINATIONS**, page 32-3) will be used.

Low gear: With regard to rear derailleurs, low gear typically means the rear cog with the greatest number of teeth. It is called low gear because it results in the lowest number when calculating gear ratios. It is confusing because the cog with the fewest number of teeth sticks up the least, and fewer teeth may seem to some to be "lower." For this reason, this book will always use the more wordy alternative, *innermost gear*, or a letter code (described in the following section **NAMING COGS AND GEAR COMBINATIONS**, page 32-3) will be used.

Bottom gear: Same as *low gear*.

Last gear (or last position): A gear is called *last gear* because it is the last one counted when counting cogs on the freewheel/freehub, this term is avoided because the outermost cog provides the highest gear ratio, which might also be called *last gear*.

Innermost gear: The cog on the rear wheel that has the most teeth and is closest to the spokes. This term will be used instead of *low gear*, *bottom gear*, or *last gear*, or a letter code (described in the section **NAMING COGS AND GEAR COMBINATIONS**, page 32-3) will be used.

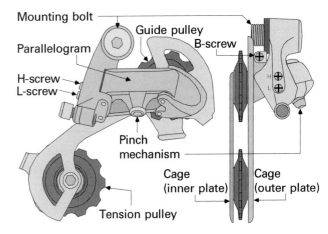

32.1 This side view and back view show the major parts of the rear derailleur.

Limit screw: Adjustable stops that are used to stop the inward and outward motion of the derailleur at points that enable the chain the shift to the innermost and outermost cogs without going too far.

H-screw: A limit screw for stopping the derailleur from shifting the chain out past the outermost cog.

L-Screw: A limit screw for stopping the derailleur from shifting the chain in past the innermost cog.

B-Screw: A screw used to adjust the spring tension on the mounting pivot, which affects the distance between the cogs and the guide pulley.

Pulley wheel: A toothed wheel in the derailleur cage that the chain runs on.

Jockey wheel: An alternate name for a pulley wheel, generally the upper one. Guide pulley will be used instead.

Guide pulley: The upper pulley wheel in the derailleur cage that guides the chain from one cog to the next.

Tension pulley: The lower pulley wheel in the derailleur cage that pulls back on the lower section of chain to keep it under tension.

Derailleur cage: The assembly at the bottom of the derailleur that encloses the chain, consisting of two plates and two toothed wheels called pulley wheels.

Outer plate: The plate in the derailleur cage that is outward of the pulley wheels.

Inner plate: The plate in the derailleur cage that is inward of the pulley wheels.

Parallelogram: With regard to the rear derailleur, this is the part of the body between the mounting pivot and the cage pivot (consisting of two arms on four pivots) that actuates to move the derailleur cage inward and outward.

Adjusting barrel: A hollow screw in the derailleur that the inner wire passes through and the housing stops against. As the adjusting barrel is screwed in and out, the relative length or tension of the cable system is changed.

Pinch mechanism: The mechanism that attaches the inner wire to the derailleur. The inner wire is usually routed through a groove in a plate on the derailleur, and a bolt or nut presses a washer or plate on top of the inner wire to trap and compress it in the groove. The groove in the plate is often hidden by the pressure washer/plate.

Indexing: This describes a type of shifting in which the shift mechanism moves in distinct increments. These increments are designed to be just the right amount to get the chain to move precisely from one gear to the next. Indexing has virtually replaced friction shifting. In friction shifting, the lever moves smoothly over its full range of motion without any incremented stops. It is up to the operator to decide what the correct amount of lever motion is to get from one gear to the next.

Derailleur hanger: The plate that the derailleur attaches to. Sometimes it is integral to the right rear dropout. Sometimes the right rear dropout is a two-piece constructions so that the hanger can be replaced. On the most inexpensive bikes, the derailleur hanger is the plate that mounts between the dropout and the wheel-retention mechanism.

Stop tab: The tab near the bottom of the derailleur hanger that stops the forward rotation of the derailleur.

Mounting bolt: The bolt through the topmost part of the derailleur that attaches the derailleur to the derailleur hanger.

Mounting pivot: The derailleur pivots around the mounting bolt at the mounting pivot. This pivoting allows the derailleur to change position to accommodate changes in gear size as the derailleur moves in and out. This pivot also allows the derailleur to be rotated back to allow rear-wheel removal.

Return spring: When the tension on the inner wire is released, this spring inside the parallelogram causes the derailleur to move out as far as the outer-limit screw will allow.

Cage pivot: The pivot that the derailleur cage rotates about. The cage rotates so that the tension pulley can move forward or backward. This keeps the chain taught when its effective length changes as it is moved to gears of different sizes.

Cage stop screw (or pin): A screw (or pin) in the outer cage plate that bumps into the cage pivot housing to keep the cage pivot spring from completely unwinding when the chain is not in the derailleur.

Over-shift: When the chain moves too far, and does not align with the intended cog.

Under-shift: When the chain does not move far enough, and does not align with the intended cog.

In-shift: Any shift to a cog that is more inward than the one that the chain is currently on.

Out-shift: Any shift to a cog that is more outward than the one that the chain is currently on.

Up-shift: This term will not be used because there are two opposite ways that it could be understood. On a rear cogset, an up-shift could be an in-shift because the chain is moving up onto a cog of larger diameter. An out-shift could also be called an up-shift because the chain is being moved to a cog that will create a higher gear ratio. The terms in-shift and out-shift will be used to avoid this confusion.

Down-shift: This term will not be used because there are two opposite ways that it could be understood. On a rear cogset, a down-shift could be an out-shift because the chain is moving down onto a cog of smaller diameter. An in-shift could also be called an down-shift because the chain is being moved to a cog that will create a lower gear ratio. The terms in-shift and out-shift will be used to avoid this confusion.

NAMING COGS AND GEAR COMBINATIONS

To perform certain adjustments, the chain needs to be in certain gear combinations. Numbering the gears to identify them does not work because rear cogsets have from 5 to 8 gears (so the innermost could be called 5, 6, 7, or 8), and cranksets have from 1 to 3 chain rings (so the innermost might be called 1, 2, or 3).

To avoid confusion, gears will be assigned codes as shown in figures 32.2 and 32.3 below.

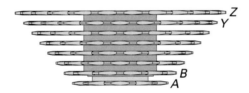

32.2 *"A" is always the outermost cog. "B" is always the next-to-outermost cog. "Y" is always the next-to-innermost cog. "Z" is always the innermost cog.*

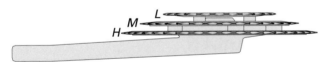

32.3 *"H" is always the outermost chainring. "M" is always the middle chainring of a triple. "L" is always the innermost chainring.*

Using the above diagrams, it should be easy to conclude that putting the chain in a gear combination of *A/M* would place the chain in the outermost position in the rear, and the middle position of a triple crank. *Y/L* would mean the chain was in the next-to-innermost position in the rear and the innermost in the front.

PREREQUISITES

Rear wheel installation

Part of a complete derailleur set-up is to align the derailleur hanger. The wheel must be installed in precise alignment to perform the derailleur-hanger alignment.

Shifter and cable installation

To adjust the rear derailleur, the shift-control mechanism and the cable system must be installed.

Chain sizing

Rear-derailleur performance is influenced by chain length. It is necessary to size the chain to optimized shift performance and to prevent derailleur damage.

INDICATIONS

Maintenance

Dirt accumulation and wear both affect derailleur performance.

The obvious dirt on the pulley wheels is a factor, but dirt hidden inside the mounting pivot and cage pivot can drastically influence shift performance. For this reason, normal maintenance of a rear derailleur should include disassembling and cleaning the entire derailleur.

Wear is a factor in the parallelogram pivots, the mounting pivot, and the cage pivot, but the most critical wear factor is a worn-out guide pulley. A normal part of derailleur service would be to replace the guide pulley. When the pivots are worn out, the derailleur must be replaced.

Changing freewheel/freehub cogset

Any time a freewheel or freehub cogset is replaced with anything other than an identical replacement, it is necessary to adjust the rear derailleur.

Replacing rear wheel

Any time a rear wheel is replaced with anything other than an identical replacement, it is necessary to adjust the rear derailleur.

Aligning rear dropouts

After aligning the rear dropouts, the derailleur-hanger alignment may have changed, which affects derailleur position and adjustment. Check and align the rear-derailleur hanger and adjust the derailleur.

Bent derailleur hanger

When bikes fall over on the right side, or when the derailleur is shifted past the Z cog and into the spokes, the derailleur hanger is likely to be significantly bent. This requires hanger alignment and derailleur adjustment.

Changing chain

Whenever a chain is changed, even if replacing a worn chain with an identical replacement, shift performance is affected. Fresh chains have less lateral flexibility than worn chains. Different chains have different performance characteristics. After replacing a chain, the derailleur adjustments should be checked.

Symptoms indicating adjustment is needed

There are a number of symptoms indicating a probable need for derailleur adjustment.

If the derailleur under-shifts or over-shifts when shifting to the A cog, or the chain makes excessive noise while on the A cog, the rear-derailleur H-screw may need adjustment.

If the derailleur under-shifts or over-shifts when shifting to the Z cog, or the chain makes excessive noise while on the Z cog, the rear-derailleur L-screw may need adjustment.

If any in-shift or out-shift to any cog between A and Z is hesitant, or results in excessive chain noise after the shift is completed, it indicates that the indexing needs adjustment.

If the shift performance is poor in several outer cogs but good in all the inner cogs, it may indicate that the B-screw or chain length need adjustment.

Symptoms indicating derailleur service is needed

There are several symptoms indicating that the derailleur should be cleaned or the guide pulley should be replaced.

Any time normal adjustments do not create acceptable shifting and all the components are known to be compatible, assume that disassembling and cleaning is needed and the guide pulley may need replacement.

When the derailleur body remains cocked back when shifting from the innermost cog out to the outermost cog, it is a good indication that the mounting pivot and cage pivot are fouled with dirt.

When the derailleur is obviously congested with dirt and gummed up, it should be disassembled and cleaned.

Symptoms indicating derailleur replacement is needed

The primary reason that derailleurs must be replaced is because they get bent. Other than adjusting barrels, pinch mechanisms, and pulley wheels, most parts are either unavailable or too costly to replace.

The most likely part of a rear derailleur to get bent is the cage. The symptom of a bent cage is that the two pulley wheels no longer share a common plane. When sighting through the central plane of one pulley wheel towards the other, the further wheel should be hidden by the closer wheel. If not, the cage is probably bent. Although it is possible to improve this condition, it is difficult to eliminate it.

It is also possible that the parallelogram arms might be bent. It may be possible to see a twist along the length of the arm, or it may appear that the plate on the back of the mounting pivot is not parallel with the portion of the outer cage plate where it mounts to the cage pivot.

After a catastrophic shift of the derailleur into the spokes or spoke guard, it is possible that either the plate on the backside of the mounting pivot, or a tab on the mounting-pivot housing may be damaged. If the plate is bent, it can often be bent back. If the tab on the mounting-pivot housing is sheared off, the derailleur needs to be replaced.

The mounting pivot, cage pivot, and parallelogram pivots may all wear out to the point that shift performance is compromised. There is no way to quantify this wear, or point to a specific symptom that proves any of these pivots are significantly worn. When everything else is fine, but shift performance remains poor, consider these points for wear. Check the wear by jerking the bottom of the derailleur cage in and out and noting the amount of free play that is evident. Compare this to a new derailleur of similar brand and quality. If there is an obvious difference, then pivot wear may be the factor that is affecting shift performance.

TOOL CHOICES

Table 32-1 (page 32-5) shows most of the tools available for rear-derailleur adjustment. Preferred choices are shown in **bold** type. Choices are preferred because of a combination among: ease of use, versatility, durability, and economy. If more than one choice of a particular tool type is **bold**, it indicates that either different tools are needed to work on equipment with different configurations, or that several tools are equally preferred.

TIME AND DIFFICULTY

Rear-derailleur adjustment, including hanger alignment and cable-system setup, is a 12–16 minute job of moderate difficulty. Rear-derailleur removal, disassembling, cleaning, installation, and adjustment is a 30–35 minute job of moderate difficulty.

COMPLICATIONS

Component compatibility problems

See the following section, **COMPONENT COMPATIBILITY**, for the numerous complications that exist.

Damaged derailleur

Bent derailleurs are somewhat common, but not always obvious. It is not unusual to spend time adjusting the derailleur, only to find that it will never work well due to damage.

Damaged hanger

Derailleur-hanger damage can be very minor, or severe. Minor damage consists of slight bends or damaged threads. Slight bends can be aligned and damaged threads can be repaired or replaced. Major bends may require replacement of the dropout by a frame builder.

The recommended procedure starts all derailleur adjustments with a derailleur-hanger check. This eliminates the problem of getting most of the way through an adjustment procedure, only to find the hanger needs alignment and the adjustments will need to be redone.

Worn components other than derailleur

Worn chains, rear cogs, cables, and shift controls can all affect derailleur adjustment. It is usually not until the attempt to adjust the derailleur fails that these other factors will get considered, resulting in duplication of effort to adjust the derailleur.

Derailleur wear

Derailleur wear can be difficult to detect. The guide pulley is the most likely part to wear out, but removal is required to tell if the bearing is worn. The derailleur-mounting pivot, cage pivot, and parallelogram pivot can all be worn out without any clear evidence, but with a significant effect on the performance of the rear derailleur.

Dirty drive train

Dirt in the derailleur cage, pulley wheels, chain, cable system, shift-control mechanism, and rear cogs can affect shift performance. Adjusting a derailleur (particularly an indexing one) without cleaning all the related components has very limited potential for success.

COMPONENT COMPATIBILITY

As a rule, it is always best to follow manufacturer's recommendations when selecting components. If not following the manufacturer's recomendations, when non-compatible components are used together, it should show up as a shifting problem. Not all prob-

REAR-DERAILLEUR TOOLS (table 32-1)

Tool	Fits and considerations
HANGER ALIGNMENT	
Campagnolo R	Sloppy pivot, not compatible with many wheel sizes
Park DAG-1	Low-play pivot, easy to use and to measure errors, fits all wheel sizes
Shimano TL-RD10	Expensive, complicated, sloppy pivot, allows hanger alignment without wheel in place in very limited circumstances
VAR 139	Even easier to use than Park DAG-1, but lacks Park's precision pivot
Wheels Mfg. GHT	Sloppy pivot, not compatible with many wheel sizes
FOURTH-HAND (CABLE-TENSION) TOOLS (These tools are same as used for front derailleurs and brakes.)	
Dia-Compe 556	Tends to let inner wire jam in tool
Hozan C356	Tends to let inner wire jam in tool
Lifu 0100	Consumer tool
Park BT-2	Least tendency for inner wire to jam in tool
VAR 233	Tends to let inner wire jam in tool

lems are immediately obvious. If using non-matched components, do not assume that there are no compatibility problems until the indexing performance has been tested. There is a section in this chapter following the derailleur adjustment section about testing indexing performance (page 32-21).

Derailleur and hanger

These days, most derailleur hangers are of a relatively-uniform design. The variations that are exist are in the thread type, the hanger length, and the angle of the stop tab on the hanger.

Almost all derailleur hangers have a 10 × 1mm thread, except Campagnolo dropouts, which have a 10mm × 26tpi thread. Fortunately, these two threads are a class B (acceptable) fit, in most cases. The problem comes if installing an aluminum mounting bolt into an aluminum hanger. The best solution is to always run a 10 × 1mm tap through the hanger before installing a derailleur or hanger-alignment tool. This will clean the threads if they already match, or convert a 10mm × 26tpi thread to the more common type.

Derailleur hangers differ in how far below the axle they position the mounting bolt of the derailleur. This affects two things: 1) The maximum-cog-size capacity of the derailleur (how large a rear cog can be accommodated). If the hanger is longer than normal, the derailleur may work with a larger cog size than it is rated for. If the hanger is shorter than normal, the derailleur may not work with the largest cog size that it is rated for. 2) The other problem created by hanger length is how it affects shift performance when it is longer than normal. An extra-long hanger will move the guide pulley further from the cogs (particularly outer ones). This means greater lateral motion of the derailleur is required for shifting, and can mean that an indexing derailleur will not perform adequately. A normal range of hanger length is approximately 24–30mm (axle-center to mounting-hole-center). Deviations from this norm are most often found on frames with aluminum dropouts.

Also, deviations in the angle of the hanger stop tab affect the distance from the guide pulley to the cogs. On many derailleurs, there is a body-angle-adjustment screw (B-screw) that compensates for these deviations. On some unorthodox dropouts, the angle of the stop tab may be beyond the capacity of the B-screw to compensate for. A normal range for this angle (measured from the vertical line through the center of the mounting hole) is 25°–35°, with larger values good for shorter hanger lengths, and smaller values good

for longer hanger lengths. Filing the stop tab can compensate for angles above 35°. Use of a longer B-screw may compensate for angles below 25°.

Derailleur and shift-control mechanism

With indexing systems, compatibility between the shift-control mechanism and derailleur is critical. This is because an indexing shifter will pull a specific amount of cable for each click. The derailleur must move in or out the right amount to line up with the next cog. If the amount of cable that is moved is wrong, then the derailleur will move the wrong amount.

The shift-control mechanism and derailleur should be brand-matched whenever possible. At the time of this writing, the only exceptions to this are a few aftermarket shift-control mechanisms that are made specifically for a different brand of derailleur, such as Grip Shift or Sachs controls made for Shimano derailleurs.

Even with brand-matching, there may be problems. Shimano Dura-Ace shift controls and derailleurs are not compatible with other models of Shimano equipment. A customer's 7-speed system may not be upgraded to 8-speed just by changing the shifter and the cogs. An 8-speed-compatible derailleur may be needed, as well.

Derailleur and cogset

In addition to being compatible with the shifter, the derailleur must be compatible with the cogset. For proper index perfromance, ideally the cogset should be a brand match with the derailleur. In addition, the derailleur needs to be suitable to the number of cogs in the cogset. In particular, 8-speed cogsets require derailleurs that have 8-speed capacity.

Inner wire and shift-control mechanism

The inner wire must be compatible with the shift-control mechanism because it is the combination of the shifter-drum diameter *and* the inner-wire thickness that determines how much cable is moved for a given amount of lever motion. See the **SHIFT-CONTROL MECHANISMS** chapter (page 30-2) for more information of shifter and inner-wire compatibility.

Maximum cog size

Every derailleur is rated for a maximum cog size. This number reflects the largest size cog that the derailleur can shift onto without jamming. The manufacturer's rating is based on an assumed derailleur-hanger length. If the actual hanger is longer than the assumed length, the derailleur may work on a cog that is a few teeth larger than the rating. If the actual hanger length is shorter than the assumed length, then the derailleur may not even work on a cog that is equal to the maximum-rated cog size.

Ratings for derailleurs can be determined in several ways.

Manufacturer's literature: There is often an instruction sheet that comes with a new derailleur. This instruction sheet normally includes the ratings for the derailleur. In addition, some manufacturers can supply literature on request.

Sutherland's Handbook for Bicycle Mechanics: This book includes ratings for a wide variety of derailleur models, but is up-to-date for only a brief time after the date of publication. It is particularly useful if trying to figure out the capacity of an older-model derailleur that is currently on a bike.

Bike'alog: This computerized source reference for bicycle parts has capacity information for currently-available derailleur models.

Test method: To test if a derailleur's maximum-cog-size capacity is being exceeded, follow this procedure: Install the derailleur and size the chain normally. Shift the chain to the *L* chainring, then the *Z* cog. If the chain will not shift to *Z* (and the limit screw is loose enough), then maximum cog size has been exceeded. If the shift is completed, then tighten the B-screw (if any) all the way in. Backpedal and push up on the cage pivot housing. If the guide pulley moves closer to the *Z* cog, maximum cog size has not been exceeded.

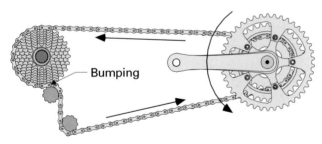

32.4 If the chain length is correct and the B-screw is as tight as possible, this symptom indicates the maximum freewheel size of the derailleur has been exceeded.

Maximum total capacity

Every derailleur is rated for maximum total capacity. This number shows the derailleur's capacity to pull up slack chain when in the *A/L* position. The number (36T, for example) indicates the maximum sum for the rear-cog tooth differential added to the front-gear tooth differential. For example, a 12–30 cogset has a differen-

tial of 18 teeth. If the chainring set was 26–36–46, its differential would be 20 teeth. The sum of these differentials would be 38T. A derailleur rated 36T would not be able to pull up all the chain slack if used on a bike with these gears.

Ratings for derailleurs can be determined in several ways.

Manufacturer's literature: There is often an instruction sheet that comes with a new derailleur. This instruction sheet normally includes the ratings for the derailleur. In addition, some manufacturers can supply literature on request.

Sutherland's Handbook for Bicycle Mechanics: This book includes ratings for a wide variety of derailleur models, but is up-to-date for only a brief time after the date of publication. It is particularly useful if trying to figure out the capacity of an older-model derailleur that is currently on a bike.

Bike'alog: This computerized source reference for bicycle parts has capacity information for currently-available derailleur models.

Test method: To test if a derailleur's maximum total capacity is being exceeded, follow this procedure: Install the derailleur and size the chain at the shortest length that will allow the chain to keep a double bend through the derailleur cage when the chain is in the *Z/H* position. Shift the chain to the *A/L* position. Check if the chain hangs slack at the bottom or touches itself or the derailleur cage an extra time on its way from the tension pulley to the chainring.

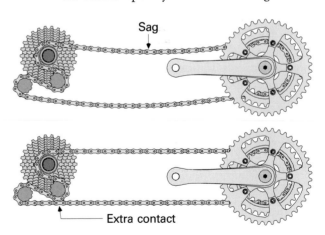

32.5 These symptoms indicate the maximum capacity has been exceeded if the chain is not too long.

Derailleur and first-cog position

The surface that the derailleur mounts to must be in a specified range of distance from the face of the *A* cog. If not, then indexing problems will be experienced. This relationship is a function of the thickness of the dropout/hanger and the right-side axle spacing. It can be adjusted by adding or subtracting spacers from the right side of the axle. In general, the shorter this dimension is, the better. The only limit is when the chain interferes with the frame or dropout when on the *A* cog, or when shifting between the *A* cog and the *B* cog. A typical distance from the face of the derailleur hanger to the face of the *A* cog is 11–14mm.

Derailleur and chain

Indexed derailleurs moved in fixed amounts. The chain must respond as expected for the shift to be completed. If the chain has more lateral flexibility than expected, then when the derailleur moves its fixed amount, the chain will not respond enough to complete the shift. Chains vary in lateral flexibility because of brand differences and wear. If manufacturer's recommendations are not adhered to, shift performance may be compromised.

Chain and cogs

The width of a chain must be suitable to the freewheel/freehub cogset or it may rub against adjacent cogs. See the **CHAINS** chapter (page 26-2).

The shaping of the side plates of the chain affects the chains ability to engage the cog teeth. When not using the manufacturer's recommended chain, shift performance may be compromised.

UNDERSTANDING HOW REAR DERAILLEURS WORK

The operation of a rear derailleur is relatively complex. By understanding what is happening in a rear derailleur, the sense of the procedures will become more apparent, and what to do when problems arise will be clearer.

How the cable moves the derailleur in and out

When the shift-control mechanism is operated in a way that pulls on the inner wire, the inner wire moves through the pieces of housing. This extra wire has to come from somewhere. That "somewhere" is the piece of exposed inner wire between the adjusting barrel and the pinch mechanism on the derailleur.

This piece of exposed wire is routed diagonally across the derailleur parallelogram. When the wire is pulled, the distance across the parallelogram is shortened, which deflects the lower end of the parallelogram inward. Figure 32.6 below shows this in a simplified form.

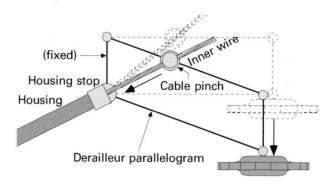

32.6 *When the inner wire is pulled through the housing, it shortens the distance from the housing stop to the pinch mechanism, which changes the distance from one end of the parallelogram to the other. This tanslates into lateral motion of the derailleur cage.*

When the tension on the cable is released, a spring in the parallelogram causes it to return in the direction of its starting point.

How limit screws work

The two limit screws are like two adjustable barricades. There is usually some projection or surface on a parallelogram arm that the limit screw butts up against. By adjusting one limit screw, the limit of the range of travel for the parallelogram in *one* direction will be altered. By loosening the H-screw, the barricade that stops the outward motion of the parallelogram is moved further out, so the parallelogram may move further out. By loosening the L-screw, the barricade that stops the inward motion of the parallelogram is moved further inward.

Changing the H-screw setting only changes the shift to the outermost cog. Changing the L-screw setting only changes the shift to the innermost cog. Figures 32.7 and 32.8 (page 32-9) shows a simplified and exaggerated model of how limit screws affect the range of motion of the parallelogram.

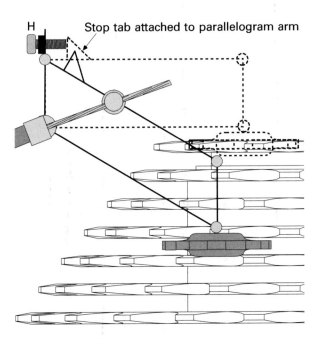

32.7 *When the derailleur moves outward, a stop fixed on one of the parallelogram arms bumps into the end of the H-screw to stop the derailleur's motion.*

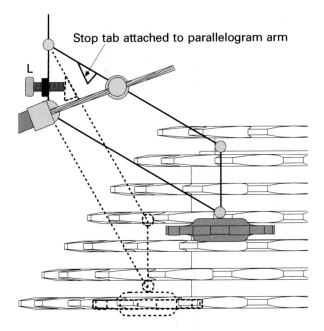

32.8 *When the derailleur moves inward, a stop fixed on one of the parallelogram arms bumps into the end of the L-screw to stop the derailleur's motion.*

Why and how the guide pulley tracks close below the cogs

One of the most important factors in shift performance is the distance from the guide pulley to the bottom of the cogs. Between the guide pulley and the cog, there is an unsupported section of chain. When the distance between the guide pulley and cog is short, it takes less lateral motion of the guide pulley to deflect the chain and get it to derail from one cog and engage another. For example: if 6mm of lateral motion of the guide pulley caused a 20° chain deflection when the length of unsupported chain was one link, then it might take 8mm of lateral motion of the guide pulley to cause a 20° chain deflection when the unsupported chain length was two links long. Consequently, for good index-shifting performance, the distance of the guide pulley from the cogs must be kept short and consistent.

This is done by a complex set of mechanical processes.

The simplest to understand is that the parallelogram is slanted. This is done so that the end of the parallelogram will move down as it moves inward towards the bottom of the larger cogs.

On most derailleurs, the center of the guide pulley is offset from the center of the cage pivot. The result of this is that as the cage rotates to take up more or less slack chain, the center of the guide pulley rotates around the cage pivot and changes its position relative to the cogs. It is this offset of the guide pulley to the cage pivot that makes chain length so important to shift performance.

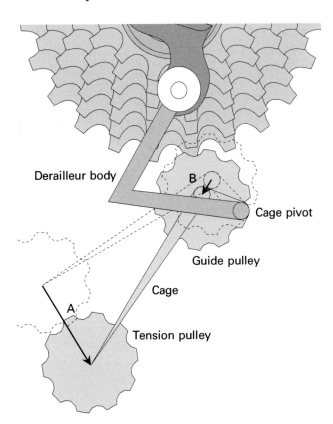

32.9 *If the chain is shortened a link or two, the tension pulley moves (A) and the pivoting cage moves the guide pulley away from the cogs (B).*

The last thing that affects guide-pulley position is the balance of the opposing springs in the mounting pivot and the cage pivot. One spring tends to move the guide pulley down, and the other moves it up. The mounting-pivot spring tension is adjustable by adjusting the B-screw. The cage-pivot spring tension is adjustable by disassembling the rear derailleur and moving the spring to a different mounting hole in the derailleur-cage plate. Consider this example: when the chain is shifted to the larger chainring, it pulls the bottom of the derailleur cage forward, which moves the guide pulley down. This counterclockwise cage rotation also increase the tension on the cage-pivot spring, which counterbalances the mounting-pivot spring more, and causes the derailleur body to rotate counterclockwise, moving the guide pulley back up.

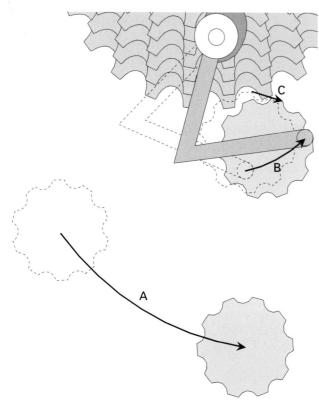

32.10 When the chain is shifted to a larger chainring, the tension pulley moves (A), this moves the cage pivot counterclockwise (B). Due to the offset between the guide pulley and the cage pivot, the guide pulley moves less (C) than the cage-pivot moved.

ABOUT THE REST OF THIS CHAPTER

The rest of this chapter is divided into seven parts. The sections are:

INSTALLATION AND ADJUSTMENT

TESTING INDEX PERFORMANCE
REAR DERAILLEUR SERVICE
DERAILLEUR-HANGER THREAD REPAIR
REAR-DERAILLEUR TROUBLESHOOTING
SHIMANO RAPID-RISE DERAILLEURS
EIGHT -AND NINE-SPEED COMPATIBILITY

INSTALLATION AND ADJUSTMENT

INSTALLATION

NOTE: before proceeding further, be sure to be acquainted with the section, NAMING COGS AND GEAR COMBINATIONS (page 32-3).

Compatibility checks

1. [ ] Check reference information to determine that derailleur and shift-control mechanism are compatible.
2. [ ] Check reference information to determine that inner wire, housing, and shift-control mechanism are compatible.
3. [ ] Check reference information to determine that shift-control mechanism is compatible with brand of cogset and number of cogs.
4. [ ] Check reference information to determine if chain is compatible with cogset.
5. [ ] Check that face of *A* cog is no more than 14mm from face of derailleur hanger.

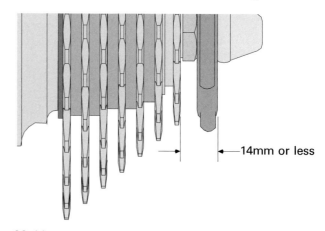

14mm or less

32.11 Measuring hanger face to A cog face.

Hanger alignment

The derailleur hanger is aligned to the plane of the rear wheel. For this to work well, the wheel should be correctly dished, reasonably true, and in the frame in good alignment. See the **WHEEL REMOVAL, REPLACEMENT, AND INSTALLATION** chapter (page 18-17) about installing wheels. To measure whether the wheel is centered between a pair of stays, butt the end of the caliper up against a stay and extend the depth gauge to the rim. Get a similar reading from the opposite side, making sure the caliper is aligned in the same way and touches the rim at the equivalent point. If the readings are 1mm or less different, the wheel is well centered. If not, try re-aligning it by moving the axle slightly in the slots. The length of the slot allows adjustment in one direction, and the fact that the slot is wider than the axle allows some limited adjustment in the other direction. Lack of precision in the rear triangle may make it impossible to achieve the desired tolerance, in which case the wheel should be left as close as possible to centered.

6. [ ] **Install correctly dished and trued rear wheel, so that there is ≤1mm centering error to seat stays and chain stays.**

When aligning the hanger, measurements will be taken at the 12:00, 3:00, 6:00, and 9:00 positions on the rim. If the bike is tipped at the wrong angle, then the chain stay may interfere with getting the tool to the 3:00 position, or the seat stay may interfere with getting the tool to the 12:00 position. If the bike is positioned with the chain stay parallel to the ground or sloping slightly up to the front, then the tool will access all the points easily.

7. [ ] **Put bike in position that puts chain stay parallel to ground or sloping up to front slightly.**

NOTE: Some bikes have replaceable derailleur hangers that are brittle and prone to failure while being aligned. Do not align replaceable hangers unless a replacement is at hand.

8. [ ] **Thread Park DAG-1 into hanger.**

The Park DAG-1 can be adjusted to reduce play at the mounting-bolt pivot. This is done by means of tightening a small set screw in the portion of the tool that houses the mounting bolt. Reducing this play is critical to the accuracy of the tool, so do not skip the following step.

9. [ ] **Check for excess play in tool pivot and adjust out play with set screw, if necessary.**

To reduce the significance of true errors, the rim will be rotated to the same four points as the tool, so that the reading is always being done to the same point on the rim. If the tire is installed, the valve stem makes a great rim reference point (RRP). If not, then put a piece of tape of the rim to make a RRP.

10. [ ] **Put a piece of tape or a mark on rim for a rim reference point (RRP), or use valve stem.**

Horizontal error is determined by measuring at the 9:00 and 3:00 positions. If there is error, there is no way to know in advance whether it will be a gap at 9:00 or 3:00. The procedure starts at 9:00, and then

goes to 3:00, anticipating that the gap will be found there. If there is a gap at 3:00, then it must be measured to determine if it is significant. If the tool indicator overlaps the rim at 3:00, then the tool should be reset at 3:00 and the gap should be checked at 9:00.

11. [ ] **Adjust DAG-1 to just contact RRP at 9:00 position.**

32.12 Set the tool to contact the RRP at 9:00.

To easily move the DAG-1 to 3:00, slide the indicator assembly in towards the tool pivot a few inches, then move the RRP and the end of the tool to 3:00. Once there, slide the indicator assembly out to the rim.

12. [ ] **Move DAG-1 and RRP to 3:00 position (if tool overlaps rim, skip to step 14).**

In the following step, use a 4mm stack of feeler gauges or a 4mm Allen wrench to check whether the gaps is more or less than 4mm. If 4mm or less, the hanger alignment in the horizontal plane is good. If more than 4mm, then the error should be corrected.

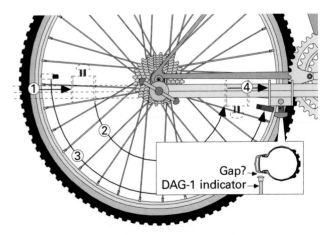

32.13 1) move the indicator assembly in towards the wheel center, 2) rotate the DAG-1 to the 3:00 position, 3) rotate the RRP to the 3:00 position, 4) move the indicator assembly until the indicator is at the rim. Now, check the gap (or overlap) between the rim and indicator.

To correct the error, slide the indicator along the main bar, away from the rim, then push in on the main bar of the tool. Keep in mind that a full correction will be done by pushing in enough to reduce the gap by half. If an over-correction is done, then the gap will switch to the position where the tool was initially set to have contact. It does not matter if the gap switches to the other position, as long as it ends up at 4mm or less.

13. If there is error, circle whether it is:

    0–4mm gap, *minor error — go to step 17*
    Overlaps rim, *go to step 14*
    >4mm gap, *continue below*:

    [ ] Correct by applying leverage to tool until gap is reduced by 50%.
    [ ] Return tool and RRP to 9:00 and reset tool to just contact.
    [ ] Return tool and RRP to 3:00 and check that gap is <4mm. (If overlap was created, correction was too much and should be reversed.)
    [ ] Repeat correction as necessary until gap is <4mm, then *go to step 17.*

NOTE: If tool did not overlap rim at 3:00 in step 13, skip step 14–16.

14. [ ] Reset tool at 3:00 position to just contact RRP.
15. [ ] Move DAG-1 and RRP to 9:00 position:
16. If there is error, circle whether it is:

    0–4mm gap, *minor error — go to step 17*
    >4mm gap, *continue below.*

    [ ] Correct by applying leverage to tool until gap is reduced by 50%.
    [ ] Return tool and RRP to 3:00 and reset tool to just contact.
    [ ] Return tool and RRP to 9:00 and check that gap is <4mm. (If overlap was created, correction was too much and should be reversed.)
    [ ] Repeat correction as necessary until gap is <4mm.

After correcting the horizontal error, the vertical error needs to be checked and corrected. The procedure is exactly the same, other than the fact the two positions are 12:00 and 6:00.

17. [ ] Adjust DAG-1 to just contact rim at 12:00 position.
18. [ ] Move DAG-1 and rim reference point (RRP) to 6:00 position. (If tool overlaps rim skip to step 20.)
19. If there is error, circle whether it is:

    0–4mm gap, *minor error, done*
    Overlaps rim, *go to step 20*
    >4mm gap, *continue below*:

    [ ] Correct by applying leverage to tool until gap is reduced by 50%.
    [ ] Return tool and RRP to 12:00 and reset tool to just contact.

    [ ] Return tool and RRP to 6:00 and check that gap is <4mm. (If overlap was created, correction was too much and should be reversed.)
    [ ] Repeat correction as necessary until gap is <4mm.

NOTE: If tool did not overlap rim at 6:00 in step 19, skip step 20–22.

20. [ ] Reset tool at 6:00 position to just contact rim.
21. [ ] Move DAG-1 and rim reference point (RRP) to 12:00 position:
22. If there is a gap, circle whether it is:

    0-4mm gap, *minor error, done*
    >4mm gap, *continue below.*

    [ ] Correct by applying leverage to tool until gap is reduced by 50%.
    [ ] Return tool and RRP to 6:00 and reset tool to just contact.
    [ ] Return tool and RRP to 12:00 and check that gap is <4mm. (If overlap was created, correction was too much and should be reversed.)
    [ ] Repeat correction as necessary until gap is <4mm.

While correcting the vertical alignment at 12:00 and 6:00, it is easy to mess up the horizontal alignment slightly. After correcting the vertical, check the horizontal again and correct whatever minor error may have been created. This need for a repeat correction can be reduced by achieving a near-perfect alignment when first doing the 3:00/9:00 alignment.

23. [ ] Recheck at 3:00 and 9:00 for a difference of 4mm or less, and correct as necessary in same fashion.

Lubrication of derailleur

24. Lubricate following points:

    [ ] Edge of each pulley-wheel dustcap.
    [ ] Both ends of all four parallelogram pivots.
    [ ] Mounting-bolt threads.
    [ ] Adjusting-barrel threads.
    [ ] Pinch-mechanism threads.

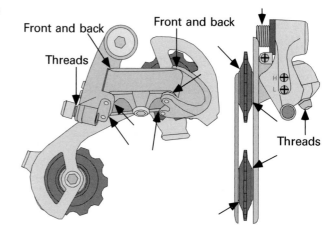

32.14 Oil at all points indicated by arrows.

Attaching derailleur to hanger

When mounting the derailleur to the hanger, it is easy to damage the derailleur or hanger if the derailleur is not lined up properly as the mounting bolt is tightened. To prevent this, rotate the derailleur considerably clockwise from its operating position, so that the stop tab or B-screw on the back of the derailleur is behind the stop tab on the bottom of the derailleur hanger.

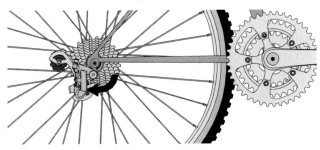

32.15 The derailleur should be kept in this position while engaging and threading the mounting bolt into the hanger.

25. [ ] **Line mounting bolt up with mounting hole in hanger.**
26. [ ] **Rotate derailleur clockwise until stop tab on mounting plate or end of B-screw is clockwise of stop tab on derailleur hanger.**
27. [ ] **Use T-handle Allen to thread mounting bolt into hanger, but do not secure.**

Although it does not matter with most modern derailleurs, the derailleur should be rotated fully counterclockwise when the bolt is being secured. Some older derailleurs would hold any position they were in at the point the mounting bolt was secured. Rather than trying to figure out whether the derailleur being installed is one of the ones that holds whatever position it is secured in, just rotate all derailleurs fully counterclockwise just before the mounting bolt begins to tighten.

32.16 The derailleur should be kept in this position while securing the mounting bolt.

28. [ ] **Rotate derailleur counterclockwise until stop tab on mounting plate or end of B-screw is against stop tab on derailleur hanger.**
29. [ ] **Secure mounting bolt to 70in-lbs (18lbs@4").**

ADJUSTMENT

The processes of describing cogs by their relative positions and describing gear combinations involving different front chainrings and rear cogs can get very wordy and awkward. For this reason, all the following procedures use a code system to name different cogs and gear combinations. This code system is described in detail in the earlier section of this chapter, **NAMING COGS AND GEAR COMBINATIONS** (page 32-3). Become acquainted with this before attempting the following procedures.

NOTE: before proceeding further, be sure to be acquainted with the section, **NAMING COGS AND GEAR COMBINATIONS** *(page 32-3).*

Pre-setting limit screws

The limit screws need to be set in a very approximate fashion before the cable and chain are installed. The purpose of this is to keep the chain from shifting off the cogset while performing the final adjustments. *Precise adjustment of the limit screws is done later; do not waste effort doing step #30 and #31 too precisely!* When the H-screw is tightened, it reduces the outward range of motion of the derailleur. When the L-screw is tightened, it reduces the inward range of motion of the rear derailleur.

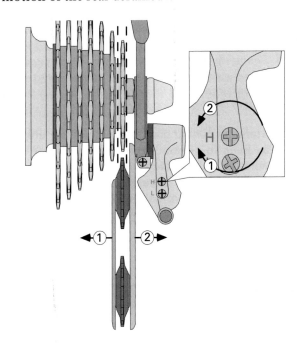

32.17 Turning the H-screw will change the derailleur's outward rest position in the direction indicated by the corresponding numbers. Adjust the screw so that the guide pulley ends up in the range indicated by the dashed lines.

30. [ ] **Standing behind bike, check whether guide pulley is lined up below A cog. Tighten H-screw to move guide pulley in, or loosen to move guide pulley out.**

and the shift happens half a pedal stroke later, that is definitely hesitation. Obviously, if the chain will not shift to the Z cog at all, then the L-screw is too tight.

48. While pedaling at approximately 60rpm, pull rear-derailleur inner wire quickly and observe whether (check one):
    [ ] Chain does not hesitate shifting to Z, L-screw should be tightened, go to step 49.
    [ ] Chain hesitates or clatters after shifting to Z, L-screw should be loosened, go to step 50.

NOTE: Skip step 49 if chain hesitated or clattered after shifting in step 48.

If there was no symptom of the L-screw being too tight in step #48, then one must be created in step #49. There is no great precision needed when creating this symptom, so half-turn adjustments of the L-screw will get quick results. Later, when eliminating the too-tight symptom, greater precision is needed, so the L-screw will be loosened by quarter-turn increments.

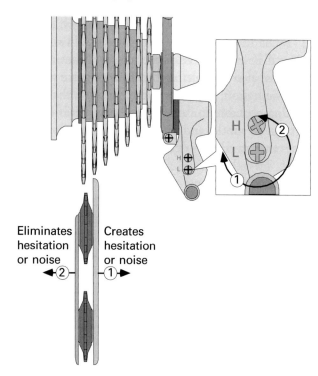

32.24 *Turning the L-screw will change the derailleur's most inward position in the direction indicated by the corresponding numbers.*

49. [ ] Turn L-screw 1/2 turn and repeat shift from Y to Z, checking for whether hesitation or post-shift clatter happens. Repeat this step as many times as necessary until either there is hesitation on the shift, or clatter after the shift.

If the too-tight H-screw symptom was experienced when first checking the shift to the Z cog in step #48, it could take any number of quarter turns of the L-screw to eliminate the symptom. On the other hand,

if the too-tight symptom was deliberately created in step #49, then it should take either one quarter turn or two quarter turns of L-screw loosening to eliminate the symptom. This is because the L-screw was turned two quarter turns to create the too-tight symptom from a setting that was not too tight in step #49.

50. [ ] Turn L-screw counterclockwise 1/4 turn and repeat shift from Y to Z, checking for whether hesitation or post-shift clatter is eliminated. Repeat this step as many times as necessary until symptoms are eliminated.

A simple double-check can be done after the completion of the L-screw adjustment to check that it is not too loose. Tighten the L-screw 1/2 turn and check the shift. Too-tight symptoms should be *obvious* at this point if the L-screw was set at the tightest good setting.

Cable stressing

A frequently used term is *cable stretch*. There is never a great enough force on the inner wire to permanently change its length (stretch). Somehow, however, cable systems develop slack rapidly after installation. This development of slack can compromise the indexing adjustment. What causes this slack is the inner wire head seats into its socket, and the housing ends and fittings seat into their sockets. This can happen gradually as shifting loads are repeatedly put on the cable systems, or it can be simulated by stressing the cable system one time at a substantially higher load than normal. This over-load stressing also tests the cable system for integrity.

Since the systems will be over-loaded, it is important that the shift-control mechanism and the derailleur be in positions that can support the load. The derailleur should be at its innermost position, supported by the L-screw. The shift-control mechanism should be at its fully-released position, supported by its own internal stop. To accomplish this, the lever must be operated to put the chain on the A cog, and then the inner wire must be pulled manually while pedaling to put the chain on the Z cog. Once the chain is in place, stop pedaling and pull out hard on the inner wire a few times. Protect the hand from damage by using a multi-folded rag between your hand and the inner wire.

51. [ ] Make sure rear shift-control mechanism is fully released.
52. [ ] While pedaling, pull on exposed inner wire at down tube or top tube until chain is on Z cog and stop pedaling.
53. [ ] With chain still on Z cog, pull hard on exposed inner wire to seat cable heads and housing ends in stops and sockets, and to test integrity of pinch mechanism and cable system.
54. [ ] Pedal crank so chain returns to A cog.

Basic cable tensioning

Coarse adjustment of the inner-wire tension is done by pulling or releasing wire through the pinch mechanism on the derailleur. Fine tuning will be done afterwards by using the adjusting barrel on the rear derailleur.

55. [ ] Loosen inner-wire pinch mechanism.

The derailleur adjusting barrel should be turned back three full turns from fully in so that it can be turned in or out to loosen or tighten the inner-wire tension.

The shift-control-mechanism adjusting barrel should be turned back one full turn from fully in so that the rider can easily adjust the wire tension tighter *or* looser while riding.

56. [ ] Set derailleur adjusting barrel so that it is three full turns out from fully in, and shift-mechanism adjusting barrel so that it is one full turn out from fully in.

The fourth-hand tool is a very convenient tool for removing inner-wire slack, but it can easily be used to make the inner wire much too tight. If the inner wire is being tightened too much by the fourth-hand tool, it will usually show up as inward motion of the derailleur parallelogram. Watch for this while squeezing the fourth-hand tool.

57. [ ] Using fourth-hand tool, *gently* pull slack out of inner wire, *being sure to stop before derailleur begins to move*.

It is easy for the inner wire to slip out of its groove in the pinch mechanism while the tension is being reset. Be sure to check that the inner wire is in place before torquing the bolt/nut. If it is out of place, then the correct torque may not keep it secure.

58. [ ] Making sure inner wire is still seated in groove in pinch mechanism, secure pinch nut/bolt to 35in-lbs (12lbs@3").

59. [ ] Put chain in *H/B* position and check shift to *A* cog. If shift hesitates, inner wire was tightened too much in step 58.

Indexing adjustment

The concept of making an index adjustment is similar to a limit-screw adjustment. There is a range of adjustments that work, but only the tightest setting is best because it allows the greatest amount of deterioration to happen before the system becomes non-functional. The fundamental approach to the adjustment, therefore, is to deliberately create symptoms that the inner wire is too tight, then loosen the adjustment by small increments until the symptom is eliminated. The complication comes from the fact that when a shift is good to one cog, there may still be symptoms of a too-tight adjustment when shift-ing to another cog. Consequently, the indexing adjustment consists of shifting into many different gear combinations, and loosening the index adjustment each time a too-tight symptom is encountered.

The index adjustment should start with the chain on the *H* chainring and the *A* cog.

60. [ ] Shift chain to *H/A* with shift-control mechanisms.

In the next step, the shift-control mechanism is used to move the chain to the *B* cog. One of three things may happen. First, the chain may fail to make the shift at all, indicating that the inner-wire slack was not adequately removed in step #57 (which should be redone). Second, the chain will complete the shift and it is time to continue with step #61. Third, the chain may shift all the way to the *C* cog, indicating that the inner wire was pulled too tight in step #57 (which should be redone).

61. [ ] While pedaling, move rear shift control one position to shift chain to *B* cog.

If the inner-wire tension was set correctly in step #57, the chain has just shifted to the *B* cog. Step #62 assumes that the chain is not rattling against the *C* cog and starts by creating that condition. If that condition exists from the beginning, just perform the portion of step #62 that loosens the adjusting barrel by 1/4 turn increments to eliminate the rattle.

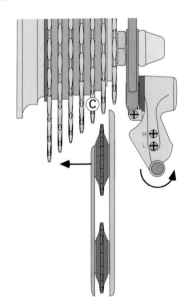

32.25 *Turning the adjusting barrel counterclockwise to cause the chain the rub against the C cog.*

62. [ ] While pedaling, turn adjusting barrel counterclockwise until chain begins to rattle against *C* cog, then turn in adjusting barrel by 1/4 turn increments to eliminate rattle. (At the point where rattle is detected, make a visual check from behind that the chain is touching the *C* cog.)

Step #63 through #65 check whether there are any too-tight symptoms when shifting the rest of the way inward on the cogset (only to the *Y* cog) and all the way back out to the *A* cog. At any point a too-tight symptom is encountered, the adjusting barrel should be turned clockwise just enough to eliminate the symptom.

63. [ ] **Shift chain to *C* cog and check for rattle against next cog inward. Turn in cable adjusting barrel by 1/4 turn increments to eliminate rattle if found.**

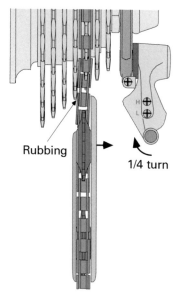

Rubbing

1/4 turn

32.26 Turn adjusting barrel 1/4 turn clockwise to eliminate rattle of chain against next cog inward. Repeat if necessary and check in all other gear combinations.

64. [ ] **Continue in-shifts one cog at a time, eliminating any rattles found with 1/4 turn adjustments of the adjusting barrel, until the chain is on *Y* cog.**
65. [ ] **Shift out one cog at a time, eliminating rattles by turning in adjusting barrel in 1/4 turn increments, until chain is on *A* cog.**

After all gear combinations with the *H* chainring have been checked and too-tight symptoms eliminated, it is time to run a similar check with the chain on the *L* chainring. The difference this time is that the chain needs to be shifted all the way to the *Z* cog.

66. [ ] **Shift chain to *L* with shift control.**
67. [ ] **Pedal and check for chain rattling on *B* cog and turn in adjusting barrel to eliminate rattle if found.**
68. [ ] **Shift chain to *B* cog and check for rattle against next cog inward. Turn in cable adjusting barrel to eliminate rattle if found.**
69. [ ] **Continue in-shifts one cog at a time, eliminating any rattles found, until the chain is on *Z* cog.**

70. [ ] **Shift out one cog at a time, eliminating rattles by turning in adjusting barrel in 1/4 turn increments, until chain is on *A* cog.**

If at any time during the index adjustment, symptoms that the cable is too loose are experienced at the same setting that creates symptoms that the inner wire is too tight, then something is set up wrong or parts are damaged, worn out, or not compatible. At this point, review the entire set up and refer to the troubleshooting information (page 32-29).

Inner-wire finish

Excess inner wire should be trimmed and finished. Excess length is unsightly and may get caught in the chain. Soldering prevents fraying, which allows reuse of the cable whether a wire cap is being used or not. Wire caps do not prevent fraying, but they do prevent someone getting poked by the wire.

The fourth hand is put on the inner wire to act as a gauge to determine how much wire to leave. This remainder does not need to be any more than the fourth hand needs to grab.

71. [ ] **Put fourth-hand tool on inner wire as if removing slack.**
72. [ ] **Trim inner wire with wire cutters just past fourth-hand tool.**

The next step suggests soldering the end of the wire. This is easy to do and prevents fraying. To solder, a soldering gun, thin 40/60 rosin-core solder, and soldering flux are needed. Put flux on the inner wire. Hold the soldering-gun tip flat against one side of the wire until the flux sizzles away. Still holding the soldering-gun tip flat against one side of the wire, hold the tip of the solder against the other side of the wire, until the heated wire causes the solder to melt and flow into the wire. Some wires have a coating or are stainless steel and will not accept solder. In these cases, the wire will melt the solder, but the solder will not flow into the wire. Instead it beads up and runs off the wire.

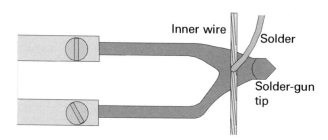

Inner wire

Solder

Solder-gun tip

32.27 Correct soldering technique.

73. [ ] **Solder inner wire end.**

Wire end caps are sometimes used instead of solder to prevent fraying. This will not work. Crimping the cap onto the wire frequently *causes* fraying. A soldered wire will not fray when the cap is crimped on. The real function of the wire cap is to cover the sharp end of the wire.

74. [ ] **Put cap on end of inner wire if desired.**

TESTING INDEX PERFORMANCE

The performance of any indexing-rear-derailleur system can be tested and measured. The procedures described above are designed to set the indexing adjustment at *the tightest setting that provides good shifting*. If the indexing system has normal performance, then there are probably looser settings for the cable that also enable shifting into all the gears. The range of adjusting-barrel positions from the tightest that provides good shifting to the loosest that will allow shifting into all the gears is called the *Functional Range of Adjustment* (or FRA).

The performance of all systems deteriorates with wear, a bent derailleur hanger, and the accumulation of dirt. When the FRA is narrow, then it will take only a small amount of riding before service is needed to restore acceptable shifting. When the FRA is extremely narrow, finding a correct adjustment at all is a challenge. When the FRA is broad, it will take much longer before service is needed. Consequently, it is to the rider's and the mechanic's advantage for the system to have a broad FRA.

There are two reasons to measure the FRA: first, it enables an accurate determination of whether parts might need replacement or cleaning on a used system; second, it permits an evaluation of whether a non-recommended part compromises indexing performance unacceptably.

There is no absolute value for an adequate amount of FRA. It varies with the brand and quality of equipment, as well as some other factors. For seven- and eight-speed systems, a FRA of at least three quarter turns of the cable adjusting barrel should be expected of new equipment. It is not unusual to get something more like four to six quarter turns.

If evaluating properly set-up used equipment that all meets manufacturer's specifications for compatibility and the FRA is not at least three quarter turns, then something in the system needs cleaning or replacement.

If evaluating any equipment, used or new, that *does not* meet manufacturer's specifications for compatibility and the FRA is not at least three quarter turns, then the non-matched equipment probably needs to be replaced.

If considering installing equipment in a system that may not be compatible, measure the FRA before the change, and again afterwards. If it is reduced, then the equipment change will downgrade shift performance. If it is still above three quarter turns, then it may be acceptable even though it is a downgrade of performance. This test process applies to mis-matching pulley wheels, chains, derailleurs and shifters, cable systems, and even mis-matching derailleurs with cogsets.

MEASURING THE FUNCTIONAL RANGE OF ADJUSTMENT (FRA)

1. [ ] **Perform an index adjustment using steps 60–65 of the *INSTALLATION AND ADJUSTMENT* procedure for rear derailleurs.**
2. [ ] **Mark adjusting barrel at 12:00 so turns of adjustment can be tracked.**
3. [ ] **Turn adjusting barrel in (clockwise) 1/4 turn.**

In the next step, a somewhat subjective evaluation of whether the adjustment is too loose must be made. As the adjustment is loosened, it is normal for performance to degrade *before* shifting actually is unacceptable. In an in-the-stand test, this loss of performance will be quite noticeable. It will even reach a point where a delay in releasing the shifter (after the click is reached) will be required to effect the shift. For the rider on the bike, this deterioration of performance will take place gradually over a long period of time, without being nearly so noticeable.

For this reason, consider a symptom of the cable adjustment being too loose to be either of the three following things: first, when an in-shift cannot be completed except by moving the shifter two positions, the cable adjustment is too loose; second, when moving the shifter one position to create an out-shift and the chain unavoidably moves two cogs, then the cable adjustment is too loose; third, if after completing a shift, the chain *clearly* is making a noise as a result of trying to shift to the next cog outward, then the cable adjustment is too loose. Before concluding that the adjustment is too loose based on chain noise after the shift, always look below the cogset to see that the chain is actually angled obviously out from the cog it is on.

4. [ ] With chain on *H* chainring, shift chain from *A*, to *B*, to *C*, etc., until cog *Y* is reached, then out one at a time until back to *A*. Pedal several crank revolutions at each cog and check for symptoms of indexing adjustment too loose (circle result).

    At 1 quarter turn in: too loose? No Yes
    At 2 quarter turns in: too loose? No Yes
    At 3 quarter turns in: too loose? No Yes
    At 4 quarter turns in: too loose? No Yes
    At 5 quarter turns in: too loose? No Yes
    At 6 quarter turns in: too loose? No Yes
    At 7 quarter turns in: too loose? No Yes
    At 8 quarter turns in: too loose? No Yes

5. [ ] With chain on *L* chainring, shift chain from *A*, to *B*, to *C*, etc., until cog *Z* is reached, then out one at a time until back to *A*. Pedal several crank revolutions at each cog and check for symptoms of indexing adjustment too loose (circle result).

    At 1 quarter turn in: too loose? No Yes
    At 2 quarter turns in: too loose? No Yes
    At 3 quarter turns in: too loose? No Yes
    At 4 quarter turns in: too loose? No Yes
    At 5 quarter turns in: too loose? No Yes
    At 6 quarter turns in: too loose? No Yes
    At 7 quarter turns in: too loose? No Yes
    At 8 quarter turns in: too loose? No Yes

6. [ ] Repeat steps 3–5 as many times as necessary until first symptom of indexing adjustment being too loose is encountered. Record how many quarter turns it takes to reach this point here: ___ quarters.

7. [ ] If comparing performance between two equipment choices, install other equipment and repeat steps 1–6, but record new number of quarter turns needed to create symptom of indexing adjustment too loose in this blank: ___ quarters.

The resulting numbers in step #6 and #7 are not the FRA because the last adjustment made the shifting non-functional. The actual functional range of adjustment would be described as 1/4 turn less than the number in either of these steps. Thus, if the first symptom of too loose showed up at three quarter turns, then the FRA would be two quarter turns (truly poor).

REAR-DERAILLEUR SERVICE

PULLEY-WHEEL REPLACEMENT AND CAGE CLEANING

The rear-derailleur cage and pulleys may need service when nothing else in the rear derailleur needs service, because of wear and the accumulation of grime that builds up in this area. This is a very simple service to do. It can be done without derailleur, cable, or chain removal; usually no adjustments are required (unless they were already needed).

Pulley-wheel removal

1. [ ] Shift chain to *A/L* position, then manually drop chain off to inside of *L* chainring so that chain rests on bottom-bracket shell.

2. [ ] Use marker or scribe to put mark on each derailleur-cage plate near bottom end so that marks line up with each other and are both visible from same side of derailleur cage.

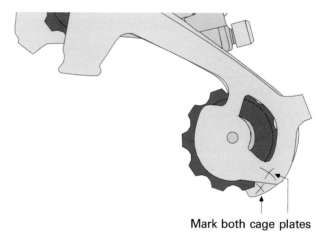

Mark both cage plates

32.28 Mark both cage plates to make it easy to restore their correct orientation.

When the tension pulley is removed (if it is an aftermarket cartridge-bearing pulley) there is a good chance that there are small washers between the pulley wheel and cage plates so that the cage plates end up correctly spaced from each other. Look carefully for these washers, as they are easy to loose and hard to replace.

3. [ ] Remove bolt through tension pulley (lower) from either front or back of cage, and catch tension pulley as it falls out of cage. (Watch carefully for any washers that might be sandwiched between tension pulley and inner faces of cage plates.)

Tension pulleys and guide pulleys are often not identical on indexing derailleurs. The word "tension" or the letter "T" may appear on the tension pulley. The

22. [ ] Using pliers to hold mounting plate by the tab that B-screw threads into, press mounting plate down until it is against upper end of mounting-pivot housing.

23. [ ] Holding mounting plate down, rotate derailleur clockwise until tab on mounting plate stops against tab on outside of mounting pivot-housing.

24. [ ] Carefully pull up mounting plate with pliers so that tab on outside of mounting-pivot housing can rotate clockwise past tab on mounting plate, then push mounting plate back in.

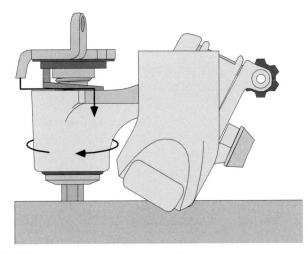

32.36 *Loading the mounting pivot spring.*

25. [ ] Insert clip in groove in mounting bolt.

In the next step, the B-screw position is restored. If it was not recorded or correct to start with, thread the B-screw in just enough to engage the threads. It will be adjusted when the derailleur is installed and adjusted.

26. [ ] Put any plastic cover over mounting plate and thread in B-screw until protrusion equals measurement in step 6.

Assembling the cage pivot

27. [ ] Insert spring into cage-pivot housing and engage end of spring in hole. Make sure that end of spring with reduced-diameter coil is facing out of cage-pivot housing.

28. [ ] Put seal in place on outer face of outer plate, or on inward end of cage-pivot housing.

29. [ ] Place outer cage pivot into hole in cage-pivot housing.

Which cage hole the spring engaged should have been recorded in step #3. Facing the outer face of the outer cage plate, the most clockwise hole is the normal position that provides less tension for the cage-return spring. The most counterclockwise hole provides a high-tension setting for the return spring that compensates for age, small cogsets, and non-standard derailleur-hanger designs.

30. [ ] Rotate cage plate to align desired hole with end of spring and engage plate to spring.

31. [ ] Push outer cage plate firmly to end of cage pivot housing.

32. [ ] Except models where removal of 2mm Allen bolt disengaged cage from derailleur body, insert small Phillips screw from back, or cage-pivot bolt from front, to retain cage to derailleur body.

33. [ ] Holding derailleur *so that outer face is visible*, rotate outer cage plate counterclockwise until cage-stop pin or mounting hole for cage-stop screw clears tab on outside of cage-pivot housing. If cage-stop pin is still fixed to cage plate, cage plate will need to be pulled away from cage-pivot housing just enough to allow cage-stop pin to clear tab on cage-pivot housing.

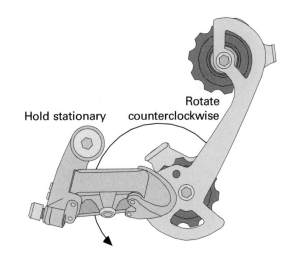

Hold stationary   Rotate counterclockwise

32.37 *Winding up the cage tension spring.*

34. [ ] Thread in cage stop pin, or 2mm Allen screw into hole in bottom of cage-pivot housing.

DERAILLEUR-HANGER REPAIR

THREAD CHASING

Derailleur-hanger threads may be fouled with contaminants, or cross-threaded, leading to difficult installation of the derailleur-mounting bolt. To solve either, use a tap of the correct size (usually 10mm × 1mm) from the back side of the hanger to clean out the threads.

THREAD REPLACEMENT

There are several brands of thread-replacement coils. These work by enlarging the hole, tapping the hole to an over-size-thread description, and then using a tool that comes with the coil kit to insert a wire coil that matches the new thread description on the outside and creates a new set of original threads on the inside. The instructions that come with the kit should be adequate, and should differ depending on the brand of thread-repair kit being used. The following steps are generic, and may not exactly match the brand of kit being used.

1. [ ] **Drill or ream hole in hanger to 13/32" diameter.**
2. [ ] **Tap hole with oversize tap provided with kit.**
3. [ ] **Treat hole threads with heaviest grade of Loctite available.**
4. [ ] **Use tool that comes in kit to thread in coil from outer face of dropout, until end of coil is flush with outer face of hanger.**
5. [ ] **Remove coil-insertion tool.**
6. [ ] **Use diagonal side cutter to clip off excess coil length on back side of hanger.**
7. [ ] **Allow Loctite to cure before installing and securing derailleur.**

SLEEVE INSERTS

Sleeve inserts to repair damaged hanger threads are sleeve nuts that go into an enlarged hanger hole. At the time of this writing, the primary product available is the Wheels Manufacturing Dropout Saver (DS-1 and DS-2). When a sleeve insert is used, the hanger is basically being sandwiched between a nut on the inside face of the hanger and the derailleur on the outside face. The sleeve inserts are effective. The worst problem with them is a tendency for them to disappear when someone unfamiliar with the repair removes the derailleur at a later time. To perform the repair, the old threads should be drilled or reamed out to 15/32" diameter. The sleeve nut should be installed from the backside. Loctite RC680 can be used to reduce the likelihood of the sleeve nut falling out when the derailleur is not mounted, but this is no guarantee.

The nut should be held with a cone wrench while the derailleur-mounting bolt is being secured or loosened.

HANGER REPLACEMENT

A number of brands of bikes with aluminum dropouts now have replaceable hangers. These are entirely brand specific and cannot be used on any frame except the original one that they were designed for. The are usually held in place by small screws or bolts. The threads should be prepared with Loctite 222 or 242.

REAR-DERAILLEUR TROUBLESHOOTING

Cause	Solution
SYMPTOM: *The shift to the A cog is slow.*	
The H-screw is too tight.	Loosen H-screw; Look for rapid improvement if the H-screw is the source of the problem.
If the H-screw is not too tight, then the inner-wire tension may be too tight.	Turn in an adjusting barrel or let more inner wire through the pinch mechanism; expect instant improvement if inner-wire tension was the source of the problem.
If none of above, the B-screw may be too tight or the chain may be too short, causing the guide pulley to be too far below the A cog.	Check B-screw adjustment and chain length. Try setting chain at longest length that works to attempt to eliminate symptom.
If none of the above, the cable system may have too much friction.	Check for poor cable routing, housing damage, inner-wire damage, inner-wire rust, dirt on inner wires, or lack of lubrication.
If none of the above, the guide pulley may be worn out.	Check guide-pulley teeth and bushing for wear.
If none of the above, the chain may be worn out.	Check chain wear.
If none of the above, dirt may be fouling the cage and/or mounting pivot, the return spring, or the parallelogram pivots; causing the guide pulley to track too low below the cogset or the parallelogram to be hesitant to return to its outermost position.	Disassemble, clean, and lubricate the derailleur.
If none of the above, the derailleur may have too little return-spring force to pull the inner wire through the housing bends. This is most likely if the derailleur and shifter are not brand and model matched.	Try installing a spring over the inner wire between the rear-derailleur adjusting barrel and the pinch mechanism. Use a compression spring 1.75" long, with a 3/8" diameter, and .035 wire gauge (or larger).
Old-style Campagnolo pulley wheels with low-profile teeth are being used with a new-style low-profile chain that does not have side plates extending above the rollers.	Change pulley wheels to Shimano type.
SYMPTOM: *There is excessive noise when the chain is on the A cog.*	
If the guide pulley is offset inward of the A cog, then H-screw or inner-wire tension is too tight.	Check guide-pulley position, then loosen H-screw and/or inner-wire tension.
If the guide pulley is offset outward of the A cog, then H-screw too loose.	Check guide-pulley position, then tighten H-screw
If the guide pulley is close to centered under the A cog, check if the chain is rubbing against the B cog where the top section of chain goes forward to the chainrings. If this is the case, then the chainline is off or the chain is a wide chain being used on a narrow-spaced cogset.	Check chainline and chain/cogset compatibility
SYMPTOM: *The chain shifts past the A cog when shifting from the B cog.*	
The H-screw is too loose.	Tighten the H-screw until the symptom goes away.
If tightening the H-screw creates the symptom that the H-screw is too tight before the original symptom goes away, the guide pulley is too far below the cog.	B-screw adjustment is too tight, chain is too short, or the mounting and cage pivots are fouled with dirt.

(continued next page)

REAR-DERAILLEUR TROUBLESHOOTING (continued)

Cause	*Solution*
SYMPTOM: *The shift to the Z cog is slow.*	
The L-screw is too tight.	Loosen the L-screw 1/4 turn at a time. Rapid improvement should happen with very little adjustment.
If derailleur is indexing and the symptom only occurs when using the shift-control mechanism, inner-wire tension is too loose.	Tighten inner-wire tension with the adjusting barrel.
The chain is on the *H* chainring.	The shift combination should be avoided.
SYMPTOM: *There is excessive noise when the chain is on the Z cog.*	
If the guide pulley appears offset inward of the Z cog, the L-screw is too loose.	Tighten the L-screw.
If the guide pulley appears offset outward of the Z cog, the L-screw is too tight.	Loosen the L-screw.
If the guide pulley appears somewhat centered under the Z cog, then the B-screw may be too loose.	Tighten the B-screw.
If the B-screw cannot be tightened enough to eliminate the symptom, the chain may be too long.	Check if the chain can be shortened without creating a too-short condition.
If the B-screw cannot be tightened enough, the chain cannot be shortened, and adjusting the L-screw is no help, the maximum cog size capacity of the derailleur may have been exceeded.	Check derailleur capacity.
SYMPTOM: *The chain shifts past the Z cog when shifting from the Y cog*	
The L-screw is too loose.	Tighten the L-screw.
If the guide pulley appears far below the Z cog, and tightening the L-screw creates a slow shift, the B-screw is too tight.	Loosen the B-screw.
If loosening the B-screw does not move the guide pulley reasonably close to the cog, then the derailleur is being used on a cogset smaller than was intended.	Use cogset with larger cogs, change derailleur, or try changing the spring tension in the cage pivot.
SYMPTOM: *Some or all in-shifts are slow (rear derailleur is indexing).*	
Inner-wire tension is too low.	Turn adjusting barrel out.
Guide pulley is worn out.	Check guide-pulley teeth and bushing for wear.
Chain is worn out.	Check chain for wear and replace if necessary.
SYMPTOM: *Some or all out-shifts are slow (rear derailleur is indexing).*	
Inner-wire tension is too high.	Turn adjusting barrel in.
Guide pulley is worn out.	Check guide-pulley teeth and bushing for wear.
Chain is worn out.	Check chain for wear and replace if necessary.
Excess cable-system friction.	Check for poor cable routing, housing damage, inner-wire damage, inner-wire rust, dirt on inner wires, or lack of lubrication.
If symptom is progressively worse as the chain is shifted further and further out, the guide pulley may be too far below the cogs.	Check for too tight a B-screw, too short a chain, or dirt in the cage and mounting pivots. Correct any problem found.

Cause	*Solution*
SYMPTOM: *The chain moves out two positions when the shift-control mechanism is moved one position.*	
Inner-wire tension is too low.	Turn adjusting barrel further out, or pull more inner wire through the pinch mechanism if the adjusting barrel is running out of threads.
Shift-control mechanism is not compatible with derailleur and/or cogset.	Check component compatibility and test shift again after replacing any suspect components.
The shift-control mechanism had already been released one position when chain wasn't moving, so it had actually been moved two positions.	Recheck the shift.
SYMPTOM: *The chain moves in two positions when the shift-control mechanism is moved one position.*	
Inner-wire tension is too high.	Turn adjusting barrel further in, or release more inner wire through the pinch mechanism if the adjusting barrel is running out of threads.
Shift-control mechanism is not compatible with derailleur and/or cogset.	Check component compatibility and test shift again after replacing any suspect components.
The shift-control mechanism had already been moved one position when the chain was not moving, so it had actually been moved two positions.	Recheck the shift.
SYMPTOM: *The chain will not move inward to the next gear when the shift-control mechanism is moved one position, or the shift-control mechanism must be moved two positions to get the chain to move inward one position.*	
Inner-wire tension is too low.	Turn adjusting barrel further out, or pull more inner wire through the pinch mechanism if the adjusting barrel is running out of threads.
Shift-control mechanism is not compatible with derailleur and/or cogset.	Check component compatibility and test shift again after replacing any suspect components.
Chain is badly worn out.	Check chain wear.
Chain and cogs are not compatible.	Check manufacturer's chain recommendations.
SYMPTOM: *With an indexing rear derailleur, the chain makes noise against the next cog inward after an in-shift to a specific cog, but not after making an out-shift to the same cog.*	
Excess cable-system friction.	Check for poor cable routing, housing damage, inner-wire damage, inner-wire rust, dirt on inner wires, or lack of lubrication.
Excess friction in the shift-control mechanism caused by wear, dirt, or lack of lubrication.	Test by temporarily installing a different shift-control mechanism. Service the shifter if the test eliminates the symptom.

(continued next page)

REAR-DERAILLEUR TROUBLESHOOTING (continued)

Cause	*Solution*
SYMPTOM: *At one cable-tension adjustment, the shifting acts as though the cable is too tight for some shifts, but acts as though the cable is too loose for other shifts.*	
Excess cable-system friction.	Check for poor cable routing, housing damage, inner-wire damage, inner-wire rust, dirt on inner wires, or lack of lubrication.
Incorrect inner wire for shift-control mechanism.	Check inner-wire compatibility.
Distance from face of derailleur hanger to face of first cog is too great.	Reduce axle spacing to move first cog as close as possible to the dropout without chain-to-frame interference.
General system congestion from dirt.	Clean cogs, chain, inside and outside of . derailleur, and inside shift-control mechanism.
General component incompatibility.	Check that shift-control mechanism, derailleur, and cogset are all compatible.
General system wear.	Check chain wear, guide-pulley wear, and derailleur-pivot wear.
SYMPTOM: *The chain shifts out one position on its own when the shift-control mechanism is not being operated.*	
If derailleur is indexing, inner-wire tension is too low.	Check and adjust inner-wire tension by turning adjusting barrel out.
If derailleur is friction-type, shift-lever friction is too light.	Adjust shift-lever friction.
SYMPTOM: *When testing the FRA, the acceptable range is very narrow.*	
Parts are dirty.	Clean drive train, derailleur, and shift-control mechanism.
Parts are worn out.	Check chain wear, guide-pulley wear, or derailleur-pivot wear.
Excess cable-system friction.	Check for poor cable routing, housing damage, inner-wire damage, inner-wire rust, dirt on inner wires, or lack of lubrication.
Non-compatible chain is being used.	Check chain compatibility.
Non-compatible guide pulley is being used.	Use only manufacturer's original pulley.
Non-compatible cable system is being used.	Use only high-quality indexing inner wires of the correct diameter, and compressionless housing.
Shift-control mechanism is not compatible with derailleur or cogset.	Check manufacturer's specifications for compatible components.

SHIMANO RAPID-RISE DERAILLEURS

OVERVIEW

Shimano Rapid-Rise rear derailleurs differ from others in that they move outward when the cable is pulled, and move inward by means of the parallelogram spring when the cable tension is released. Their motion is the opposite of conventional derailleurs.

For many purposes, these derailleurs are no different to install, adjust, or service than regular derailleurs, but some of the sequences in which things are done need to be changed to make the procedures easier. The following procedure is very generalized for the purpose of illustrating the correct sequence to go through derailleur setup and adjustment. The assumption of this procedure is that you are already familiar with all the details of proper setup and adjustment as they are done on conventional derailleurs.

RAPID-RISE PROCEDURES

Derailleur, cable, and chain installation

1. [ ] Align hanger, lubricate derailleur and install.
2. [ ] With derailleur at rest under *Z* cog, pull down on derailleur cage to allow upper pulley to clear cog, then preset L screw so pulley is centered under cog.
3. [ ] Pull outward on derailleur to move upper pulley under *A* cog, then check if pulley stops centered under cog and preset H screw as necessary.
4. [ ] With upper pulley pulled out to *A* cog and parallelogram positioned parallel to chain stay, size housing loop to rear derailleur.
5. [ ] With derailleur at rest position under *Z* cog (pull down on cage if upper pulley catches against outer face of cog), install cable system, pull slack out of cable with fingers, then secure pinch mechanism.
6. [ ] Using shift mechanism, move derailleur so upper pulley is under *A* cog, then install and size chain normally.

Limit screw and indexing adjustments

7. [ ] To set H screw, use shifters to put chain in *Z/H* combo, then pull on exposed wire to shift chain from *B* to *A* cog. Adjust limit normally, but pull on cable to check shift to *A* instead of releasing cable.

8. [ ] To set L screw, use shifters to put chain in *Z/M* combo (*Z/L* if double chainring), then pull on exposed wire to shift chain from *Z* to *Y* cog. Adjust limit normally, but release cable to check shift to *Z* instead of pulling cable.

Setting the cable tension and adjusting the indexing are where the most significant differences between Rapid-Rise and conventional derailleurs are found. Everything involving the cable is exactly reversed with Rapid-Rise. Consequently, the slack is removed when the chain is on the *Z* cog instead of the *A* cog. Less obvious is the fact that when the indexing is adjusted, the adjusting barrel should always be turned the opposite way from normal to correct any symptom.

9. [ ] Use shifter to put chain on *Z* cog, then pull on exposed inner wire while pedaling until chain reaches *A* cog, then stop pedaling and stress cable system.
10. [ ] Pedal until chain returns to *Z* cog, then release pinch mechanism, set adjusting barrels, pull slack from inner wire, and secure pinch mechanism.

As always, the best indexing adjustment is the tightest good setting. With Rapid-Rise, however, the tightest good adjustment is one just short of the point where the chain tends to shift outward one cog if the cable is tightened further (opposite of normal).

11. [ ] Adjust indexing to tightest good setting, turning adjusting barrel out (ccl) to improve shifts outward and in (cl) to improve shifts inward (opposite of adjusting conventional derailleur).

EIGHT- AND NINE-SPEED COMPATIBILITY

Because nine-speed derailleurs have the same actuation ratio (the amount the derailleur moves for a specific amount of inner-wire travel) as derailleurs that are not nine-speed, they are technically acceptable to mix. However, Shimano made other changes coincidental with introducing nine-speed systems that also affect interchangeability. The primary concern is the derailleur capacity. Most Shimano nine-speed MTB derailleurs work with up to a 34T rear cog. Most pre-nine-speed derailleurs have a maximum capacity of 32T. Consequently, if the bike has a nine-speed cog set with a 34T cog, a nine-speed derailleur must be used. Otherwise, there are no derailleur compatibility issues.

When replacing pulley wheels, it is important to be aware that there are nine-speed-specific pulleys. The significant difference is not the thickness of the pulley, but the number of teeth. Using a pulley wheel with the wrong number of teeth can adversely affect the capacities of the derailleur. If the teeth numbers match, the pulleys are generally compatible.

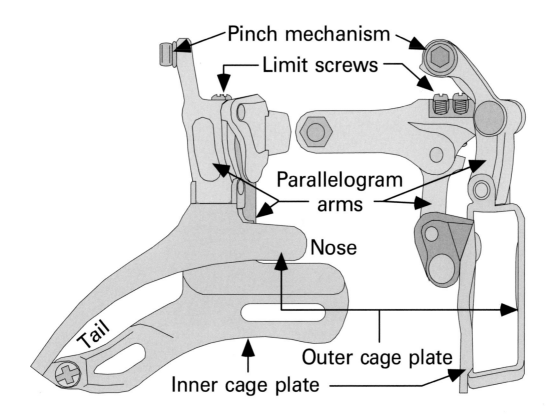

Pinch mechanism

Limit screws

Parallelogram arms

Nose

Tail

Outer cage plate

Inner cage plate

33 – FRONT DERAILLEURS

33 – FRONT DERAILLEURS

ABOUT THIS CHAPTER

This chapter is about installing, adjusting, and servicing front derailleurs. The procedures for installation and adjustment make references to installing the chain, shifter, and cable. These items are covered in the **CHAINS**, **SHIFT-CONTROL MECHANISMS**, and **DERAILLEUR-CABLE SYSTEMS** chapters.

The front derailleur procedure assumes that the rear derailleur is already installed. The rear derailleur need not be precisely adjusted, but must be able to move the chain to the innermost and outermost cogs. It may seem like a good idea to install and adjust the rear derailleur first, because of this. However, the rear-derailleur procedure requires that the front derailleur be able to shift the chain to the innermost and outermost positions, as well. Whichever is done first, to complete one derailleur adjustment it is necessary to do at least some preliminary work on the other derailleur.

There is some confusing and contradictory terminology used regarding derailleurs, so be sure to review the terminology section to become clear on the terms used by *this* book.

GENERAL INFORMATION

TERMINOLOGY

High gear: On front derailleurs, high gear refers to the chainring furthest from the frame. It is called high gear because using it results in the highest number when calculating gear ratios, not because the top of this chainring is higher than the other chainrings (as is commonly assumed). These two explanations of the term are consistent with each other, but if this same system is used with rear gears it can be confusing. For this reason, this book will always use the more wordy alternative, *outermost chainring*, or a letter code that is described in **NAMING COGS AND GEAR COMBINATIONS** (page 33-2).

Outermost chainring: The one that has the most teeth and is furthest from the frame.

Top gear: Same as *high gear*.

Low gear: On front derailleurs, low gear refers to the chainring closest to the frame. It is called low gear because using it results in the lowest number when cal-

culating gear ratios, not because the top of this chainring is lower than the other chainrings (as is commonly assumed). These two explanations of the term are consistent with each other, but if this same system is used with rear gears it can be confusing. For this reason this book will always use the more wordy alternative, *innermost chainring*, or a letter code that is described in **NAMING COGS AND GEAR COMBINATIONS** (page 33-2).

Bottom gear: Same as *low gear*.

Innermost chainring: The one that has the least teeth and is closest to the frame.

Limit screws: Adjustable stops that are used to stop the inward and outward motion of the derailleur at points that enable the chain to shift to the innermost and outermost chainrings without going too far.

H-screw: A limit screw for stopping the derailleur from shifting the chain out past the outermost chainring.

L-Screw: A limit screw for stopping the derailleur from shifting the chain in past the innermost chainring.

Derailleur cage: The assembly that surrounds and moves the chain.

Outer plate: The plate in the derailleur cage that is on the outward side of the chain.

Inner plate: The plate in the derailleur cage that is on the inward side of the chain.

Cage or plate tail: The rear end of the derailleur cage or of one of the cage plates.

Cage or plate nose: The front end of the derailleur cage or of one of the cage plates.

Parallelogram: In regard to the front derailleur, this is the part of the body (consisting of two arms on four pivots, between the mounting clamp and the cage) that moves the derailleur cage inward and outward.

Adjusting barrel: A hollow screw in the shift-control mechanism (and rarely, in the derailleur) that the inner wire passes through and the housing stops against. As it is screwed in and out, the relative length or tension of the cable system is changed.

Pinch mechanism: This is the mechanism that attaches the inner wire to the derailleur. The inner wire is usually routed through a groove in a plate on the derailleur, and a bolt or nut presses a washer or plate on top of the inner wire to trap and compress it in the groove. The groove in the plate is often hidden by the pressure washer/plate.

Indexing: The type of shifting in which the shift mechanism moves in distinct increments. These increments are designed to precisely move the chain from one chainring to the next. Indexing has virtually replaced friction shifting. In friction shifting, the lever moves smoothly over its full range of motion without any incremented stops. It is up to the operator to decide what the correct amount of lever motion is to get from one chainring to the next.

Mounting bolt: This is the bolt through the derailleur clamp that attaches the derailleur to the seat tube.

Return spring: A spring inside the parallelogram that causes the derailleur to move in as far as the inner-limit screw will allow, when the tension on the inner wire is released.

Over-shift: When the chain moves too far to shift to, and align with, the intended chainring.

Under-shift: When the chain does not move far enough to shift to, and align with, the intended chainring.

In-shift: A shift to a chainring that is further inward than the one that the chain is currently on.

Out-shift: A shift to a chainring that is further outward than the one that the chain is currently on.

Up-shift: This is a term that will *not* be used, because it is an imprecise phrase.

Down-shift: This is a term that will *not* be used, because it too is imprecise.

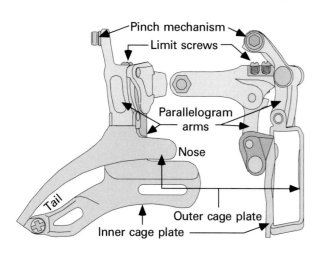

33.1 Back and face views of a front derailleur.

NAMING COGS AND GEAR COMBINATIONS

To perform certain adjustments, the chain needs to be in certain gear combinations. Numbering the gears to identify them does not work, because rear-cog sets have between 5 and 8 gears (so the innermost could be called 5, 6, 7, or 8), and cranksets have between 1 and 3 chainrings (so the innermost might be called 1, 2, or 3).

To avoid confusion, gears will be assigned codes as shown in figures 33.2 and 33.3 (below).

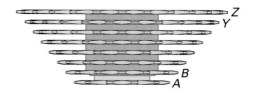

33.2 "A" is always the outermost cog. "B" is always the next-to-outermost cog. "Y" is always the next-to-innermost cog. "Z" is always the innermost cog.

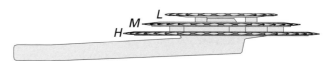

33.3 "H" is always the outermost chainring. "M" is always the middle chainring of a triple. "L" is always the innermost chainring.

Using the above diagrams, it should be easy to conclude that putting the chain in a gear combination of *A/M* would place the chain in the outermost position in the rear, and the middle position of a triple crank. *Y/L* would mean the chain was in the next-to-innermost position in the rear and the innermost in the front.

PREREQUISITES

Shifter and cable installation

In order too adjust the front derailleur, the shift-control mechanism and cable system must be installed.

INDICATIONS

Maintenance

Dirt and wear both affect derailleur performance.

Dirt in the parallelogram can affect shifts. This can be cleaned by immersing the fully-assembled derailleur in solvent, which can quickly remove the dirt.

Wear can adversely affect the parallelogram pivots. When the pivots are worn out, the derailleur must be replaced.

Changing chainrings, right crank arm, or bottom bracket

Any time a chainring, the right crank arm, or a bottom bracket is changed, it is necessary to check the front derailleur adjustment.

Changing chain

Whenever a chain is replaced, shift performance is affected. Fresh chains have less lateral flexibility than worn chains. Different chains have different performance characteristics. After replacing a chain, the derailleur should be checked and readjusted if necessary.

Symptoms indicating adjustment is needed

There are a number of symptoms indicating a probable need for derailleur adjustment.

If the derailleur under- or over-shifts when shifting to the H chainring, or the cage rubs the chain while on the H chainring, the front-derailleur H-screw may need adjustment, or the derailleur height and rotation may be wrong.

If the derailleur under- or over-shifts when shifting to the L chainring, or the cage rubs the chain while on the L chainring, the front-derailleur L-screw may need adjustment, or the derailleur height and rotation may be wrong.

If any shift feels hesitant or results in the cage rubbing the chain after the shift is completed, the indexing needs adjustment.

Symptoms indicating derailleur service is needed

If the derailleur is dirty and the inward action is sluggish, the derailleur should be removed and cleaned, then installed and adjusted.

Symptoms indicating derailleur replacement is needed

The inner plate of the cage can get gouged and worn out from trying to shift when the derailleur is not properly adjusted. If the inner cage plate is gouged or scarred in any way, the derailleur should be replaced.

The derailleur cage can get bent from abusive shifting, crashes, or failure to secure the derailleur. Minor bends can be realigned, but sometimes the derailleur needs to be replaced.

Parallelogram pivots wear out, resulting in excess play in the derailleur. This excess play would show up by wiggling the tail of the cage in and out.

TOOL CHOICES

Table 33-1 (below) shows most of the tools available for front-derailleur adjustment. Most of them are the same tools used for rear derailleurs. Preferred choices are shown in **bold** type. These highlighted tools are recommended because of a balance among: ease of use, versatility, durability, and economy.

TIME AND DIFFICULTY

Front-derailleur adjustment, including hanger alignment and cable-system setup, is a 12–16 minute job of moderately-high difficulty. Front-derailleur removal, cleaning, installation, and adjustment is a 25–30 minute job of moderately-high difficulty.

COMPLICATIONS

Wobbling chainrings

Wobbling chainrings make it difficult to find a limit-screw setting that enables the shift, without ending up with the chain rubbing on the derailleur cage.

FRONT-DERAILLEUR TOOLS (table 33-1)

Tool	Fits and considerations
CAGE ALIGNMENT	
Park BT-3	Actually a brake tool for aligning caliper arms, this tool works well for bending the front-derailleur cage.
FOURTH-HAND (CABLE TENSION) TOOLS (These tools are same as those used for rear derailleurs and brakes.)	
Dia-Compe 556	Tends to let inner wire jam in tool
Hozan C356	Tends to let inner wire jam in tool
Lifu 0100	Consumer tool
Park BT-2	Least tendency for inner wire to jam in tool
VAR 233	Tends to let inner wire jam in tool

railleurs. Instead of numerical ratings, there may simply be a reference to "alpine," "cross-over," or "half-step."

Test method: To test if a derailleur's minimum capacity is being exceeded, follow this procedure. Install the derailleur to the correct height on the seat tube. Swing the derailleur out far enough that the inner plate swings over the top of the next-to-outermost chainring. If the inner plate clears, then the minimum capacity has not been exceeded.

Measurement method: If the bottom edge of the inner cage plate is never more than 10mm below the bottom edge of the outer cage plate, then the derailleur is half-step compatible. If the offset is greater than 10mm at any point, then the derailleur cannot be used with half-step chainrings.

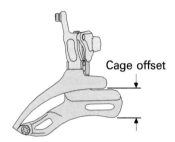

33.6 *Measure cage-plate offset here.*

Derailleur and chainring-set position

It is possible for the chainring set to end up too close to the frame for the front derailleur to work. This can happen even though chainline is acceptable and chainring-to-frame clearance is adequate. When the chainrings are too close to the frame, the moving part of the derailleur may bump into the seat tube or itself before the cage has moved enough to complete the shift. The best solution to this is to change the bottom bracket to move the chainrings as far out as the chainline will allow. At times, it may be necessary to re-space the rear hub *and* move the chainring set, so that the chainrings and rear cog set can both be moved out together to maintain the chainline.

Derailleur and chain

Indexed derailleurs moved in fixed amounts. The chain must respond as expected for the shift to be completed. If the chain has more lateral flexibility than expected, when the derailleur moves its fixed amount, then the chain will not respond enough to complete the shift. Chains vary in lateral flexibility because of

brand differences and wear. If the derailleur manufacturer's recommendations are not followed, shift performance may be compromised.

Chain and chainrings

The width of a chain must be suitable to the chainring set or it may rub against adjacent chainrings. See the **CHAINS** chapter (page 26-2 and 26-16).

The shaping of the side plates of the chain affects a chain's ability to engage the chainring's teeth. When not using the manufacturer's recommended chain, shift performance may be compromised.

UNDERSTANDING HOW FRONT DERAILLEURS WORK

The operation of a front derailleur is relatively complex. By understanding what is happening in a front derailleur, the installation and adjustment procedures outlined here will become clearer.

How a cable moves the derailleur in and out

Most shift-control mechanisms operate by pulling the inner wire through one or more lengths of housing. The mechanism takes up excess inner wire and pulls the derailleur to its outermost position. Figure 33.7 shows this in a simplified form.

The piece of exposed wire closest to the derailleur is attached to an arm that serves as an extension of one of the parallelogram arms. When this lever is rotated about its pivot, the whole parallelogram structure changes shape so that it expands or contracts, moving the derailleur cage out or in.

When the tension on the cable is released, a spring in the parallelogram causes it to return toward its original position.

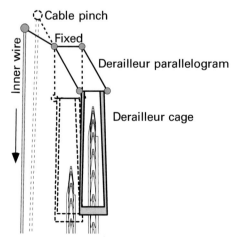

33.7 *How a derailleur parallelogram is deformed across its diagonal, to deflect it laterally to a more outward position.*

How limit screws work

The two limit screws act like two adjustable barricades. There is usually some projection or surface on a parallelogram arm that the limit screw butts up against. By adjusting one limit screw, the range of travel for the parallelogram in one direction will be changed. In other words, by loosening the H-screw, the barricade that stops the outward motion of the parallelogram is changed so the parallelogram can move further out. By loosening the L-screw, the barricade that stops the inward motion of the parallelogram is changed and the derailleur can move further in.

Changing one limit screw does not affect the other. Changing the H-screw setting only changes the shift to the outermost cog. Changing the L-screw only changes the shift to the innermost cog. Figures 33.8 and 33.9 show a simplified and exaggerated model of how limit screws affect the range of motion of the parallelogram.

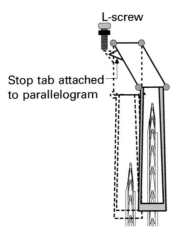

33.8 A stop tab attached to the parallelogram bumps into the H-screw to stop the derailleur's outward motion.

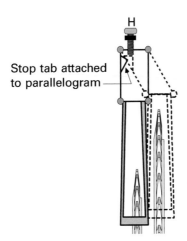

33.9 A stop tab attached to the parallelogram bumps into the L-screw to stop the derailleur's inward motion.

The importance of derailleur height

One of the most important factors affecting front shifting performance is the distance from the derailleur cage to the chainrings. Consider the point that the cage pushes on the chain to be the *deflection point* (see figure 33.10). Consider the point that the chain engages the chainring to be the *engagement point* (see figure 33.11). The engagement point is always at the top dead center of the chainring; it never moves. As the derailleur moves up, the deflection point on the chain moves further back in the derailleur cage. Consequently, as the derailleur moves up, the distance between the engagement point and the deflection point increases. The greater this distance is, the more derailleur motion is needed to deflect the chain enough to cause it to disengage one chainring and engage another. Figures 33.10 and 33.11 show in an exaggerated fashion how moving the derailleur up increases the distance from the engagement point to the deflection point.

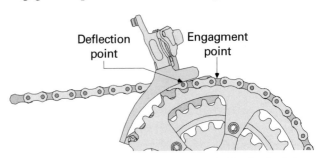

33.10 With the derailleur at the recommended height, the deflection point is only two and a half links behind the engagement point.

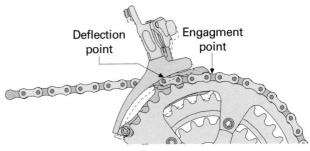

33.11 Note how the deflection point has moved to three and a half links behind the engagment point now that the derailleur height has moved up.

What happens when the derailleur shifts the chain from the outermost chainring inward to the next chainring

Before reading this, put a bike in the stand and shift the chain off of the outermost chainring. As you shift, turn the crank very slowly and move the derailleur in very slowly. Observe exactly what is happening with the chain and derailleur cage for the duration of the shift.

When the derailleur moves inward, the nose of the outer plate deflects the chain just behind the engagement point. Since the distance between the deflection point and the engagement point is very small, only minimal cage motion is needed to cause the chain to derail to the inside of the outermost chainring.

Once the chain disengages from the outer chainring, it is moving inward. Something has to stop the chain from moving too far. That is accomplished by the inner plate of the cage. The rest position of the inner plate is determined either by the derailleur's L-screw on a double-chainring set, or by the indexing adjustment of the cable on a triple-chainring set. If either the L-screw or the cable-tension adjustment is too loose, then the derailleur cage will move too far inward.

After the nose of the outer plate starts the chain derailment and inward motion, two things can add to this inward motion. One is the angle of the chain coming from the rear cogs, and the other is the motion of the tail of outer plate.

Chains naturally want to run straight, rather than in the S-shaped curve that is required when the chain is on two gears that are not in line with each other. When the chain is on an inward cog in the rear, and the chain gets released from the chainring, it tries to straighten itself out. This straightening tends to move the chain inward. The opposite is true if the chain is on one of the outermost cogs when the shift in from the outermost chainring occurs. Since the chain is fixed to a rear cog that is already further out than to where the chain is being pushed, the tendency of the chain to straighten out actually resists the inward motion of the chain. Consequently, when a chain is on an inward cog in the rear, the inward shift of the chain in front is enhanced; when the chain is on an outward cog in the rear, the inward shift of the chain is restricted. Whenever chainline is off, one of these two tendencies becomes exaggerated. If the chainrings are too far out relative to the rear cogs, then the chain has a tendency to shift too far in the front, when being shifted in. If the chainrings are too far in relative to the rear cogs, then the chain resists inward shifts in the front.

The tail of the outer cage plate also affects the inward motion of the chain. When the in-shift starts, the chain is high on the outermost chainring and is being pushed by the highest, most forward, part of the outer plate. Once the chain derails, the chain begins to drop to the smaller chainring. At this point, it

is lower and further back in the derailleur cage. This is when the motion of the tail of the derailleur cage affects the shift inward from the outermost chainring.

Two things determine the range of motion of the tail of the outer plate. One is the L-screw setting (double-chainring sets) or cable tension (triple-chainring sets). The less the whole mechanism is allowed to travel inward, the less the outer plate will move. The primary function of the L-screw or cable tension setting, however, is to position the inner plate so that it will stop the chain from moving too far.

The second factor that influences the inward range of motion of the outer plate is the shape of the derailleur cage. If the tail of the cage is wide, the tail of the outer plate will not end up as far in when the inner plate arrives at its innermost position. If the tail of the cage is narrow, the tail of the outer plate will end up further inward when the inner plate stops at the same point. The width of a derailleur-cage tail can be modified by bending the plates or by changing spacers between the tail ends of the two plates.

What happens when the derailleur shifts the chain from a middle chainring to the innermost chainring

Before reading this, put a bike in the stand and shift the chain from the middle chainring in. As you shift, turn the crank very slowly and shift the derailleur in very slowly. Observe exactly what is happening with the chain and derailleur cage for the duration of the shift.

This is a more difficult shift than the shift from an outer chainring to a middle or inner chainring. The reason is that the top of the middle chainring is much further below the derailleur, so the deflection point is way back on the outer cage plate. This difference is what led Shimano to redesign their chainring teeth to make it easier for the chain to derail inward. This way, the outer plate does not have to move as far to achieve chain derailment.

Other than the fact that this shift naturally demands more of the derailleur, the principles are the same as the shift from the outer chainring.

What happens when the derailleur shifts the chain out to the outer chainring

Before reading this, put a bike in the stand and shift the chain from the next-to-outermost chainring out. As you shift, turn the crank very slowly and move the derailleur cage out slowly. Observe exactly what is happening with the chain and derailleur cage for the duration of the shift.

With this shift, the inner plate moves the chain and the outer plate prevents it from going too far. The shift starts when the tail of the inner plate contacts the chain and pushes it outward. The next thing to happen is that the teeth of the outer chainring (at about the 10:00 position), begin to catch the chain, causing it to rise. As the chain begins to rise, it moves in the derailleur cage and the deflection point moves forward. The nose of the inner plate completes the shift by pressing the chain the rest of the way onto the chainring, close to the engagement point. Because of the short distance between the nose of the inner plate and the engagement point, small changes in the nose position can make big differences in shift performance. Although it is the tail of the inner plate that begins the shift, the final position of the nose of the inner plate is the most critical factor affecting the completion of the shift to the outermost chainring.

Two factors influence the final position of the nose of the inner plate. These are: the H-screw setting and the width of the nose of the cage.

When the H-screw is set, it determines the range of motion of the entire cage. The function of this screw is to position the outer cage plate close enough to the outer chainring so that it is impossible for the chain to move out past the chainring. Consequently, the H-screw cannot be used to adjust the final position of the nose of the inner plate.

Unlike in-shifts, the width of the tail is relatively unimportant to out-shifts. It is the cage width at the nose that is the most important factor. This is controlled by toeing the nose of the inner plate. The final position of the nose of the inner plate is adjusted by bending the nose towards or away from the chain. This is called *toeing* the nose. These days, most derailleurs already come with a good amount of toe, but toeing can be used to speed up the shift to the outer chainring anytime it is sluggish.

Chain angle and load on the chain dramatically affect this shift. As in the case of in-shifting, the position of the chain in the rear affects the tendency of the chain to move one direction or the other. When the chain is in an inward position in the rear, it resists outward motion at the chainrings. When the chain is in an outward position in the rear, it encourages the outward motion of the chain. Load is important because the rising teeth on the chainring being shifted to must help the chain rise by just brushing against the chain. When there is load on the chain, it keeps the chain down.

What happens when the derailleur shifts the chain from an inner chainring to a middle chainring

Before reading this, put a bike in the stand and shift the chain from the innermost chainring to the middle chainring. As you do this, turn the crankset very slowly and move the derailleur cage out slowly, and observe exactly what is happening with the chain and derailleur cage for the duration of the shift.

Like the shift to the outermost chainring, this shift is initiated by the contact of the tail of the inner plate to the chain. This occurs at a considerable distance from the engagement point. Consequently, a great deal of lateral motion is required to move the chain enough to engage the middle chainring. As in the case of a shift to the outermost chainring, the teeth of the middle chainring intersect the chain, and cause it to rise. Unlike the shift to the outermost chainring, the chain never rises enough to engage the nose of the inner plate. This means that the deflection point never gets very close to the engagement point. The only way to keep the chain moving out is to move the inner plate outward more. Consequently, a lot more outward motion is required to shift out to a middle chainring than is required to shift out to an outer chainring. This is perhaps the most demanding shift for a front derailleur to make.

The amount of outward motion of the cage is controlled by the operator on a friction system. It is controlled by the cable-tension adjustment on an indexing system. It is the difficulty of this shift that led Shimano to develop the HyperDrive chainring design, which features an extra set of teeth on the inner face of the middle chainring. These extra teeth help pick up the chain. The HyperDrive chainring's primary teeth are also designed to make it easier for the chain to engage.

The importance of the rotational alignment of the cage

Rotational alignment of the derailleur cage (adjusted by rotating the derailleur mount around the seat tube), controls two important things. It affects the relative angles of the cage plates to the chain, and it affects the relative width of the cage.

Rotational alignment affects the relative angle of the cage plates to the chain. This is most critical when looking at the relationship between the chain and the outer cage plate, when the chain is on the large chainring. If the chain is on an outer rear cog, the outward motion of the chain is enhanced; the chance of the chain shifting out past the outer chainring is at its greatest. Consequently, it is at this time that it is most important to keep the nose of the outer plate as close to the outer chainring as possible. The chain angles out to the outermost cog. The outer plate should remain in a position so that it stays parallel to the chain when the chain is on the outermost chainring and rear cog. Make certain that the outer plate is parallel to the chain, and not the chainrings. Otherwise, there will be large gap between the chain and the nose of the outer plate at the point the chain just clears the tail of the cage. This reduces the effectiveness of the outer plate in preventing an over-shift.

Rotational alignment also affects the effective width of the derailleur cage. Think of the opening in the back of the cage like a window opening in a wall. If you are facing the wall directly and the window is right in front of you, then the full width of the window is apparent, and it would be relatively easy to throw a ball through the window. On the other hand, if the wall is rotated so that you are no longer facing the window squarely, its apparent width is reduced, and it becomes much more challenging to throw the ball through the opening. When a derailleur cage is not rotated correctly, it is effectively narrower, and it is a lot more likely that the chain will end up rubbing the cage in some gear combination.

ABOUT THE REST OF THIS CHAPTER

The rest of this chapter is divided into five parts:
INSTALLATION AND ADJUSTMENT
TESTING INDEX PERFORMANCE
FRONT-DERAILLEUR SERVICE
FRONT-DERAILLEUR TROUBLESHOOTING
EIGHT -AND NINE-SPEED COMPATIBILITY

INSTALLATION AND ADJUSTMENT

INSTALLATION

NOTE: Before proceeding further, be sure to be acquainted with the section, NAMING COGS AND GEAR COMBINATIONS (page 33-2).

Compatibility checks

1. [ ] Check reference information to determine that derailleur and shift-control mechanism are compatible.

2. [ ] Check reference information to determine that inner wire, housing, and shift-control mechanism are compatible.

3. [ ] Check reference information to determine that shift-control mechanism is compatible with brand of crankset and number of chainrings.

4. [ ] Check reference information to determine if chain is compatible with chainring set.

Lubrication

5. Lubricate following points:
   [ ] Both ends of all four parallelogram pivots.
   [ ] Mounting bolt threads.
   [ ] Pinch mechanism threads.

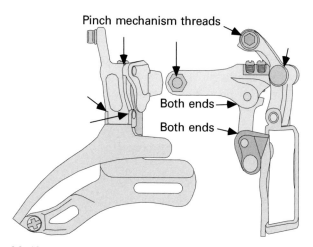

Pinch mechanism threads

Both ends

Both ends

33.12 Oil at all these points.

Setting derailleur height

The derailleur height is critical to the performance of the front derailleur. The height is ideal when the outer cage plate clears the teeth on the outer chainring by 2mm, as it passes over the teeth. The height is acceptable within a clearance range of 1–3mm.

There are several complications to setting the height. The derailleur cage moves upward as it moves out, so if the height is checked when the outer plate is not exactly over the teeth of the outer chainring, then the setting will not be accurate. Another complication is that all the teeth on the outer chainring may not be all equal in height. This may be because the chainring is deliberately not round, or it may be because some teeth are shaped differently to facilitate shifting. When setting the derailleur height, make sure that the crank is rotated to position the tallest teeth under the derailleur cage. The last complication is that the curve of the bottom edge of the outer plate may not be concentric to the curve created by the tips of the chainring teeth. This means that the clearance between the bottom edge of the outer plate and the teeth may not be uniform over the whole length of the outer plate. When setting the height, be sure the clearance is being checked at the point that the bottom edge of the outer plate comes closest to the chainring teeth.

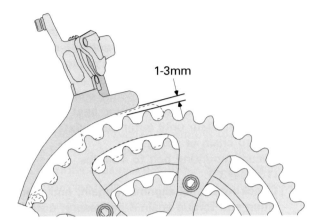

33.13 The correct range of derailleur height.

6. [ ] **Place derailleur clamp around seat tube, then install and gently secure mounting bolt (enough so derailleur will not slide down tube).**

7. [ ] **Check that outer plate is close to parallel to outer chainring, and reposition derailleur if it is not.**

8. **Perform one of following steps, depending on whether the derailleur is just being installed, or already has cable attached.**
   [ ] **If cable is attached to derailleur, use shifter to position derailleur so that outer plate is directly above outer chainring teeth (raise derailleur if necessary).**
   [ ] **If cable is not attached, use fingers to move derailleur cage out until outer plate is directly of outer chainring teeth (raise derailleur if necessary).**

9. [ ] **Turn L-screw in (usually innermost screw) until it supports derailleur so that the outer plate is held directly over teeth of outer chainring (release shifter at this time, if cable is attached).**

10. [ ] **Rotate crank so that tallest teeth are underneath derailleur cage and find point on outer plate that chainring teeth come closest to bottom edge of outer cage plate.**

11. [ ] **Arrange stack of feeler gauges until they total close to 2mm thickness.**

12. **Insert stack of feeler gauges between teeth and bottom edge of outer cage plate and determine if they:**
    [ ] **just fit, height is good**
    [ ] **fit loosely, derailleur should be lowered**
    [ ] **fit too tight, derailleur should be raised.**

13. [ ] **Leave, lower, or raise derailleur on seat tube as determined in previous step, then recheck height.**

Setting derailleur rotation

The derailleur's rotational alignment is critical to the shifting performance. The rotational alignment is ideal when the portion of the outer plate that overlaps the chain is parallel to the chain (when the chain is on the outermost chainring and outermost rear cog).

There are several items to consider when to setting rotational alignment.

One important consideration is that the outer plate of the derailleur cage is rarely a simple flat shape. Add to that the fact that the chain is not flat. Consequently, it is difficult to say that the two are parallel, or not parallel. Furthermore, the whole length of the outer plate does not overlap the chain all at one. The nose is generally above the chain and from the midpoint to the tail, the outer plate is generally below the chain. The only portion of the cage plate that matters is the short section that would rub the chain if the cage plate were moved in far enough to contact the chain (the overlap zone, see figure 33.14, next page).

Another consideration is the fact that the derailleur tends to move while the mounting bolt is being secured.

Finally, it makes a difference whether the chain is already installed, or the derailleur is being installed before the chain. With the chain already in place, the outer plate must be aligned to the chain. That can be somewhat awkward. With the chain not in place yet, a simple and superior substitute for the chain is used to align the derailleur.

This simple substitute for the chain must be hand-made. It cannot be purchased. The materials needed are two short sections of chain and some string. It works best if you use elastic string. Try a store that sells fabric and sewing supplies. One section of chain (3–4") will sit on top of the outer chainring. The other section of chain (3–4") will sit on top of the outermost rear cog. The string needs to be attached to both chain sections. If it is elastic, the length should be set so that it must be stretched slightly for the two segments of the chain to end up where they need to be.

To use the string tool, clamp or tie the wheel and the crank so that they cannot rotate. Place one piece of the chain on the outermost chainring so that the end with the string attached is close to 12:00. Place the other piece of chain on the outermost rear cog so that the slack is pulled out of the string. It is important that the string attaches to both sections of chain in the same way. If the string lines up with a chain roller on one section, it should line up with a chain

20. [ ] **Use procedures in DERAILLEUR-CABLE SYSTEMS chapter (page 31-3) to install cable system.**
21. [ ] **Put front-derailleur shift-control mechanism in fully released position.**
22. [ ] **Loosen or disassemble pinch mechanism to find groove covered by pinch plate or washer.**

Routing the inner wire through the pinch mechanism correctly can be counter-intuitive. The best procedure is to disassemble the pinch mechanism in order to find the groove that the inner wire sits in. The inner wire usually does not maintain a straight line as it goes through the pinch mechanism, but it bends to go over the top of the pinch mechanism. See the illustration below for examples of normal and incorrect cable routing.

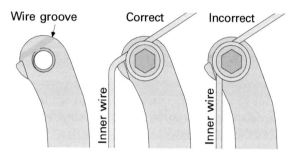

Wire groove   Correct   Incorrect

Inner wire   Inner wire

33.20 Routing the inner wire through the pinch mechanism.

23. [ ] **Lay inner wire into groove and gently secure pinch bolt/nut just enough to keep wire from falling out or slipping. If the pinch plate has a narrow tab that folds over edge of plate with groove, narrow tab always goes counterclockwise of section of wire entering pinch mechanism.**

The inner wire needs slack removed, but not too much or it will interfere with the setting of the L-screw (particularly if the preliminary setting of the L-screw was too tight). In the next step, pull *most* of the slack out of the inner wire before torquing the pinch nut/bolt.

24. [ ] **Pull of slack out of inner wire by hand and secure pinch mechanism to 35in-lbs (12lbs@3") (check that inner wire is still in groove).**
NOTE: Install rear derailleur and attach rear cable system at this time, if not already installed.

Checking chainring wobble

If the chainrings wobble, it interferes with limit-screw setting. The next steps checks for wobble and refer to other chapters for correction of wobble.

25. [ ] **Align nose of outer cage plate directly over teeth of outer chainring.**
26. [ ] **Rotate crank and observe whether outer chainring wobbles >.5mm.**
27. [ ] **See CHAINRINGS chapter (page23-12) and TAPER-FIT CRANKARMS chapter (page 20-10) for procedures for aligning chainrings.**

Chain installation and derailleur-capacity checks

The derailleur should be checked for whether its maximum or minimum capacities have been exceeded.

28. [ ] **Install chain and size by procedure in CHAINS chapter (page 26-10).**
29. [ ] **Put chain in *A/L* position, put load on chain, then check if chain touches cross-piece at tail of front-derailleur cage. If so, maximum capacity has been exceeded.**
30. [ ] **Shift front derailleur until inner cage plate is just above next-to-outermost chainring. If interference with teeth occurs, minimum capacity has been exceeded.**

H-screw setting

Set the H-screw to stop the outward motion of the derailleur cage at a point where the outer plate clears the chain by .5–1.0mm (with chain in *A/H* position).

This is complicated by chainring wobble and chain wiggle. The crank must be turned for several revolutions, and stopped at the point that there is the least clearance between the chain and the outer cage plate. If the chainrings don't wobble much and the chain doesn't wiggle much, then the 1.0mm clearance should be safe. On the other hand, if there is a lot of lateral motion of the chain while the cranks are turning, once the closest point is found, the H-screw should be set closer to .5mm of clearance.

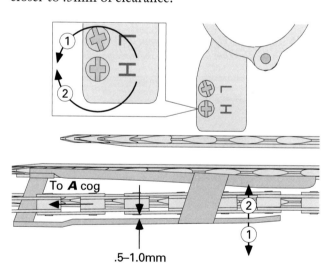

To *A* cog

.5–1.0mm

33.21 Set the H-screw so that this clearance is achieved when the derailleur stops its outward motion.

The best way to check clearance is to insert a feeler gauge between the cage plate and the chain.

31. [ ] **Shift chain to *A* position in rear.**
32. [ ] **While turning crank, pull on exposed section of inner wire to move front derailleur out as far as it will go, then hold it at this position.**

33. [ ] Rotate crank several revolutions and stop at point where least clearance occurs between chain and outer cage plate.

34. [ ] Insert feeler gauge to check clearance between chain and outer cage plate.

35. Correct clearance error by one of following methods:

[ ] Clearance is .5–1.0mm, no change necessary.

[ ] Clearance is <.5mm, turn H-screw counterclockwise about 1/8 turn.

[ ] Clearance is >1.0mm, turn H-screw clockwise about 1/8 turn.

36. [ ] After making adjustment of H-screw, repeat steps 33–35.

L-screw setting

Set the L-screw to stop the inward motion of the derailleur cage at a point where the inner plate clears the chain by .5–1.0mm (with chain in *Z/L* position).

This is complicated by chainring wobble and chain wiggle. The crank must be turned for several revolutions, then stopped at the point that there is the least clearance between the chain and the inner cage plate. If the chainrings don't wobble much and the chain doesn't wiggle much, then the 1.0mm clearance should be safe. On the other hand, if there is a lot of lateral motion of the chain while the cranks are turning, once the closest point is found, the L-screw should be set to get something more like the .5mm clearance.

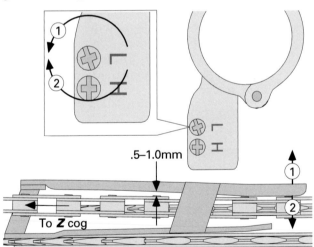

33.22 Set the L-screw so that this clearance is achieved when the derailleur stops its inward motion.

The best way to check clearance is to insert a feeler gauge between the cage plate and the chain.

NOTE: If inner-wire is too tight, L-screw cannot be set.

37. [ ] Shift chain to *Z/L* position.

38. [ ] Rotate crank several revolutions and stop at point where least clearance occurs between chain and inner cage plate.

39. [ ] Make sure shift-control mechanism is fully released.

40. [ ] Insert feeler gauge to check clearance between chain and inner cage plate.

41. Correct clearance error by one of following methods:

[ ] Clearance is .5–1.0mm, no change necessary.

[ ] Clearance is <.5mm, turn L-screw counterclockwise about 1/8 turn.

[ ] Clearance is >1.0mm, turn L-screw clockwise about 1/8 turn.

42. [ ] After making adjustment of L-screw, repeat steps 39–41.

Fine-tuning shift to outer chainring

Once the H-screw is set, the chain should shift effortlessly to the *H* chainring. In some cases, the shift may be slow or hesitant. In this case, some further adjustment is needed, but not of the H-screw. Instead, the angle of the nose of the inner cage plate must be changed.

When the chain is in a more inward position in the rear, the angle of the chain retards out-shifting at the chainrings. Consequently, to test whether further tuning is needed, the chain should be on the most inward cog it would normally be on when shifting to the *H* chainring. This is the *Y* cog. The shift to the *H* chainring should always be made from the adjacent inward chainring, which would be the *L* chainring on a double-chainring set, or the *M* chainring on a triple-chainring set.

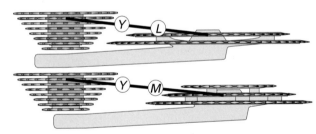

33.23 Correct chain position when checking the shift to the *H* chainring.

43. [ ] Put the chain in the *Y/L* position (double-chainring sets), or *Y/M* position (triple-chainring sets).

When the rider shifts to the *H* chainring, it is usually because the pedaling speed is getting too high in the current chainring. It is a false test to check the shift to this chainring while pedaling slowly. For this test, the minimum pedaling speed should be 60rpm and there is nothing unrealistic about testing the shift at 80rpm.

44. [ ] While pedaling at 60rpm or better, shift chain to *H* chainring and observe whether chain shifts promptly, or with clatter and/or hesitation.

45. [ ] If shift is too slow, use Park BT-3 to bend nose of inner cage plate closer to chain (without bending it far enough that it will rub when chain is on *H* chainring).

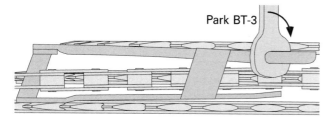

Park BT-3

33.24 Bending the nose of the inner plate closer to the chain to improve the shift to the H chainring.

46. [ ] Shift chain in one chainring and check shift to *H* chainring again. If shift hesitates, toe nose further and check shift again.

Cable stressing

Cable stretch is a commonly misused term. There is really never enough force on the inner wire to actually stretch it. Somehow, however, cable systems develop slack rapidly after installation. This development of slack can compromise the indexing adjustment. What causes this slack is: the inner-wire head seats into its socket, and the housing ends and fittings seat into theirs. This can happen gradually as shifting loads are repeatedly put on the cable systems, or it can be simulated by stressing the cable system one time at a substantially higher load than normal. This over-load stressing also tests the cable system for integrity.

Since the systems will be over-loaded, it is important that the shift-control mechanism and the derailleur be in positions that can support the load. The derailleur should be at its outermost position, supported by the H-screw. The shift-control mechanism should be at its fully released position, supported by its own internal stop. To accomplish this, the lever must be operated to put the chain on the *L* chainring, and then the inner wire must be pulled manually (while pedaling) to put the chain on the *H* chainring. Once the chain is in place, stop pedaling and pull out hard on the inner wire a few times. Protect your hand from damage by using a multi-folded rag between your hand and the inner wire.

47. [ ] Make sure front shift control mechanism is fully released.

48. [ ] While pedaling, pull on exposed inner wire at down tube or top tube until chain is on *H* chainring and stop pedaling.

49. [ ] With chain still on *H* chainring, pull hard on exposed inner wire to seat cable heads and housing ends in stops and sockets, and to test integrity of pinch mechanism and cable system.

Basic cable tensioning

Coarse adjustment of the inner-wire tension is done by pulling or releasing wire through the pinch mechanism on the derailleur. Fine tuning will be done afterwards, by using the adjusting barrel on the shift-control mechanism.

50. [ ] Loosen pinch mechanism.

Before starting, the shift-control-mechanism adjusting barrel should be two full turns out from fully in, so that it can be turned in or out to loosen or tighten the inner-wire tension.

51. [ ] Set shift-control-mechanism adjusting barrel so that it is two full turns out from fully in.

The *fourth hand* is a very convenient tool for removing inner-wire slack, but it can easily make the inner wire much too tight. Watch for any outward motion of the derailleur, indicating the fourth hand tool is being squeezed too tightly.

52. [ ] Using fourth hand tool, *gently* pull slack out of inner wire, *being sure to stop before derailleur begins to move*.

It is easy for the inner wire to slip out of its groove in the pinch mechanism while the tension is being reset. Be certain that the inner wire is in place before torquing the bolt/nut. If it is out of place, then the correct torque may not keep it secure.

53. [ ] Making sure inner wire is still seated in groove in pinch mechanism, secure pinch nut/bolt to 35in-lbs (12lbs@3").

54. [ ] Put chain in *B/H* position (double-chainring sets), or the *B/M* position (triple-chainring sets), then check shift to *L* chainring. If shift hesitates, inner wire was tightened too much in step 52.

Indexing adjustment

The concept of making an index adjustment is similar to a limit-screw adjustment. There is a range of adjustments that work, but the tightest setting is best, since that allows for the greatest amount of deterioration to happen before the system becomes non-functional. The most effective approach to adjustment, therefore, is to deliberately create symptoms that the inner wire is too tight, then loosen the adjustment by small increments until the symptom is eliminated.

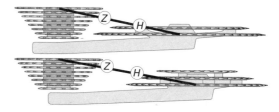

33.25 Starting chain position when checking the indexing adjustment.

55. [ ] Shift chain to *Z/H* position.
56. [ ] Shift chain to next chainring inward.

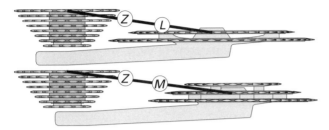

33.26 *Final chain position when checking the indexing adjustment.*

57. Check clearance between chain and inner cage plate and check one of following choices:
[ ] Chain rubs derailleur-cage inner plate, cable-adjusting barrel needs to be turned clockwise 1/4 turn.
[ ] Clearance is >.5mm, cable-adjusting barrel needs to be turned counterclockwise 1/4 turn.
[ ] Clearance is >0mm and ≤.5mm, cable tension is correct.

58. [ ] Shift chain back to *H* chainring.
59. [ ] Repeat steps 56–58 until clearance is >0mm and ≤.5mm.

Inner-wire finish

Excess inner wire should be trimmed and finished. Excess length is unsightly and may get caught in the chain. Soldering prevents fraying, and, therefore, allows the cable to be reused whether a wire cap is used or not. Wire caps do not prevent fraying, but they do prevent someone getting poked by the wire.

The fourth hand is place on the inner wire to act as a gauge to determine how much wire to leave. This remaining wire does not need to be any more than what the fourth hand needs to grab.

60. [ ] Put fourth hand tool on inner wire as if removing slack.
61. [ ] Trim inner wire with wire cutters just past fourth-hand tool.

The next step suggests soldering the end of the wire. This is easy to do and prevents fraying. To solder, a soldering gun, thin 40/60 rosin-core solder, and soldering flux are needed. Put flux on the inner wire. Hold the soldering gun tip flat against one side of the wire until the flux sizzles away. Still holding the soldering gun tip flat against one side of the wire, hold the tip of the solder against the other side of the wire until the heated wire causes the solder to melt and flow into the wire. Some wires have are specially coated or made of stainless steel and will not accept solder. In these cases the wire will melt the solder, but the solder will not flow into the wire. Instead, it beads up and runs off the wire.

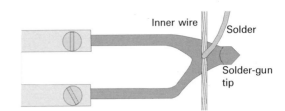

33.27 *Correct soldering technique.*

As an easier alternative to using soldering wire, consider using a flux/solder paste mix (Galaxy Fluxo 50/50, or similar). Apply like flux, heat up until flux stops bubbling, then wipe off while still hot. This method will work on some coated wires and stainless-steel wires that the solder-wire method does not work on.

62. [ ] Solder inner-wire end.

Wire-end caps are sometimes used instead of solder to prevent fraying. This will not work. Crimping the cap onto the wire frequently *causes* fraying. A soldered wire will not fray when the cap is crimped on. The real function of the wire cap is to cover the sharp end of the wire.

63. [ ] Put cap on end of inner wire if desired.

Fine-tuning shift to inner chainring

Occasionally, additional adjustment is needed to get the chain to shift quickly to the innermost chainring. The normal way to improve this shift is to sacrifice the .5–1.0mm clearance between the chain and the inner cage plate that has been set with the L-screw. Be careful; the clearance should never exceed 4mm.

The most difficult time for the chain to shift to the innermost chainring is when the chain is on the outermost portion of the rear cog set. The *B* cog is the furthest-out position that is normal for the chain to be in when shifting to the *L* chainring. When testing the shift to the *L* chainring, the correct starting position is with the chain in the *B/H* position (double-chainring sets), or the *B/M* position (triple-chainring sets).

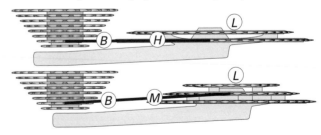

33.28 *Correct chain position to check the shift to the L chainring.*

64. [ ] Put chain in *B/H* position (double-chainring sets), or *B/M* position (triple-chainring sets).

The rider will usually shift to the *L* chainring because the pedaling speed is too slow. It is unrealistic to check if the shift is too slow if the test is performed at a high pedaling speed. Too slow a pedaling speed is also unrealistic. Keep the pedaling speed close to 60rpm for the following test.

65. [ ] While pedaling at no more than 60rpm, check shift to *L* chainring.

66. Check one of following results:
   [ ] Shift hesitated, or chain did not complete shift to *L* chainring, L-screw needs to be turned 1/8 turn counterclockwise.
   [ ] Shift was good, no further L-screw adjustment needed.

Often it is not possible to fully eliminate hesitation in the shift to the *L* chainring. There are three limits to how much the L screw can be loosened. First, part of the derailleur may bump into itself or the frame, in which case further loosening of the limit screw will not result in additional inward motion of the derailleur. Second, the cable tension, which has already been set for optimal indexing, may create an inner limit that is more restrictive than the screw. Consider a slightly looser indexing adjustment to allow a looser L-screw setting. In both these cases, stop adjusting the screw when the derailleur stops responding with additional inward motion. If the shift is still unacceptable, examine other factors, such as derailleur height and rotation. Third, if the inside clearance in the *Z/L* gear combination exceeds 4mm, stop loosening the screw, because more clearance than 4mm is certain to cause an overshift to occur.

67. [ ] Repeat step 65, and 66 if necessary, until shift is good. Stop if derailleur does not move further, or if chain/inner-cage-plate clearance reaches 4mm (with chain in *Z/L* position).

After loosening the L-screw to improve a hesitant shift to the *L* chainring, it is important to check that the chain does not then over-shift when in other gear combinations. If the L-screw is too loose, the chain will try to shift in past the *L* chainring. This is most likely to occur when the chain is on the inner portion of the rear cog set, because this position for the chain encourages inward motion of the chain. Put the chain in the *Z/H* position (double-chainring sets), or the *Z/M* position (triple-chainring sets) to test the chain's tendency to shift in past the *L* chainring.

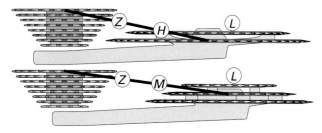

33.29 Correct chain position when checking for an over-shift to the L chainring.

68. [ ] Shift chain to *Z/H* position (double-chainring sets), or to *Z/M* position (triple-chainring sets).

69. [ ] While pedaling at no more than 60rpm, shift chain repeatedly to *L* chainring to check for tendency of chain to shift too far.

If there is not an L-screw setting that eliminates slow shifting without introducing over-shifting, then there is a likely problem with chainline (chainrings are too far out). It could also be that the tail of the derailleur cage needs to be customized (widened) to reduce the tendency to over-shift.

70. Check one of following options:
   [ ] Chain shows no tendency to over-shift in step 69, L-screw setting is final.
   [ ] Chain does show tendency to over-shift in step 69, chainline should be checked and modifying width of tail of derailleur cage should be considered.

TESTING INDEX PERFORMANCE

The performance of any indexing front-derailleur system can be tested and measured. The procedures described above are designed to set the indexing adjustment at *the tightest setting that allows for good shifting*. If the indexing system has normal performance, then there are probably looser settings for the cable that also allow proper shifts into all the gears. The range of adjusting-barrel positions from the tightest that provides good shifting to the loosest that will allow shifting into all the gears is called the *Functional Range of Adjustment* (or FRA).

The performance of all systems deteriorates with wear and the accumulation of dirt. When the FRA is narrow, it will take only a small amount of riding before service is needed to restore acceptable shifting. When the FRA is extremely narrow, finding a correct adjustment at all is challenging. When the FRA is broad, it will take much longer before service is needed. Therefore, it is to the rider's and the mechanic's advantage for the system to have a broad FRA.

There are two reasons to measure the FRA. First, it enables an accurate determination of whether parts might need replacement or cleaning on a used system. Second, it permits an evaluation of whether a non-recommended part negatively affects indexing performance.

There is no absolute value for an appropriate FRA. It varies with the brand and quality of equipment, as well as some other factors. For popular systems, an FRA of about two quarter turns of the cable-adjusting barrel should be expected of new equipment. One of the most critical things to getting a decent FRA is proper rotational alignment of the derailleur.

If evaluating properly set-up used equipment that all meets manufacturer's specifications for compatibility, and the FRA is not at least two quarter turns, then something in the system needs to be cleaned or replaced.

If evaluating any equipment, used or new, that *does not* meet manufacturer's specifications for compatibility and the FRA is not at least two quarter turns, then the non-matched equipment probably needs to be replaced.

If considering installing equipment on a system that may not be compatible, measure the FRA before the change, and again afterwards. If it is reduced, then the equipment change will downgrade shift performance. If it is still above one quarter turn, then it may be acceptable even though it is a downgrade of performance. This test process applies to mis-matching chains, derailleurs and shifters, cable systems, and even derailleurs with chainring sets.

MEASURING THE FUNCTIONAL RANGE OF ADJUSTMENT (FRA)

1. [ ] Perform an index adjustment using steps 55–59 of the *INSTALLATION AND ADJUSTMENT* procedure for front derailleurs (page 33-17).

2. [ ] Turn cable-adjusting barrel in 1/4 turn.
3. [ ] Shift chain to *A/H* position.
4. **Check for chain rubbing outer cage plate and check one of following options:**
    [ ] No rub, shift chain back to *M* chainring and repeat steps 2–4.
    [ ] Chain rubs, inner-wire tension is too loose, record number of turns to create too loose symptom here: _____ quarter turns.
5. [ ] If measuring FRA to evaluate a component change, install new component and repeats steps 1–4.

FRONT-DERAILLEUR SERVICE

The only service performed on front derailleurs is removal and cleaning of the fully-assembled derailleur; most front derailleurs are not designed to be disassembled to any significant degree. It is a good idea to perform a few inspections before installing the derailleur. Before installing the derailleur, inspect for cracks in the mounting clamp and roughness or gouges in the inner cage plate.

FRONT-DERAILLEUR TROUBLESHOOTING

Cause	*Solution*
SYMPTOM: *The shift to the H chainring is slow.*	
Inner wire is not tight enough.	Shift to *L* chainring and check inner-wire tension.
The inner-cage-plate nose needs toe adjustment.	Trying bending inner cage-plate nose toward chain.
The H-screw is too tight. This is only the cause if the chain is also rubbing the outer cage plate when the chain is in the *A/H* position.	Loosen H-screw only enough to create up to 1.0mm clearance between chain and outer cage plate (when the chain is in the *A/H* position).
The derailleur is mounted too high.	Check and correct derailleur height.
The chainring teeth are worn out.	Compare teeth to a new chainring of the same type.
The inner cage plate is chewed up.	Inspect plate and replace the derailleur if the cage plate is damaged.
SYMPTOM: *The chain is shifting past the H chainring.*	
If the derailleur rotation is correct, then the H-screw is too loose.	Check derailleur rotation, and tighten H-screw to create no more than 1.0mm clearance between the cage and the outer cage plate (when the chain is in the *A/H* position).
If the clearance between the chain and the outer cage plate is correct, then the derailleur is positioned with the tail rotated too far in.	Check and correct derailleur rotation, then set limit screws and cable tension again.

(Continued next page)

FRONT-DERAILLEUR TROUBLESHOOTING (continued)

Cause	Solution
SYMPTOM: *The chain rubs the inner cage plate after shifting to the M chainring (the derailleur is indexing).*	
Inner-wire tension is too tight if the derailleur is indexing.	Check the indexing adjustment of the front derailleur.
There is excess friction in the cable system.	Remove, inspect, and correct problems in cable system.
The derailleur is fouled with dirt.	Remove and clean the derailleur.
SYMPTOM: *The chain rubs the outer cage plate when the chain is on the M chainring and is shifted to one of the outer rear cogs.*	
If the derailleur is indexing, the inner-wire tension is too low.	Check and correct the indexing adjustment.
The derailleur's rotational alignment is off, with the tail too far in compared to the nose.	Check and align the derailleur's rotation so that the outer cage plate is parallel to the chain (when the chain is in the A/H position).
If the derailleur is non-indexing, it may not be designed to clear the chain in all gear combinations without its position being manually trimmed.	The operator needs to trim the cage position with the shift-control mechanism.
The tail of the derailleur cage is too narrow for the gear set-up and bike.	Add spacers to the tail of the cage, or deform the outer plate at the tail end to widen the tail end of the cage.
SYMPTOM: *There is a tick once per crank revolution, whenever the chain is on the H chainring.*	
The tail of the derailleur cage is interfering with the crank arm.	The H-screw is too loose, or the derailleur is rotated with the tail too far out.
SYMPTOM: *The tail of the derailleur cage hits the crank arm when the derailleur is properly rotated and the H-screw setting is correct.*	
The crankset does not provide enough clearance between the arm and the outer chainring for the derailleur being used.	Change derailleurs to one with a flatter outer cage plate (no tail offset), or compromise the rotational alignment of the derailleur (check for ill consequences if the compromise is made).
SYMPTOM: *There is a continuous scraping sound when the chain is on the H chainring, but the chain is not rubbing either cage plate.*	
The minimum capacity of the derailleur has been exceeded, and the teeth of the next-to-outermost chainring are rubbing on the inner cage plate.	Change the derailleur or the size of the next-to-outermost chainring.
The outer cage plate is rubbing on a chainring guard.	Remove the chainring guard or compromise the derailleur height or rotation (check for ill consequences if the compromise is made).
SYMPTOM: *The chain drags over the cross-piece at the tail of the derailleur cage when the chain is in the A/L position.*	
Chain is dangling when there is no load.	If the symptom only occurs when chain is not under load, it is not a problem.
Derailleur is mounted too high.	Check and correct derailleur-mounting height.
If symptom occurs when derailleur height is correct and there is load on the chain, the maximum capacity of derailleur has been exceeded.	Change the derailleur to one that can handle the difference in largest and smallest chainring sizes, or change size of chainrings so that the difference is within the capacity of the derailleur being used.

EIGHT- AND NINE-SPEED COMPATIBILITY

COMPONENT COMPATIBILITY

The narrower chain and chainring spacing used in the Shimano nine-speed drive trains requires a narrower front derailleur cage for optimal performance. Therefore, Shimano derailleurs marked "Mega-9" are not fully interchangeable with other Shimano derailleurs.

Mega-9 front derailleurs have the same actuation ratio (the amount the derailleur moves for a given amount of cable movement), so there is full compatibility between all Shimano MTB front derailleurs and Shimano MTB front shift levers.

While there is no problem mixing shift levers and derailleurs there is a problem with mixing a Mega-9 front derailleur with a chain that is not nine-speed type. Obvious rubbing will occur that cannot be eliminated by any adjustment.

As long as the chain is changed also, excellent results can be attained when using a Mega-9 front derailleur on a Shimano chainring set that is not nine-speed spacing. Since the nine-speed chain works with all cog sets, this is a very acceptable mix of components.

The reverse combination of using a front derailleur that is not Mega-9 on a full nine-speed drive train will work, but you should expect a compromise in performance. In particular, the shift from the middle chainring to the inner chainring will be slow and unpredictable.

CHAINRING SIZE CAPACITY

In addition to the component compatibility issues, it is important to keep in mind that Mega-9 models of derailleurs sometimes have different minimum and maximum-tooth-difference ratings than the earlier version of the same derailleur. This is due to the fact that at the same time that Shimano introduced nine-speed drive trains, they also switched from compact chainring sets to "Mega" sized chainring sets. For example, the older seven- or eight-speed Deore LX model FD-M567 is rated for a minimum chainring size difference of 10 teeth and the matching crankset is a 22-32-42 configuration, but the more current Mega-9 type Deore LX model FD-M570 is rated for a minimum difference of 12 teeth. Consequently, the FD-M570 will not work on the older crankset, regardless of nine-speed issues.

Pull-up nut: The nut that the pull-up bolt threads into.

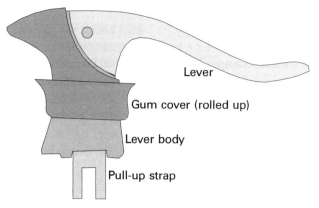

34.3 A typical brake lever for drop bars on a road bike.

Strap clamp: This is like a cast clamp with a hinge or hook on one end, but the separate part that wraps around the side of the handlebar opposite the lever body is a semi-flexible plate of metal, rather than a rigid casting. The strap clamp is found most often on BMX/freestyle bikes, and on bikes with upright bars such as are found on classic 3-speeds.

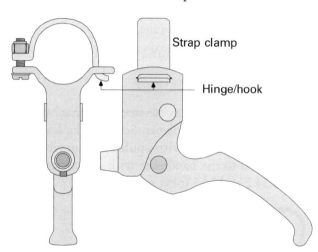

34.4 An inexpensive BMX/freestyle lever. More expensive BMX/ freestyle levers are similar in design to MTB levers.

Cable anchor: The part of the lever arm to which the brake inner-wire attaches. It might be a simple socket in the body of the lever arm, or it may be a pivoting mechanism (with a socket for the inner-wire head) attached to the lever arm.

Inner wire: The wire that attaches to the lever arm, passes through the lever body and adjusting barrel, through the cable housing, and attaches to the brake.

Cable housing: The outer sheath of the cable system. It stops against the adjusting barrel or a non-adjustable fitting on the lever body.

Ferrule: Any of a wide variety of shapes of fittings that adapt the end of the cable housing to fit to the socket in the lever body or adjusting barrel.

PREREQUISITES

To install a brake lever, it is necessary to know how to adjust the brake. In many cases it is also necessary to know how to install handlebar coverings, such as tape or grips.

INDICATIONS

Symptoms indicating a brake lever should be replaced

Brake levers need to be replaced for four reasons: bends in the lever at any point, cracks in any part of the lever, stripped threads for the mounting bolt in the cast body, or excessive play in the lever pivot that cannot be adjusted out or repaired by replacing pivot bushings.

Symptoms indicating brake levers need service

Brake levers need service for many reasons:
- Pull-up mechanisms fail and need to be replaced.
- Levers operate roughly because of dirt in the pivots.
- Levers operate roughly because of lack of lubrication in the pivots.
- Jerky brake operation or squeaks indicate that the cable anchors need lubrication.
- Bent adjusting barrels should be replaced.
- Slop in the lever pivots indicates that the pivots need adjustment or that the bushings need to be replaced.
- In some types of levers, sticky lever action might indicate that a bent pivot stud might need replacement.

Symptoms indicating a brake lever needs to be repositioned

The position of the brake levers is critical to the safe operation of the brakes. The brake levers need to be readily accessible from any normal riding position, and they should be positioned so that the rider can operate the levers with a minimum of hand and wrist contortion.

One way to identify whether brake levers need to be repositioned is to ride the bike and operate the levers from all normal hand positions on the handlebar. If some hand positions provide dramatically easier access to the levers than others, then the levers should be repositioned. If the wrist must be cocked too close to its limit of range of motion to operate the brake lever, then a better position should be found.

You should also review the positioning guidelines offered in this chapter.

Symptoms indicating a brake lever needs to be secured

The issues of lever security are different for brake levers on road bikes with drop bars and for brake levers on off-road bikes. On drop-bar road bikes, the lever bodies are often used like handlebar extensions and twisted with great force, but on all other types of bikes the lever bodies are never grasped. For this reason, brake levers on drop bars should be virtually rigid on the handlebar. Any time the lever rotates easily around a drop handlebar, the lever should be secured to the limit of the equipment. For all other brake-lever types, there is a desireable degree of freedom to rotate; freedom to rotate prevents damage to the brake levers when they experience impact. More details on lever security are provided in the instructions for lever installation.

Handlebar and stem replacement

To replace a stem, at least one brake lever must be removed, and then properly installed on the bars. To replace the handlebars, both levers must be removed, and then properly installed on the bars.

General brake service

Any time a mechanic services the brakes in any way, the brake levers should be given a thorough inspection. If the levers are damaged they should be replaced. If misaligned they should be aligned. The levers should be torqued to the recommended torque and checked for security. If operating roughly, the levers should be cleaned or lubricated.

TOOL CHOICES

The only special tool recommended for brake lever service is a Park SD-1. This is a T-handled screwdriver with a hollow-ground tip. This tool is essential for the proper installation of slotted-head pull-up bolts.

TIME AND DIFFICULTY

Installing or servicing a brake lever is a relatively easy job of that should only take 1–2 minutes. The real work is the work comes as a result of installing a lever: adjusting the brakes or covering the bars.

COMPLICATIONS

Fit of brake levers to different-size bars

For most types of brake levers, fit to the handlebar is simple. For example, if installing a brake lever on an MTB handlebar, use an MTB brake lever; fit is assured. Brake levers that fit on road-bike handlebars are more complicated. There are three basic sizes of drop bars, and different pull-up straps available to fit the different sizes of bars. For more information on the sizes of straps and handlebars, see table 34-1 (page 34-6).

Interference with shift-control mechanisms

Brake levers and shift-control mechanisms are often mounted close together on MTB handlebars. The manufacturers of each cannot anticipate all the designs that might exist or be created. Consequently, there is sometimes interference between the brake lever and the shift-control mechanism even if both are mounted correctly. Sometimes a minor change in the position of the shift-control mechanism is all that is needed. Do not compromise the brake lever position. On rare occasions, it might be necessary to change either the brake lever or the shift-control mechanism to eliminate this interference.

Compatibility with brake calipers

Brake levers may be incompatible with some brake calipers. The distance from the center of the lever pivot to the center of the cable anchor determines the amount of inner wire that will be moved per degree of lever arm motion. If a replacement brake lever has a significantly larger dimension between the lever pivot and cable anchor, then the lever will move the pads much more quickly to the braking surface. This will result in greater maximum power, but less ability to modulate the brake. If a replacement brake lever has a significantly smaller dimension between the lever pivot and cable anchor, then the lever will move the pads much less quickly to the braking surface. This will result in less maximum power, but greater ability to modulate the brake.

Failure of pull-up-strap system

Pull-up-strap systems are prone to several types of failure that prevent the lever from securing fully.

Some types of pull-up nuts are not fixed to the pull-up strap. When the system has too much slack, the pull-up nut can disengage, resulting in a failure of the lever to secure, and damage to the pull-up strap. The strap is damaged because the nut usually remains engaged to one end of the strap; when the nut is pulled up, only one end of the strap is pulled, which destroys its symmetry.

A pull-up strap can crack or break where it joins the pull-up nut. This damage cannot be seen except when the brake lever is off the bar and disassembled.

The threads on the pull-up nut or pull-up bolt often strip. This damage is hidden inside the lever.

Levers will not secure

Levers may fail to secure for a variety of reasons due to fit problems or parts failure. In some cases, the lever will fail to secure adequately even when everything is the correct size and nothing has failed. This can be caused by two things. Plastic lever bodies do not offer enough friction against the bar to prevent slippage. Chrome-plated-steel bars are more slippery than aluminum bars and can keep levers from properly securing. The combination of a plastic lever body and a chrome-plated-steel handlebar is certain to be a problem. Without changing the equipment, there is no solution. The mechanic must make sure that everything is in working order and the maximum allowable torque is used.

ABOUT THE REST OF THIS CHAPTER

The rest of this chapter is divided into five sections. The first section is *MTB-BRAKE LEVERS*. It is followed, in order, by *DROP-BAR BRAKE LEVERS*, *BMX/FREESTYLE-BRAKE LEVERS*, *UPRIGHT-BAR BRAKE LEVERS*, and finally *BRAKE-LEVER TROUBLESHOOTING*.

Detailed information about removal, installation, inspection, and installation is provided about MTB brake levers and brake levers for drop-bars on road bikes. For BMX/freestyle levers and levers for upright-bars, only significant differences from the other types of levers are covered. The **BRAKE-CABLE SYSTEMS** chapter covers setup of the cable system. Individual chapters about different types of brake calipers cover the setup of the calipers and attachment of the cable system.

MTB-BRAKE LEVERS

For purposes of installation and removal, MTB-brake levers come in several varieties. These are closed-clamp types, open-clamp types, closed-strap types, and open-strap types. The open-clamp and open-strap types can be removed and installed without sliding the lever over the end of the bar. The closed-clamp and closed-strap varieties must be slid off and on the end of the bar. Since the vast majority of MTB-brake levers are of the "closed" variety, the following procedure assumes this type.

NOTE: If working on a bike with already-installed levers, go to the section of this procedure called INSPECTION *for used bikes, or* LUBRICATION *for new bikes.*

REMOVAL

1. [ ] **Remove grip(s).**
2. [ ] **If mounted outward from brake lever, remove shift-control mechanism.**
3. [ ] **Unhook cable system from brake caliper(s).**
4. [ ] **Align slots in lever body, adjusting barrel, and barrel locknut.**
5. [ ] **Pull housing out of end of adjusting barrel and drop inner wire through slots in lever body, adjusting barrel, and barrel locknut.**
6. [ ] **Pull lever arm toward handlebar, align inner wire with slot in cable anchor, then pull inner-wire head out of cable anchor.**
7. [ ] **Loosen mounting bolt or pull-up bolt.**
8. [ ] **Slide lever off end of handlebar.**

INSPECTION

9. [ ] **Inspect lever body and lever arm for cracks.**
10. [ ] **Inspect lever arm for bends.**

Loose lever pivots detract from the rider's feeling of control. Wiggle the end of the lever arm side-to-side to check for excessive play. A couple of millimeters is normal, but more than that should be eliminated, if possible. Some MTB lever pivots are adjustable, and some are not. If the pivot bolt threads into a nut in a socket, then the lever pivot is probably not adjustable. If the nut is exposed, then the pivot is adjustable. To adjust, loosen the nut, turn the pivot bolt clockwise, then secure the nut while holding the bolt stationary. If the adjustment is made too tight, then the lever will not return when released (once the brake system is fully set up).

11. [ ] **Inspect lever pivot for looseness and adjust if possible.**

LUBRICATION

12. [ ] **Oil both sides of lever arm at lever pivot.**
13. [ ] **Oil cable-anchor pivots, or inside cable-head socket in lever arm if socket is in aluminum casting.**
14. [ ] **Grease adjusting-barrel threads if not already obviously greased.**

If the lever will be secured, it is critical that the mounting-bolt/pull-up-bolt threads are lubricated, because the recommended torques are based on the assumption that the threads are lubricated. If the threads are visible and clearly have lubrication on them, it is reasonable to assume that no more need be added. If the threads are not visible, or no lubrication can be seen, even if it means removing the bolt, the threads should be lubricated.

15. [ ] **Oil mounting-bolt/pull-up-bolt threads if not obviously lubricated already.**

INSTALLATION, ALIGNMENT AND SECURITY

There are right and left brake levers for MTBs. When the lever is on the correct side, the mounting bolt will be on the back/bottom face of the lever. If the wire head is installed in a socket that is on one face of the lever arm, this socket also will be on the back/bottom face of the lever.

16. [ ] **If shift-control mechanism is to be mounted inward of brake lever (most non-integral shift-control mechanisms except twist grips), install it on bar first, but do not secure.**
17. [ ] **Slide brake lever over end of handlebar.**
18. [ ] **Install twist-grip-type shift-control mechanism onto handlebar (if any).**
19. [ ] **Install grip fully onto bar.**
20. [ ] **Position brake lever as far outward as grip (and twist grip) will allow. (Some old-style brake levers are so long that this positioning would place the tip of the lever arm past the outward end of the grip. In this case, position the brake lever as far outward as possible without the tip of the lever extending beyond the outward end of the grip.)**

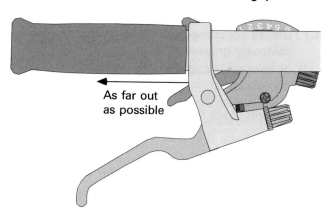

As far out as possible

34.5 *Set the lateral position of the brake lever as close to the grip as possible.*

21. [ ] **Gently secure mounting-bolt/pull-up-bolt. (Lever should still easily rotate around bar.)**

To properly align the brake levers, the bike needs to be at the angle that it would be when sitting on level ground. This can be done several ways. If the bike is known to have a level top tube, then use a dial protractor to check that the top tube is parallel to the ground. If it is not known whether the top tube is level, or it is known that it is not, then use a tape

measure to measure from the center of each axle to the ground. If the axles are equidistant from the ground, then the bike is in the "on-ground" position.

22. [ ] **Put bike at angle it would be when sitting on level ground.**
23. [ ] **Place dial protractor on lever body so that dial is visible from side of bike (if lever body has no flat surface, hold protractor so that its base is parallel to the plane in which the lever arm swings).**
24. [ ] **Adjust lever position until protractor reads 45° (±5° is acceptable range).**

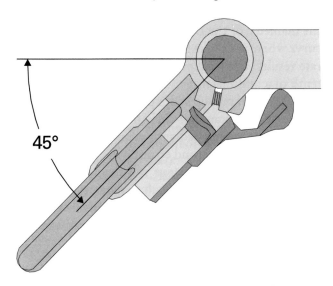

45°

34.6 *Set the rotational position of the lever so that the plane that the lever swings in is 45° down from flat.*

25. [ ] ***Lever with cast clamp:* Secure mounting bolt to 35–60in-lbs (12–20lbs@3").**
    ***Lever body held on by pull-up strap:* Secure pull-up bolt to 60–70in-lbs (20–24lbs@3").**
26. [ ] **Viewing from rider's perspective, check that both levers extend in front of handlebar equally, indicating that their rotational positions match.**

INNER-WIRE ATTACHMENT

27. [ ] **Align slots in adjusting barrel and barrel locknut with slot in bottom of lever body.**
28. [ ] **Pull lever to grip and place inner-wire head in cable anchor.**
29. [ ] **Swing wire up into slots in lever body, adjusting barrel, and barrel locknut.**
30. [ ] **Turn adjusting barrel or locknut so that slot no longer lines up with slot in lever body.**

Sizing and routing the left-brake-lever housing loop

The housing loop from the left brake lever usually goes directly to the brake, but is sometimes routed down through the center of the stem.

If the loop of housing goes directly to the brake, the brake pads must be held to the rim while sizing the housing loop. The loop should be a gentle curve that is as short as possible, without creating any abrupt bends at either end. The housing should stay in front of the handlebar.

If the housing is routed into the center of the stem, the loop should be a gentle curve that is as short as possible, without creating any abrupt bends at either end. The housing should stay in front of the handlebar.

UPRIGHT-BAR BRAKE-LEVER HOUSING LOOPS

The housing loop from the right lever should be set up in the same fashion as on an MTB right lever. The housing loop for the left lever should be set up in the same fashion as a BMX/freestyle left lever that has housing routed directly to the brake.

REAR-HOUSING-STOP LOOPS

The loop can go around either side of the seat post/seat tube, except that it should be on the opposite side of any seat post quick-release lever. The length of the loop should be set to minimize abrupt bends where the housing enters the stops, and to minimize double bends. If the housing stop is a hanger mounted to the seat-post binder, the angle of the hanger might need to be adjusted. The hanger position should be set so that the inner wire will come out of the hanger parallel to the line of the hanger or any adjusting barrel on the hanger.

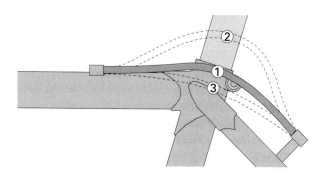

35.10 When housing is the correct length (1), it enters the stop straight. When it is too long (2) or too short (3), then it bends at the point it enters the stop..

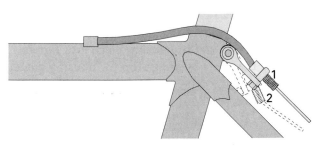

35.11 When an adjustable cable hanger is correctly aligned (position 1), then the inner wire leaves the adjusting barrel without a bend. If the hanger is incorrectly aligned (position 2), the inner wire changes direction as soon as it exits the adjusting barrel.

REAR-CALIPER HOUSING LOOPS

The position of the housing stop on a caliper changes as the caliper opens and closes. The small amount of motion that occurs under normal operation of the caliper is not an issue; however, when the caliper is not hooked up, the housing stop will move a significant distance from its operating position. For this reason, the brake pads should always be held to the rim when sizing a loop of housing that goes to the caliper. The length of the loop should be set to minimize abrupt bends where the housing enters the stops, and to minimize double bends.

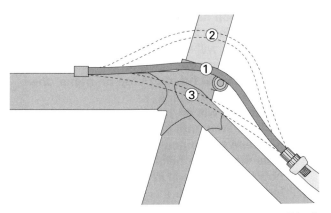

35.12 When the length of the housing loop to a rear sidepull brake is correct (1), then it enters the adjusting barrel in a straight line. If the length is too long (2), or too short (3), then the housing bends as it enters the adjusting barrel.

TOOL CHOICES

Some brake tools are virtually universal, while others are specific to certain brands and models of brakes. Table 36-1 covers all the tools for the job. The preferred choices are in **bold**. A tool is preferred for a balance among: ease of use, quality, versatility, and economy. When more than one tool for one function is **bold**, it means that several tools are required for different configurations of parts.

BRAKE TOOLS (table 36-1)

Tool	Fits and considerations
THIRD-HAND TOOLS (for holding pads to rim)	
Park BT-1	Inexpensive, not universally effective
Park BT-4	Inexpensive, works on some cantilevers
Park BT-5	Expensive "universal" tool that is not truly universal
Pocket Pro Velcro	Velcro strap, not universally effective
United Bicycle Tool WB-BRK	A truly universal third-hand tool borrowed from the carpentry trade (called Quick Grip, also)
VAR 02	Expensive, not universally effective
VAR 939	Expensive, not universally effective
Wire-types, various manufacturers	Inexpensive consumer tools, not universally effective
FOURTH-HAND TOOLS (for pulling slack from brake inner wire, same tool used for derailleurs)	
Dia-Compe 556	Tends to let inner wire jam in tool
Hozan C356	Tends to let inner wire jam in tool
Lifu 0100	Consumer tool
Park BT-2	Least tendency for inner wire to jam in tool
VAR 233	Tends to let inner wire jam in tool
SIDEPULL-CALIPER TOOLS	
Dia-Compe 445	Set, includes: 10mm open with 8mm box, and 10mm box with 9mm box: thin wrenches for brake-pivot nuts
Dia-Compe 446	Set, includes: 13mm open with 12mm box, 10mm open with 9mm box, 8mm open with10mm box: thin wrenches for brake-pivot nuts
Park BT-3 (pair)	Used for twisting ends of caliper arms to toe brake pads
Park CBW-6	Set (includes CBW-1 thru CBW-5) of thin 8mm, 9mm, 10mm, and 11mm wrenches for brake-pivot nuts
Park OBW-1	10mm & 13mm thin offset wrench for brake centering and pivot adjustment
Park OBW-2	11mm & 12mm thin offset wrench for brake centering and pivot adjustment
Park OBW-3	14mm thin offset wrench for brake centering and pivot adjustment, with pronged end for muscling caliper springs to adjust centering
Scura Centering Tool	Fits in the coils of a sidepull spring so that spring can be muscled
Weinmann 682/683/693	Set, includes: 9mm/10mm box, 11mm open, 8mm box with 10mm open: thin wrenches for brake nuts
Weinmann 685 & 687	4mm & 5mm sockets for hex fitting on end of pivot bolt on old Weinmann brakes (for centering)
United Bicycle Tool Langley Fifth Hand	Very useful for disengaging and engaging caliper springs
CANTILEVER-CALIPER TOOLS	
Bicycle Research BM-1	Mill for repairing pivot-stud damage and cleaning paint off pivot stud
Shimano TL-CB-10	Set of 6 tools for setting up Shimano Pro-Set type brakes with link-wires

THREADED-STUD/CURVED-WASHER PAD ALIGNMENT

This type of pad-alignment system is primarily found on cantilever brakes and U-brakes. It is also found on upgrade pad sets that can be used with any caliper that comes with a simple threaded-stud pad-alignment system. A threaded-stud on the brake shoe fits in a slot in the caliper arm. Height and tangent of the pad are fully adjustable (in the same way as the simple threaded-stud system), but alignment washers between the shoe and the caliper arm permit simultaneous alignment of the toe and vertical angle of the pad face.

Toe alignment

Brake pads need toe to reduce squeal, particularly when the pads are new. When a pad is properly toed, the exit-end of the pad should reach the rim before the entry-end of the pad. If both brakes were at the 12:00 position on the wheel, toe could be described as having the front ends of the brake pads reach the rim before the rear ends reach the rim. If pads have broken in properly to the rim, no toe should be needed, unless the pads squeal on a test ride.

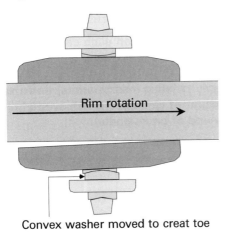

Convex washer moved to creat toe

36.13 When the convex washer is moved forward or backward, the end of the pad moves in or out.

The curved washer between the inside face of the caliper arm and the brake shoe enables toe adjustment. When this washer is pushed one way, the forward end of the pad moves in. When the washer is pushed the other way, the forward end of the pad moves out. Some mechanics find it easiest to manipulate the washer to align the pad. For other mechanics, the easiest approach is to manipulate the pad in order to position the washer. If the mounting nuts are loose and the cable is adjusted so that the caliper arms are pressing the pads against the rim, the pads will automatically align to have no toe. To adjust pad toe, a spacer can be put between the entry-end of the pad and the rim to space it further out. A #4 (1/2") thumb tack pressed into the face of the entry-end of the pad makes a good spacer. With this thumb tack (henceforth called *toe-tack*) in place, toe adjustment is semi-automatic. Moving the toe-tack closer to the exit-end of the brake pad increases the amount of toe. Manipulation of the washer may be necessary to finesse the alignment.

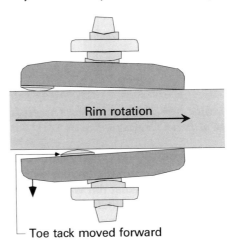

Toe tack moved forward

36.14 Toe tacks can be moved toward the exit-end of the pad to increase the toe.

1. [ ] Complete **ATTACH CABLE TO CALIPER** procedure for the type of cable system being used.
2. [ ] Check that toe-tack and exit-end of brake pad are both contacting rim simultaneously, and manipulate curved washer between arm and shoe to improve toe as necessary.

Vertical-angle alignment

Vertical-angle alignment can also be affected by changing the position of the curved washer against the inside face of the caliper arm. When this washer is pushed in one direction, the pad face angles down. When the washer is pushed in the other direction, the pad face angles up. Some mechanics find it easier to manipulate the washer to align the pad. Other mechanics, find the easier approach is to manipulate the pad to position the washer. The procedure for setting the toe usually also sets the vertical-angle alignment, but it may need additional fine tuning.

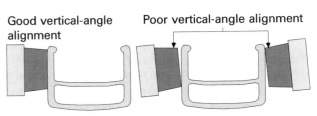

Good vertical-angle alignment   Poor vertical-angle alignment

36.15 The vertical angle of the pad face should closely match the vertical angle of the rim's braking surface.

When manipulating the washer or pad to improve the vertical angle of the pad face, it is not unusual for the height of the pad to end up too high or too low. The height is adjusted later, so do not compromise the vertical-angle alignment at this time in order to maintain acceptable height.

3. [ ] **Inspect at either end of brake pad to see if vertical angle of pad face is parallel to vertical angle of rim face, then manipulate washer between caliper arm and shoe up or down to fine-tune alignment.**

Tangent alignment

4. [ ] **View brake pad from side of bike and move viewpoint up or down, until top corners of brake shoe are even with top edge of rim.**
5. [ ] **Twist brake shoe around axis of shoe stud, until front and back corners of pad are simultaneously even with top edge of rim.**

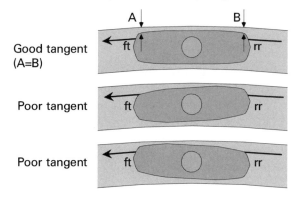

36.16 *When pad tangent alignment is correct, the upper front and rear corners of the pad are equidistant from the top of the rim.*

Height adjustment

6. [ ] **Slide shoe stud up/down in slot until desired height setting is achieved. If acceptable height cannot be achieved, compromise vertical angle just enough to enable setting of height.**

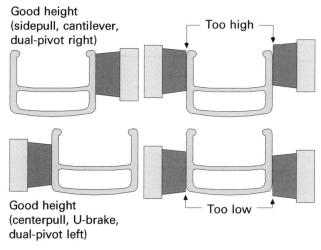

36.17 *Proper pad height varies with the type of brake.*

7. [ ] **Gently secure mounting nut/bolt.**
8. [ ] **Stabilize shoe with fingers or adjustable wrench while tightening mounting nut to 50–60in-lbs (17–20lbs@3').**
9. [ ] **Check that all alignments were maintained during securing of mounting nut.**

SMOOTH-STUD/CURVED-WASHER PAD ALIGNMENT

This type of alignment system is found on most Shimano cantilevers, many other cantilevers, and some U-brakes. The front of the caliper arm has a curved face against which an oppositely-curved washer is nestled. The shoe stud is inserted through a hole in a shoe-anchor bolt. The stud of the shoe-anchor bolt is inserted through the curved washer and the slot in the face of the caliper arm. Like other pad-alignment systems, height is adjusted by moving the bolt up and down in the slot (see figure 36.18, below). Tangent is aligned by rotating the shoe about the axis of its stud. Toe is adjusted by means of moving the curved washer in the face of the caliper arm (see figure 36.19, page 36-12), which enables the end of the shoe anchor to twist in or out (relative to the rim). Vertical angle of the pad is adjusted by rotating the shoe-anchor bolt about its axis (see figure 36.21, page 36-12).

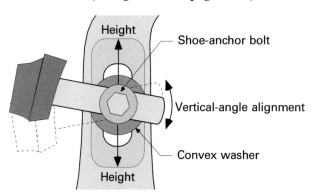

36.18 *Height is adjusted by moving the shoe-anchor bolt up or down in the slot. Vertical-angle alignment is done by rotating the shoe-anchor bolt around its axis.*

Toe alignment

Brake pads need toe in order to reduce squeal. This is particularly true when the pads are new. When a pad is properly toed, the exit-end of the pad should reach the rim before the entry-end of the pad. If both brakes were at the 12:00 position on the wheel, toe could be described as having the front ends of the brake pads reach the rim before the rear ends reach the rim. If pads have broken in properly to the rim, no toe should be needed, unless the pads squeal on a test ride.

The curved washer between the face of the caliper arm and the shoe-anchor bolt enables toe adjustment, by allowing the head of the shoe-anchor bolt to pivot toward or away from the rim. When the head of the shoe-anchor bolt pivot moves out from the rim, the exit-end of the pad moves in. Conversely, when the head of the shoe anchor bolt pivot moves in toward the rim, the exit-end of the pad moves out. Some mechanics find it easier to align the pad by manipulating the shoe anchor. For other mechanics, the easier approach is to position the shoe-anchor bolt by manipulating the pad. If the shoe-anchor nut is loose and the shoe stud is pushed to press the pad against the rim, the pads will automatically align to have no toe. To adjust pad toe, a spacer can be put between the entry-end of the pad and the rim to space it further out. A #4 (1/2") thumb tack pressed into the face of the entry-end of the pad makes a good spacer. With this thumb tack (henceforth called *toe-tack*) in place, toe adjustment is almost automatic. Moving the toe-tack closer to the exit-end of the brake pad increases the amount of toe. Manipulation of the washer may be necessary to finesse the alignment.

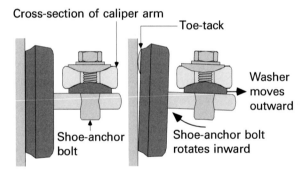

36.19 *When a toe-tack is put between the entry end of the pad and the rim, it cause the head of the shoe-anchor bolt to rotate toward the rim and the convex washer to twist and move outward.*

Some Shimano calipers have an automatic-toeing system called *Easy-Set*. With the Easy-Set system, there is no need to use toe-tacks, or any other system that creates toe alignment before the shoe-anchor nut is tightened. This system, instead, relies on a special washer between the shoe stud and the curved washer to automatically create toe. The washer sits inside a plastic housing that fits flat against the curved washer. It appears flat but has a distinctly sloped face that faces out from the brake caliper. The washer is designed to collapse on one side, but not on the other. The side of the washer that collapses is in the lower portion of the plastic housing. When the low side of the plastic housing is on the rim-side of the shoe-anchor bolt, the end of the pad

that is in front of the face of the caliper arm moves closer to the rim. When the low side of the plastic housing is on the non-rim-side of the shoe-anchor bolt, the end of the pad that is in back of the face of the caliper arm moves closer to the rim. Use the figure 36.20 as a guide to positioning the plastic housings.

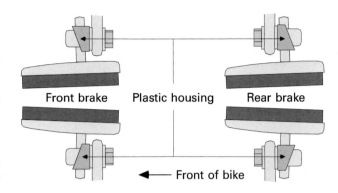

36.20 *The plastic housings reverse orientation on front and rear brakes.*

1. [ ] Complete **ATTACH CABLE TO CALIPER** procedure for the type of cable system being used.
2. [ ] Push in on shoe stud to press pad against rim, then check that toe-tack and exit-end of brake pad are both contacting rim simultaneously; manipulate shoe-anchor-bolt head in or out to improve toe as necessary.

Vertical-angle alignment

Vertical-angle adjustment is also enabled by changing the position of the shoe-anchor bolt, but in this case it is done by rotating the shoe-anchor bolt around its axis. When the bolt is rotated in one direction, the pad face angles down and when it is rotated in the other, the pad face angles up. Some mechanics find it easier to align the pad by manipulating the bolt. For other mechanics, the easiest approach is to manipulate the pad in order to position the bolt. If done properly, the procedure for setting the toe usually also sets the vertical-angle alignment. If it does, it may still need fine tuning.

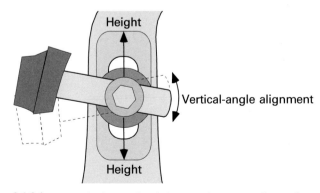

36.21 *Rotate the shoe-anchor bolt around its axis to change the vertical-angle alignment.*

When rotating the shoe-anchor bolt to improve the vertical angle of the pad face, it is not unusual for the pad to end up too high or too low. The height is adjusted later, so do not compromise the vertical-angle alignment at this time.

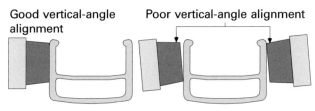

36.22 *The vertical angle of the pad face should closely match the vertical angle of the rim's braking surface.*

3. [ ] Inspect at both ends of brake pad to see if vertical angle of pad face is parallel to vertical angle of rim face, then rotate shoe anchor bolt around its axis to fine-tune alignment.

Tangent alignment

4. [ ] View brake pad from side of bike and move viewpoint up or down until top corners of brake shoe are even with top edge of rim.

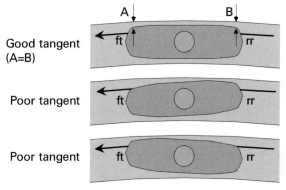

36.23 *When pad tangent alignment is correct, the upper front and rear corners of the pad are equidistant from the top of the rim.*

5. [ ] Twist brake shoe around axis of shoe stud until front and back corners of pad are simultaneously even with top edge of rim.

Height adjustment

6. [ ] Slide shoe stud up/down in slot until desired height setting is achieved. If acceptable height cannot be achieved, compromise vertical angle just enough to enable setting of height (see figure 36.24).

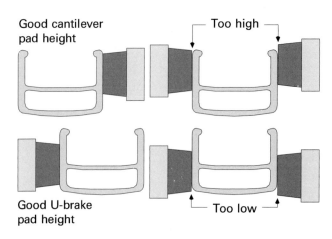

36.24 *Correct pad height varies depending on the type of brake caliper.*

7. [ ] Stabilize shoe-anchor bolt with Allen wrench and tighten shoe-anchor nut to 70–80in-lbs (23–27lbs@3").

8. [ ] Check that all alignments were maintained during securing of shoe anchor nut.

SMOOTH-STUD/SLOPED-WASHER PAD ALIGNMENT

This type of alignment system is commonly found on older Shimano cantilevers and on many after-market cantilevers. The front of the caliper arm has a flat face. The shoe stud is inserted through a hole in a shoe-anchor bolt. The stud of the shoe-anchor bolt is inserted through the sloped washer and through the slot in the face of the caliper arm. The sloped washer has a tab at its perimeter. Like some other pad-alignment systems, height is adjusted by moving the shoe anchor bolt up and down in the slot, and tangent is aligned by rotating the shoe about the axis of its stud. Toe is adjusted by moving the tab on the sloped-washer between the 10:00 and 2:00 position. That enables the end of the shoe anchor to twist in or out (relative to the rim). Vertical angle of the pad is adjusted by rotating the shoe anchor bolt around its axis. (See figure 36.25, page 36-14.)

Toe alignment

Brake pads need toe in order to reduce squeal. This is particularly true when the pads are new. When a pad is properly toed, the exit-end of the pad should reach the rim before the entry-end of the pad. If both brakes were at the 12:00 position on the wheel, toe could be described as having the front ends of the brake pads reach the rim before the rear ends reach the rim. If pads have broken in properly to the rim, no toe should be needed, unless the pads squeal on a test ride.

The sloped-washer between the face of the caliper arm and the shoe-anchor bolt enables toe adjustment, by allowing the head of the shoe-anchor bolt to pivot toward or away from the rim. When the head of the shoe-anchor bolt pivots out from the rim, the exit-end of the pad moves in. Conversely, when the head of the shoe-anchor bolt pivots in toward the rim, the exit-end of the pad moves out. The only way to align the toe is to rotate the sloped washer.

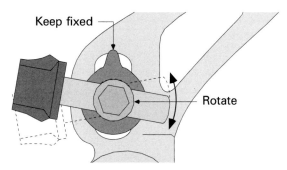

36.26 The vertical-angle alignment is adjusted by rotating the shoe-anchor bolt around its axis.

When rotating the shoe-anchor bolt to improve the vertical angle of the pad face, it is not unusual for the pad to end up too high or too low. The height is adjusted later, so do not compromise the vertical-angle alignment at this time.

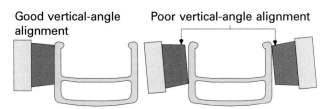

36.27 The vertical angle of the pad face should closely match the vertical angle of the rim's braking surface.

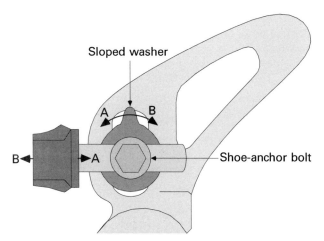

36.25 When the tab on the sloped washer is rotated back and forth, the end of the pad moves in or out.

1. [ ] Complete **ATTACH CABLE TO CALIPER** procedure for the type of cable system being used.
2. [ ] Push on end of shoe stud to move pad to rim, then check that toe-tack and exit-end of brake pad are both contacting rim simultaneously; manipulate sloped-washer tab in or out to improve toe as necessary.

Vertical-angle alignment

Vertical-angle alignment is also enabled by changing the position of the shoe-anchor bolt, but in this case it is done by rotating the shoe-anchor bolt around its axis. When the bolt is rotated in one direction, the pad face angles down and when it is rotated in the other, the pad face angles up. Rotating the shoe-anchor bolt changes the effective position of the sloped washer; it is likely the toe will need fine-tuning if the shoe-anchor bolt needs rotation to adjust the vertical-angle alignment.

3. [ ] Inspect at either end of brake pad to see if the vertical angle of the pad face is parallel to the vertical angle of the rim face, then rotate shoe-anchor bolt around its axis to fine-tune alignment.

Tangent alignment

4. [ ] View brake pad from side of bike and move viewpoint up or down until top corners of brake shoe are even with top edge of rim.
5. [ ] Twist brake shoe around axis of shoe stud until front and back corners of pad are simultaneously even with top edge of rim.

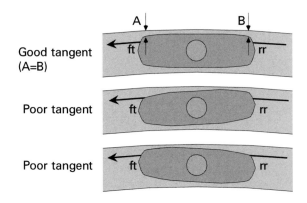

36.28 When pad tangent alignment is correct, the upper front and rear corners of the pad are equidistant from the top of the rim.

Height adjustment

6. [ ] **Slide shoe stud up/down in slot until desired height setting is achieved. If acceptable height cannot be achieved, compromise vertical angle just enough to enable setting of height.**

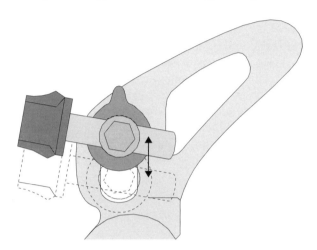

36.29 To adjust pad height, move the shoe-anchor bolt up and down in the slot in the caliper arm.

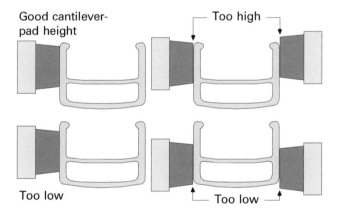

36.30 Correct cantilever brake-pad height.

7. [ ] **Stabilize shoe-anchor bolt with Allen wrench and tighten shoe anchor nut to 70–80in-lbs (23–27lbs@3').**
8. [ ] **Check that all alignments were maintained during securing of shoe-anchor nut.**

CANTILEVER CALIPERS

This section covers cantilevers equipped with several different cable systems, including straddle-wire systems, link-wire systems (such as Shimano Pro-Set models), link-unit systems (such as Shimano M-system brakes), and transverse-wire systems (such as Shimano V-brakes). Several different pad-alignment systems are found on cantilever brakes; the following procedure defines the alignment tolerances, but it is expected that you will refer back to *PAD-ALIGNMENT SYSTEMS* for the alignment procedure.

CALIPER-ARM INSTALLATION

If working on a bike with the caliper arms already installed , it is still a good idea to remove and reinstall them using the following procedure. *Pivot cleaning, pivot greasing, pivot-stud inspection, and spring greasing are very important and should not be taken for granted!*

When installing caliper arms, it is a good idea to check the pads for proper orientation. Usually, a left-rear caliper arm and a right-front caliper arm are interchangeable, except that the pads might be facing in the wrong direction were you to switch the arms from one end of the bike to the other.

Brake pads often have distinctly different top and bottom sides. If the pad is curved over its length, it should be clear which is the top. Obviously, the curve of the pad should match the curve of the rim. Pads that are not curved may, nonetheless, still have distinct top and bottom sides. Usually, if there is a manufacturer's name on only one side of the pad, that would be the top side. If it is not clear which side of the pad should face up, then determine whether there is a front or back end (front or back of bike), whether the pad should face in any direction in regard to the rim's rotation (exit-end or entry-end), or whether there are any other indications that a pad is a left or right pad.

Some pads are specifically designed to work only on the front or back of the bike. This is often done so that a longer pad can be used. Longer pads often come with the stud off-center. The shorter end of the pad always faces the frame or fork, so that the pad will clear the frame or work when the brakes are released.

It is not unusual for a pad to be specifically designed for its orientation to the rim's rotation. If the shoe is open at one end so that the pad rubber can be slid in or out, then the open end *must* be the entry-end, and the closed end would consequently be the exit-end. This orientation prevents the pad from sliding out of the shoe. When a manufacturer marks a pad with the word *forward*, the end that is *forward* would be the exit-end of the pad.

Some pads are marked for left and right usage. Shimano has done this for years, putting an L or R directly on the pad. Usually, however, it is unlikely that a pad will be marked this way. A combination of other markings may, in effect, make a pad a left or right pad. If a pad were marked for the front of the bike, curved so that it had a specific top side, and marked with an arrow or the word *forward* (for direction of rim rotation), then it could *only* go on one side of the front brake to meet all these criteria.

1. [ ] **Check for any indications of: which side of each brake pad is top side, which end of each pad should point to direction rim rotates, whether pads are specific to front or rear of bike, and for any markings that indicate pads are specific to left or right side of the bike.**

The next step suggests installing toe-tacks in the face of the brake shoes. Toe-tacks are simply #4 thumb tacks. Placing toe tacks in the pad face is a convenient way to set the toe adjustment. The amount of toe can be controlled by how deep the toe-tack is pressed in, and by how far the toe-tack is installed from the entry-end of the brake pad. Rubber bands wrapped around the entry-end of the pad are alternative method for creating toe. Brake pads that are well broken-in to the rim, and brake pads on Shimano V-brakes, may not need any toe; if this is the case, the next step should be skipped.

2. [ ] **Install toe-tacks in face of entry-end of pad so that they do not extend beyond pad face.**

Before preparing to install the caliper arms on the pivot studs, it is a good idea to test fit the caliper arms on the pivot studs. If the fit is difficult, it could be caused by several things. Paint or rust on a pivot stud can make it a tight fit; these conditions can easily be repaired by using some medium-grit emery cloth on the pivot stud. Pivot studs could be mushroomed on the end, if caliper-mounting bolts have been over-tightened. This mushrooming damage is harder to repair with emery cloth. A Bicycle Research BM1 is a simple and effective tool that will repair mushrooming, as well as remove paint with ease.

If the bike is used, it is a good idea to inspect the pivot studs for bends or cracks at the base. It is *not* a good idea to bend pivot studs back into alignment. Cracked studs are a safety and liability risk that no one should take. If the pivot stud is not replaceable, it may still be possible to repair it without brazing. Some types of brazed-on pivot studs can be repaired with a replacement retained by a bolt that attaches to the original pivot-stud base.

3. [ ] **Grease outside of pivot studs.**
4. [ ] **Grease outside of any bushings to be installed over pivot studs.**

It is very critical that the caliper arms be well-secured, but the design of pivot studs prevents using high torques on the mounting bolts (mushrooming of the pivot stud may occur). The solution to this is to use Loctite #242 to retain the mounting bolt securely without relying on high torque. The Loctite should be put inside the pivot stud, *not* on the mounting bolt threads; Loctite on the bolt threads has a tendency to back out of the pivot-stud hole and get into the space between the pivot stud and the caliper arm. The factory often puts dry Loctite on the mounting bolt that is good for several installations. If the bolt can be threaded in by hand, then fresh Loctite is needed.

5. [ ] **Use Loctite 242 inside pivot-stud threads unless mounting bolts have dry factory Loctite in good condition (or nylon insert) on threads.**
6. [ ] **Grease any coil springs that will be enclosed inside caliper arms.**

There are springs specific to the left and right caliper arms. When a spring is on the correct side, it will always coil tighter as the caliper arm moves the pad closer to the rim, and uncoil as the pad moves away from the rim. Over the years, Shimano has remained very consistent and used a silver spring in the right caliper arm, and a gold spring in the left caliper arm (left and right when facing front of caliper, not in regard to side of bike).

Coil springs often have one leg that fits into a hole in the spring-mounting plate at the base of the pivot stud, and another leg that goes in a hole in the caliper arm. When a spring has legs of different length, the longer leg almost always fits into the spring-mounting plate at the base of the pivot stud.

Certain vintages of Shimano brakes had multiple holes inside the caliper arm into which the spring leg installs. This was done to offer the option of setting up the brake with a soft (SLR) feel, or firmer (NORMAL) feel. After putting the spring into one of the holes, a dustcap is placed over the spring. The triangular indicator on the caliper arm points either to the SLR or NORMAL notation on the dustcap, depending into which hole in the caliper arm the spring was installed. These SLR/NORMAL-marked dustcaps were also marked for left and right side of the brake with an L or R. Particularly as the brakes are getting older, it is a good idea to select the spring hole that sets the brake at the NORMAL setting.

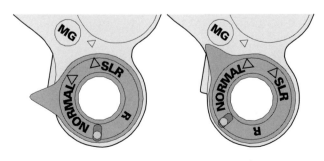

36.31 Shimano SLR and NORMAL spring and dustcap orientations.

7. [ ] Select spring for each side so that spring will coil tighter as brake pad moves in towards rim, and install spring in caliper.

8. [ ] Put any dustcaps or spring-adjusting nuts (if any) on backside of caliper, and any removable bushings (greased) inside of caliper hole.

9. [ ] Slide caliper assembly onto pivot stud. If there are multiple spring holes in spring-mounting plate, make sure springs go in middle holes.

10. [ ] If caliper is Dia-Compe 984 or similar (with spring-tension-adjusting nut on front of caliper), install nut on face of caliper.

11. [ ] Install, but do not tighten, mounting bolts.

All caliper arms have a bushing that fits between the pivot stud and the caliper arm to act as a bearing. In some cases, the bushing is a fixed and permanent part of the caliper arm. In other cases, the bushings is either removable or can be rotated in the caliper arm. If a caliper arm has a fixed bushing, the head of the mounting bolt presses against the end of the pivot stud. In these cases, low torque is needed to prevent mushrooming the pivot stud. If the caliper arm has an independent bushing (removable or free-rotating), then the head of the mounting bolt presses against the bushing. In these cases, the bushing can take higher torque than the pivot stud, and the bushing needs higher torque to prevent it from turning. Inspect the caliper arm to determine whether it has a fixed, or independent, bushing.

Some caliper arms have a nut (or plate) that is installed in front of or behind the caliper arm, to which the spring is attached. This is seen on some Dia-Compe and SunTour brakes. This feature is usually found on one caliper arm. This spring-tension-adjusting nut (or plate) will stay at the position it is set when the mounting bolt is secured. When securing the mounting bolt in the next step, position the spring tension nut so that the positions of the caliper arms on each side of the wheel are symmetrical.

12. [ ] *Fixed-bushing caliper(s):* Secure to 25in-lbs (8lbs@3").
    Independent-bushing caliper(s): Secure to 50–60in-lbs (17–20lbs@3").

If the brake uses a link-wire or link-unit cable-attachment system, the brake pads can interfere with getting the cable-attachment system set up properly. For this reason, if the brake has one of these cable systems, the next step requires positioning the pads so that they will miss the rim when the caliper arms move in. On the other hand, brakes with straddle-wires or transverse wires require that the pads are in a normal position in order to attach the cable system to the caliper arms. The pads should be set up close to their final position, but precision adjustment is done later.

13. [ ] *Link-wire and Link-unit systems:* Position pads so that they will go below rim when caliper arms move in.
    Straddle-wire systems and Shimano V-brake: Position pads on caliper to approximately correct height, tangent, and toe. Leave nuts/bolts just tight enough to keep shoe in place.

ATTACH CABLE TO CALIPER

At this point, determine whether the brake system uses a straddle-wire, a link-wire, a link-unit, or a transverse cable. Once this is determined, use the appropriate following section for attaching the cable system to the calipers.

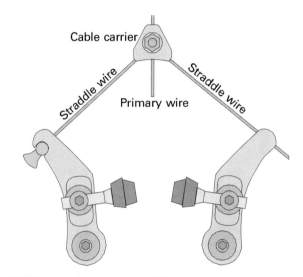

36.32 A cantilever with a straddle-wire.

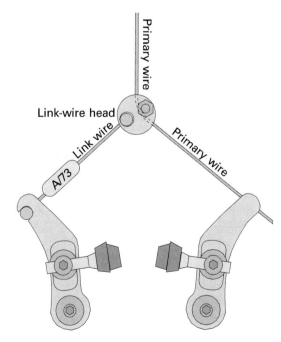

36.33 A cantilever with a link-wire.

14. [ ] Hold shoes to rim with third-hand tool.
15. [ ] Loosen shoe-anchor nuts.
16. [ ] Move calipers/Pro-Set tool assembly to one side or other until equal amounts of shoe stud protrude from each shoe-anchor bolt, then gently secure one shoe-anchor nut. *NOTE: Side with loose shoe-anchor nut will be first side to adjust pad alignment on.*
17. [ ] Remove third-hand tool, but *do not remove Pro-Set tool* at this time.

Link-unit systems

Shimano invented the link-unit system to replace the link-wire system. Link-units are used on a Shimano brakes called M-system brakes. The link-unit serves all the purposes and functions of the link-wire system, but does not require the use of Pro-Set tools to set it up. A link-unit consists of a link-wire, a link-wire head, and a piece of housing attached to the head that goes to the caliper arm with the pinch mechanism. The piece of housing fixes the distance of the head from the right caliper arm and eliminates the need for the Pro-Set tool.

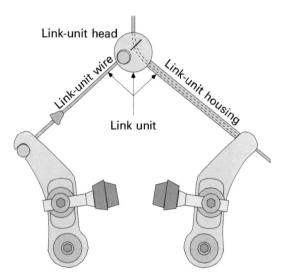

36.38 A link-unit system.

1. [ ] Install brake lever and cable system, if not already installed.
2. [ ] Set cable-system adjusting barrel to 3 full turns out from fully-in position.

Link-units come in a variety of sizes. They may be marked with letters A, B , C, or D. The A and B sizes are the most common. When replacing a link-unit, try to match the existing size. If a longer link-unit is used, watch out for the link-unit head end up too close to the housing stop. A clearance of at least 20mm is required between the link-unit head and the housing stop.

3. [ ] Lubricate threads of pinch mechanism on caliper arm.
4. [ ] Thread primary wire through link-unit head and then through link-unit housing.
5. [ ] Move primary wire over ramp and into working slot in link-unit head.

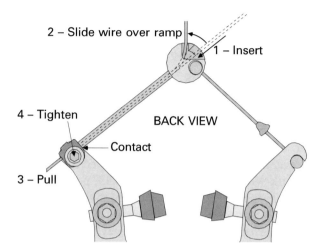

36.39 Installing the primary wire into the link-unit.

6. [ ] Hook lead bead on link-unit into caliper arm.
7. [ ] Insert primary wire through pinch mechanism on right caliper arm, then tighten pinch bolt just enough so that cable can still slide through pinch mechanism.
8. [ ] Push on link-unit head until link-unit housing stops against caliper arm.
9. [ ] Move primary wire through link-unit housing with fourth-hand tool, to align alignment line in link-unit head so that groove is aligned to link-unit wire. (Use straight edge to extend alignment line to make alignment easier to see.)

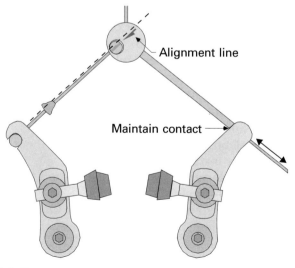

36.40 Use a fourth hand on the primary wire to align the alignment line with the link-unit wire.

10. [ ] Torque caliper-arm pinch to 50–70in-lbs (17–23lbs@3").

11. [ ] Use cable-adjusting barrel to raise link-unit head up until alignment line points to position A in figure 36.41. (Use straight edge to extend alignment line to make alignment easier to sight.)

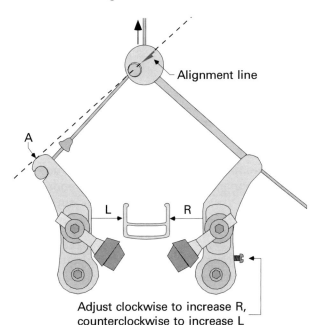

Adjust clockwise to increase R, counterclockwise to increase L

36.41 *Use adjusting barrel to move link-unit head up until alignment line points to A.*

12. [ ] Use adjusting screw in side of right caliper arm to center arms to rim to <1mm difference. Measure from each caliper to rim as shown in figure 36.41.

Shimano V-brake (transverse wire)

The Shimano V-brake system differs in appearance from a cantilever, but acts in essentially the same fashion. It is simpler to set up than most cantilever brakes, because the primary wire attaches directly to the caliper arms, much like a sidepull brake.

1. [ ] Install brake lever and cable system, if not already installed.
2. [ ] Set cable-system adjusting barrel to 3 full turns out from fully-in position.
3. [ ] Lubricate threads of pinch mechanism on right caliper arm.
4. [ ] Hold pads to rim with third-hand tool.

It is possible to set up a Shimano V-brake so that the ends of the caliper arms actually end up touching under certain conditions. That, of course, makes the application of additional brake force impossible. To ensure that this does not happen, Shimano provides washers that can be moved to different locations to compensate for different combinations of rim and

pivot-stud width. The washers are the same concave types used for pad alignments. There is one 6mm-thick concave washer, and another that is 3mm. They can be switched back and forth between their positions inward and outward of the caliper arm to change the distance between the ends of the caliper arm when the pads meet the rim. See figure 36.42, and try switching the washers if the dimension is less than 39mm.

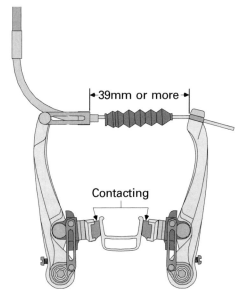

36.42 *If the dimension shown is less than 39mm, switch the positions of the 3m and 6mm concave washers in the pad-mounting hardware.*

5. [ ] Measure from end of bracket that holds cable-guide tube, to edge of pinch-bolt head.
6. [ ] If dimension in previous step is <39mm, re-install pads with 6mm concave washers between caliper arm and brake shoe, and 3mm concave washers between caliper arm and mounting nut.
7. [ ] Insert cable-guide tube into bracket in left arm.
8. [ ] Insert inner wire through cable-guide tube and through pinch mechanism.
9. [ ] Pull slack wire through pinch mechanism until pads are against rim, then torque pinch bolt to 50–70in-lbs (17–23lbs@3").

PAD-ALIGNMENT PREPARATION

1. [ ] Loosen shoe-mounting bolts/nuts just enough so that shoe alignment can be manipulated with your fingers (except link-wire and link-unit brakes; this step is already done).

Determine the type of pad-alignment system used on the calipers. Use the procedures in the earlier section for **SIMPLE THREADED-STUD-PAD ALIGNMENT** (page 36-8), **THREADED-STUD/CURVED-WASHER PAD ALIGNMENT** (page

4. [ ] Operate brake and check whether pad clearance is uniform on both sides. If not, repeat adjustment of spring-tension-adjusting screw.

Changing shoe-stud engagement

When setting up brakes with smooth-stud brake shoes, the objective is to have the same amount of shoe stud protruding out past both anchor bolts. If the centering methods described above do not get the pads equally centered, check whether the shoe studs are protruding evenly. If not, the shoe alignments should be redone. Be certain to set the shoe studs equally.

If the shoe-stud engagements are equal, the cable system is set up properly, and the brakes still cannot be centered, there are usually other problems with the brakes. These problems could be sticky caliper-arm pivots, damaged springs, mis-installed springs, or simply that the wheel is poorly centered between the pivot studs. If any of these problems are found, they should be addressed. If there is still a problem equalizing pad clearance, then shoe-stud engagement in the shoe anchor bolts can be deliberately *offset* to improve pad-clearance symmetry.

FINISHING

See the section called **FINISHING** (page 36-43) for cable finish, rim cleaning, and test-ride procedures.

SIDEPULL CALIPERS

This section contains the following sub-sections, which may all be used, or can be used in part:

DOUBLE-NUT PIVOT SERVICE
SAFETY-PIVOT SERVICE
CALIPER ATTACHMENT AND LUBRICATION
PAD ADJUSTMENT
CABLE ATTACHMENT AND CLEARANCE ADJUSTMENT
CENTERING ADJUSTMENT

Even if the brake caliper is not being disassembled as part of the brake service, it is nonetheless a good idea to readjust the pivots. Loose pivots cause brake squeal and "grabby" feeling brakes. It is important to remember that loose pivot-adjusting nuts on a double-nut-type pivot *can cause the brake to come apart!*

The **PAD ADJUSTMENT** section provides alignment tolerances only. You must refer back to the earlier section, **PAD-ALIGNMENT SYSTEMS**, to use the procedure for aligning the pads. (Page numbers are provided in the procedure when needed.)

DOUBLE-NUT-PIVOT SERVICE

The double-nut-pivot type of sidepull caliper is characterized by two nuts that are locked to each other on the face of the caliper. These nuts are used to adjust the pivot. The other common type of pivot design is the safety-pivot type, which has a bolt head on the front of the pivot, instead of the two nuts.

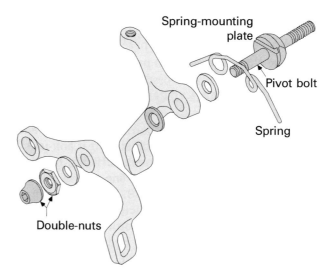

36.49 *Blow-up of a typical double-nut-pivot assembly.*

Disassembly

1. [ ] Grasp back end of pivot/mounting bolt in soft jaws of bench vise.
2. [ ] Disconnect springs from caliper arms by popping them out of their mounts with screwdriver, or Langley fifth-hand tool.
3. [ ] Hold inner nut stationary while turning outer nut counterclockwise, until removed.
4. [ ] Remove inner nut.
5. [ ] Remove front washer(s) and note orientation(s).
6. [ ] Remove front caliper arm, and look for washers stuck on back side of arm.
7. [ ] Remove any washers between front and back caliper arms. Shimano Dura-Ace caliper #BR7400 may have central washer that is sandwich of plastic washer (contains 14-2mm ball bearings) between two metal washers. Be careful when separating washers so that balls do not drop out.
8. [ ] Remove back caliper arm and look for washer stuck on backside of arm. Note orientation of washer.
9. [ ] Remove any washer left on pivot bolt and note its orientation.
10. [ ] Note orientation of spring and remove it from slot in spring-mounting plate.

If you are disassembling front and rear calipers at the same time, it is critical that you do not mix up the arms. They may be different lengths, or they may have been twisted to create the pad-toe adjustment. When caliper arms have been twisted for toe adjustment, the direction of twist on the front is opposite of that used on rear calipers. Use a scribe to mark the back face of each caliper arm. A single scribe mark can be used to indicate a front caliper arm, and a double scribe mark can indicate a rear caliper arm.

11. [ ] **If disassembling front and rear brakes, mark front and rear arms with different marks.**

Brake pads that have broken-in to the rim should always be reinstalled at their original locations and orientations, even if there were no original orientation guidelines on the pads. A convenient way to mark pads is to use the corner edge of a file to put a groove in the *back* and *bottom* edge of the pad. This location for the groove is well hidden from view when the pad is on the bike and has no effect on braking quality. By putting the groove on the back *and* bottom edge, there is no way the pad can be installed incorrectly. See figure 36.53 (page 36-29) for clarification as to where the pads should be marked. Once again, one mark can be used to signify front brake, and two marks to signify rear brake.

12. [ ] **Remove brake pads for replacement or cleaning. Note front and back ends of pads, and mark pads so that they will not be switched between front and back of bike.**

Cleaning and inspection

13. [ ] **Clean all parts in solvent.**
14. [ ] **Inspect pivot bolt for bends.**
15. [ ] **Inspect caliper arms for bends.**
16. [ ] **Inspect pivot bolt and adjusting nuts for damaged threads.**
17. [ ] **Inspect adjusting nuts for damaged flats.**
18. [ ] **Inspect spring for stiffness (should be too stiff to remove or install without tools, except when lever has return spring).**

Assembly and lubrication

19. [ ] **Grasp pivot bolt by mounting end in soft jaws of vise.**
20. [ ] **Lubricate pivot and threads in front of spring-mounting plate only.**

In the next step, the spring is put into the spring-mounting plate. Be careful, it is easy to install the spring incorrectly. The spring should be oriented so that coils protrude back from mounting point and the coils are beside the mounting plate (not above or below). Most calipers are designed so that the slot in the spring-mounting plate should be above the pivot bolt. If, however, mounting the spring above the pivot bolt causes the coils to rise above the caliper arms, then the slot in the spring-mounting plate belongs below the pivot bolt.

21. [ ] **Place spring in spring-mounting plate.**
22. [ ] **Place back washer in its correct orientation on pivot.**
23. [ ] **Oil front and back of rear caliper arm at pivot.**
24. [ ] **Place rear caliper arm on pivot, but do not engage spring.**
25. [ ] **Place middle washer(s) on pivot. (Oil bearings in Shimano Dura-Ace #BR-7400 middle washer.)**
26. [ ] **Oil front and back of front caliper arm at pivot.**
27. [ ] **Place front caliper arm on pivot, making sure that cable-pinch-mechanism end of arm is below housing stop end of rear caliper arm. Do not engage spring ends at this time.**
28. [ ] **Place front washer(s) on pivot in correct orientation.**
29. [ ] **Thread on two front nuts.**
30. [ ] **Engage spring ends to posts on back face of caliper arms, and lubricate points at which they bear against arms. Additional oil may be needed in coils themselves, between coils and spring-mounting plate, and between spring and rear caliper arm.**
31. [ ] **If shoes have been removed, oil mounting threads and mount shoes securely.**
32. [ ] **Additional oiling should be done on pinch-mechanism threads, cable-adjusting-barrel threads, and quick-release-mechanism pivots.**

Pivot adjustment

Adjustment can be accomplished with the brake still mounted on the bike, as long as it is secure, The adjustment can also be done with the mounting bolt secure in a vise with soft jaws.

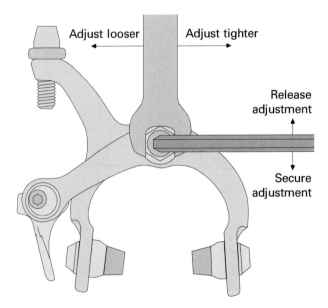

36.51 *Proper setup for adjusting the pivot on a double-nut-type pivot. The adjustment can be done with the caliper on the bike, or mounted in the vise.*

33. [ ] If brake was not just oiled, oil front and back of each caliper arm at pivot and at points at which spring ends bear against caliper arms.

34. [ ] If brake adjusting nuts are still locked together, hold inner one stationary and break loose outer nut.

35. [ ] Turn inner nut clockwise until it bears against caliper arms, then turn it counter-clockwise 90°.

36. [ ] Holding inner nut stationary, tighten outer nut to torque of 50–70in-lbs (13–18lbs@4").

37. [ ] Grasp bottoms of caliper arms and jerk them vigorously forward and back to check for any knocking sensation that indicates adjustment is too loose.

For the proper directions to turn the inner nut and outer nut for adjusting and securing the pivot adjustment, see figure 36.51 (page 36-27).

38. [ ] To tighten adjustment, hold inner nut stationary while breaking loose outer nut, then turn inner nut 10° clockwise (about 3/4" at end of 4.5" wrench), and hold it at this position while re-securing outer nut.

In the next step, it is important to eliminate all play from the pivot adjustment. Loose pivot adjustments cause grabby brakes and squealing brakes.

39. [ ] Check for knocking again, and repeat adjustment as many times as necessary to eliminate knocking that indicates pivot adjustment is loose.

In the next step, the pivot adjustment is checked for excessive tightness. It can appear that the adjustment is too tight because the spring is too soft. The spring should be stiff enough so that it cannot be removed or installed comfortably by hand (unless lever has return spring). Soft springs should be replaced. Soft springs can be stiffened, if necessary, by bending the ends further away from each other. Use a pair of Langley fifth-hand brake tools (or pliers on each end of spring) to spread the spring ends further apart.

40. [ ] To check for too-tight pivot adjustment, squeeze caliper arms together about 1/2", then release them slowly. If they do not open all way by themselves, adjustment may be too tight, or spring too soft. Check spring before loosening adjustment.

41. [ ] To loosen adjustment, hold inner nut stationary while breaking loose outer nut, then turn inner nut 10° counterclockwise (about 3/4" at end of 4.5" wrench), and hold it at this position while re-securing outer nut. Repeat adjustment until knocking is detected, then return to last setting.

SAFETY-PIVOT SERVICE

Disassembly

The safety-pivot type of sidepull caliper is distinguished by the fact that the pivot bolt has a head on the front of the caliper, unlike the double-nut type which has two nuts threaded onto the pivot bolt at the front of the caliper. The adjustment nut and locknut are located between the caliper and the mounting point on the frame or fork. On some models, there is no adjustment locknut and the adjustment must be done with the caliper mounted on the bike (the mounting nut serves as the adjustment locknut).

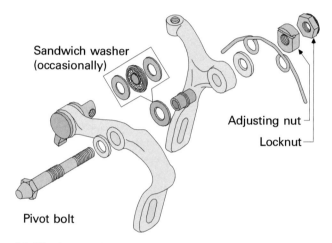

36.52 Blow-up of a safety-pivot-design sidepull caliper.

1. [ ] **Remove brake from bike.**
2. [ ] **Disengage spring. With many models, spring needs to be rotated up for wrench access to adjusting nut (nut closest to caliper).**

The adjustment locknut (outer nut) on some models of Shimano brakes is a 12-point nut that is fit only by a 13mm or 14mm box-end wrench. In the next step, the end of the pivot bolt is grasped in the vise; the box-end wrench needs to be placed over the end of the pivot bolt first.

3. [ ] **Mount pivot bolt in soft jaws of vise.**
4. [ ] **Facing caliper from its back, hold inner nut stationary with cone wrench, then turn outer nut counterclockwise to break it loose.**
5. [ ] **With caliper in hand (not in vise), hold nuts and arms stationary while turning pivot-bolt head counterclockwise to unthread it from nuts. Note order and orientation of each nut as it comes off.**

In the next step, a simple washer may be found between the caliper arms. There may also be a more complex thrust washer with bearings. The thrust washer is a sandwich with a plastic retainer containing 14 tiny 2mm bearings. Because the bearings are easily lost, be careful when separating the metal washer from either face of the plastic retainer.

6. [ ] **Remove caliper arms and washers, noting order and orientation of each.**

If you are disassembling front and rear calipers at the same time, it is critical that you do not mix up the arms. They may be different lengths, or they may have been twisted to create the pad-toe adjustment. When caliper arms have been twisted for toe adjustment, the direction of twist on the front is opposite of that used on rear calipers. Use a scribe to mark the back face of each caliper arm. A single scribe mark can be used to indicate a front caliper arm, and a double scribe mark can indicate a rear caliper arm.

7. [ ] **If disassembling front and rear brakes, mark front and rear arms with different marks.**

Brake pads that have broken-in to the rim should always be reinstalled at their original locations and orientations, even if there were no original orientation guidelines on the pads. A convenient way to mark pads is to use the corner edge of a file to put a groove in the *back* and *bottom* edge of the pad. This location for the groove is well hidden from view when the pad is on the bike and has no effect on braking quality. By putting the groove on the back *and* bottom edge, there is no way the pad can be installed incorrectly. See figure 36.53 for clarification as to where the pads should be marked. Once again, one mark can be used to signify front brake, and two marks to signify rear brake.

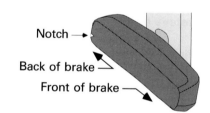

Notch →
Back of brake
Front of brake →

36.53 *Notch the back-bottom edge of the pad. Use one notch for front-brake pads, or two notches for rear-brake pads.*

8. [ ] **Remove brake pads for replacement or cleaning. Note front and back ends of pads, and mark pads so that they will not be switched between front and back of bike.**

Cleaning and inspection

9. [ ] **Clean all parts in solvent.**
10. [ ] **Inspect pivot bolt for bends.**
11. [ ] **Inspect caliper arms for bends.**
12. [ ] **Inspect pivot bolt and adjusting nuts for damaged threads.**
13. [ ] **Inspect adjusting nuts for damaged flats.**

14. [ ] **Inspect spring for stiffness (should be too stiff to remove or install without tools except when lever has return spring).**

Assembly and lubrication

15. [ ] **Oil pivot area of pivot bolt.**
16. [ ] **Oil threads for adjusting nut(s).**
17. [ ] **Install front washer on pivot.**
18. [ ] **Oil front and rear face of front caliper arm at pivot point.**
19. [ ] **Install front caliper arm on pivot.**
20. [ ] **Install middle washer(s) and bushing (if any). Oil bearings in Shimano sandwich washer with bearings.**
21. [ ] **Oil front and rear face of rear caliper arm at pivot point.**
22. [ ] **Install rear caliper arm on pivot.**
23. [ ] **Install rear washer.**

In the next step, the spring is put into the spring-mounting plate. Be careful, it is easy to install the spring in incorrectly. The spring should be oriented so that coils protrude back from mounting point and the coils are beside the mounting plate (not above or below). Most calipers are designed so that the slot in the spring-mounting plate should be above the pivot bolt. If, however, mounting the spring above the pivot bolt causes the coils to rise above the caliper arms, then the slot in the spring-mounting plate belongs below the pivot bolt.

24. [ ] **Thread on spring-mounting plate in correct orientation, until it is just close enough to caliper to allow installation of spring. Then install spring.**
25. [ ] **Thread pivot bolt rest of way into spring-mounting plate.**
26. [ ] **Install outer nut.**

Pivot adjustment

The pivot adjustment on a safety-pivot caliper has to be done with the caliper removed from the bike.

27. [ ] **Mount pivot bolt in soft jaws of vise.**
28. [ ] **Flip spring up out of way if it prevents access to inner nut with wrench from above.**
29. [ ] **If brake was not just oiled, oil front and back of each caliper arm, and points at which spring ends bear against caliper arms.**

In the next step, make the adjustment while viewing the caliper from its back face.

30. [ ] **If brake adjusting nuts are still locked together, hold inner nut (spring-mounting plate) stationary while turning outer nut counterclockwise.**
31. [ ] **Turn inner nut clockwise until it bears against caliper arms. Then turn it counterclockwise 90°.**
32. [ ] **Holding inner nut stationary, tighten outer nut to torque of 50–70in-lbs (13–18lbs@4").**

CABLE-OPERATED RIM-BRAKE-CALIPER TROUBLESHOOTING

Cause	*Solution*
SYMPTOM: *Brake squeals when applied hard or softly.*	
Loose pivot(s).	Adjust pivot(s) if adjustable, and/or replace pivot bushings. Condition is not always correctable, particularly with cantilever brakes.
Contamination on rims (oil or dirt).	Clean rims with solvent or heavy-duty cleanser that leaves no residue.
Brakes shoes need toe adjustment.	Toe pads to a maximum clearance of 1.5mm at tail end of pad.
Caliper arms are flexing.	Long and/or skinny caliper arms are prone to flexing, which can only be prevented by using higher-quality, stiffer arms.
Humidity conditions.	Changes in humidity may change a brake's tendency to squeal; there is no solution.
Contamination on pad faces.	Replace pads or regrind pad face(s).
Pads incompatible with rim.	Changing brands of pads may reduce squeal.
Pads not broken-in to rim.	New pads may squeal under high braking force only, then not squeal once they have conformed to the shape of the rim. Recheck all pad alignments, or run emery cloth between the pads and the rim while applying the brakes gently, to accelerate pad break-in.
SYMPTOM: *Brake mechanism(s) squeak when applied and/or released.*	
Lever pivot(s) need oil.	Oil lever pivots.
Cable-anchor pivots in lever need oil.	Oil cable-anchor pivots.
Cable-end socket for barrel-ended cable needs oil in lever.	Oil cable-end socket.
Spring ends need oil where they brace against caliper arms.	Oil spring ends.
Spring coils need oil.	Oil spring coils.
SYMPTOM: *Sidepull caliper will not hold its center adjustment.*	
Caliper-mounting nut not secure.	Secure caliper-mounting nut.
Spring not fixed securely in slot in spring-mounting plate.	Peen down slot in spring-mounting plate to eliminate play between spring and spring-mounting plate.
Caliper pivots need oil.	Oil caliper pivots.
Spring ends need oil.	Oil spring ends.
Spring is fatigued.	Replace spring.
SYMPTOM: *Properly centered sidepull caliper has one arm that moves in before the other.*	
Cable housing resists motion of only one caliper arm.	This is a normal response and needs no correction. The arms act uniformly once both pads reach the rim.
Housing loop to rear brake may be too short, particularly on BMX bikes, so that it loses all bow before the pad contacts the rim.	Lengthen housing loop.

(continued next page)

Cause	*Solution*
SYMPTOM: *Sidepull-caliper-pivot adjustment does not stay correctly adjusted.*	
Improper centering technique.	See section on sidepull-caliper-centering adjustment.
Inadequate adjustment security.	Reset adjustment and secure adequately.
Heavy-duty use.	Treat adjustment nut and adjustment-locknut threads with Loctite #222 and reset adjustment.
SYMPTOM: *Sidepull-caliper-pivot adjustment remains too tight no matter how it is adjusted.*	
Adjustment nut or pivot-bolt threads are stripped.	Inspect and replace damaged parts.
Return spring is fatigued.	Check and replace spring.
SYMPTOM: *Sidepull caliper will not release completely after release of the lever.*	
Pivot needs oil.	Oil pivot.
Pivot too tight.	Adjust pivot to eliminate bind and/or play.
Spring fatigued.	Check and replace spring.
Friction in cable system.	Inspect for poor cable routing, the remove cable system and inspect for rust, kinks, improperly finished housing ends, and lack of lubrication.
Sticky lever.	See **BRAKE LEVERS** chapter (page 34-9).
SYMPTOM: *Centerpull caliper will not hold its centering adjustment.*	
Mounting nut not secure.	Secure mounting nut.
SYMPTOM: *Cantilever brakes cannot be properly centered.*	
Wheel out-of-center in frame/fork.	Check and correct wheel centering.
Pivot studs in need of grease.	Remove calipers and grease pivot studs.
Link-wire improperly setup.	Setup again, using proper Pro-Set tool and technique.
Primary wire approaches brake from off-center approach.	It may be necessary to deviate from standard setup procedures to center brake when frame manufacturer forces primary wire to approach brake from off-center.
Caliper arm not pivoting freely on damaged (flared) pivot stud.	Remove arm and use Bicycle Research BM1 pivot-stud mill (or emery cloth) to reduce flare.
Pivot bushing of caliper arm longer than pivot stud.	File caliper-pivot bushing shorter.
Deformed mounting washer pressing against face of caliper arm.	Replace washer.
Depth of shoe stud in each anchor bolt not equal.	Reset shoe-stud depth.
Damaged, mis-matched, or mis-installed springs.	Disassemble caliper and inspect springs.
Springs not engaged in equal hole positions in multiple-hole braze-ons.	Reposition springs.
Braze-ons mis-positioned.	Not correctable.

(continued next page)

CABLE-OPERATED RIM-BRAKE-CALIPER
TROUBLESHOOTING (continued)

Cause	Solution
SYMPTOM: *Cantilever arm is not pivoting freely.*	
Pivot stud needs grease.	Grease pivot stud.
Pivot stud flared from over-tight mounting bolt.	Remove arm and use Bicycle Research BM1 pivot-stud mill (or emery cloth) to reduce flare.
Rust on pivot stud.	Clean with emery cloth and grease.
Caliper-arm-pivot bushing longer than pivot stud.	File bushing shorter.
Deformed mounting washer pressing against face of caliper arm.	Replace washer.
SYMPTOM: *Cantilever pads force their way to below the rim.*	
Pads adjusted too low on rim.	Reset pads to as high as possible on rim face.
Poor vertical-angle alignment causes pads to travel too far.	Align vertical angle of pad face to match vertical angle of rim face.
V-shaped rim cross-section incompatible with cantilever brakes.	– Use firm pads to reduce deflection. – Switch rim to more vertical or inverted-slope face.
SYMPTOM: *Cantilever pads cannot be adjusted to have proper height and vertical-angle alignment at the same time.*	
Improper pivot-stud position in relation to rim.	– No complete solution possible; sacrifice proper alignment for best possible height. – Wider rim, narrower rim, or rim with taller braking surface may help.
Caliper arm with threaded-stud/curved-washer pad-alignment system is having to swing too far to reach rim.	If available, switch fat washers from outboard of caliper arm to between caliper arm and brake shoe.
SYMPTOM: *U-Brake will not release completely when hooked up, even though there is no problem with the cables detached.*	
Straddle wire too short.	Lengthen straddle wire.
SYMPTOM: *Shimano U-Brake cannot be centered using the correct technique on the adjustment screw.*	
Pivot stud rusty or needing lube.	Remove, clean and lube.
Improper mounting.	Loosen mounting bolts and resecure with both caliper arms open fully, to reset basic spring tension.
Rim cannot be centered to pivot studs.	Loosen mounting bolt on side where clearance is greater, and re-secure caliper arm with pad rotated closer to rim.
Poorly matched springs.	Reset the basic spring tension to be higher or lower as necessary on just one side.

(continued next page)

Cause	Solution
SYMPTOM: *Brake levers bottom-out easily when pads are set at minimal clearance to the rims.*	
Excess housing-loop length.	Shorten housing loops to minimum recommended length.
Spongy housing.	Upgrade housing.
Poorly finished housing ends and/or lack of end caps where they might improve fit.	Finish properly and use end caps.
Light-duty inner wires.	Upgrade inner wires.
Levers mis-positioned on handlebars.	Reposition levers to recommended guidelines.
Mismatched leverage ratio of lever and caliper arms.	Replace one or the other, using brand- and model-matched equipment whenever possible.
Poor vertical-angle pad alignment on cantilever brakes.	Realign vertical-angle alignment of pads.
SYMPTOM: *Brake has inadequate stopping power, but levers are not bottoming out on handlebars.*	
Excess cable friction.	Set housing-loop lengths properly, lubricate cables, finish ends properly, and use end caps where appropriate.
Poor pad alignment.	Realign pads to improve contact to rim.
Pad surfaces hardened from overheating or age.	Replace pads.
Cable carrier, link-wire head, or link-unit head is bumping into housing stop.	Check that there is 20mm clearance between cable carrier, link-wire head, or link-unit head and housing stop.
Straddle wire too long.	Shorten straddle wire to minimum recommended length.
Oil on rim.	Clean rim and replace pads.
Water on rim.	Use high-performance brake pads.
SYMPTOM: *Brake levers require a very high force to start motion, or when pulled gently, they seem to move as though indexed (jerky, not smooth).*	
Excess cable friction.	Set housing-loop lengths properly, lubricate cables, finish ends properly, and use end caps where appropriate.
Adjustable pivot adjusted too tight.	Check pivot adjustment.
Caliper pivot(s) need lubrication.	Lubricate caliper pivots.
Cable-anchor pivot in lever sticking.	Oil cable-anchor pivot.
Barrel-type cable end sticking in lever socket.	Lubricate cable-end socket.
SYMPTOM: *Levers require excess force to pull.*	
Dual-pivot caliper is off-center, causing rim to deflect laterally before second pad will contact.	Check and correct pad centering.
Excess cable friction.	Set housing-loop lengths properly, lubricate cables, finish ends properly and use end caps where appropriate.
Caliper-spring tension set too high.	Reset caliper-spring tension.
Lever pivots and caliper pivots sticky.	Oil all pivots.
SYMPTOM: *Cable frays where it leaves brake lever.*	
Bent or kinked cable housing.	Replace or trim housing.

(continued next page)

The Gustav M brake has no adjustments for pad clearance. It is not problematic if it rubs lightly at times, similar to motorcycle and automotive disc brakes.

NOTE: For frames or forks with Hayes-type post mounting (bolt holes aligned parallel to bike, rather than perpendicular to bike), an adapter plate must be mounted first. Install adapter and secure bolts to 55–70in-lbs.

9. [ ] Remove plastic pad spacer (if any) from between brake pads, then slide caliper over rotor and align bolt holes in caliper with mounting holes of fork or frame.

10. [ ] If caliper-mounting bolts are being reused, treat threads with Loctite 242 (not needed for first-time installation).

11. [ ] **Install and gently snug caliper-mounting bolts. Check clearance between rotor and slot in caliper mount. Rotor should be centered in slot. If rotor is closer to inside edge of slot, adjust clearance by remounting caliper with .2mm shim washer between caliper and each fork/ frame mount. then check centering again.**

12. [ ] **Once centering is adequate, secure caliper-mounting bolts to 50in-lbs.**

13. [ ] **Secure hose to frame and/or fork, then turn handlebars and/or move suspension through its full range to check for interference with hose.**

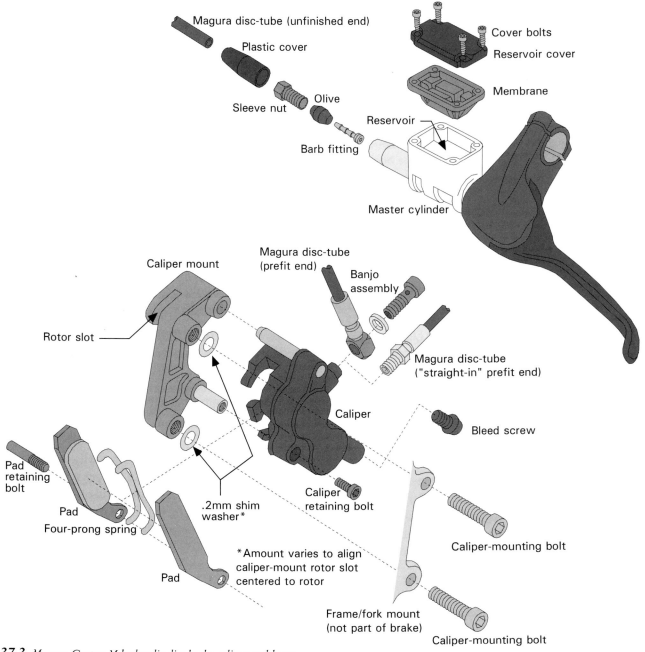

Magura disc-tube (unfinished end)
Plastic cover
Sleeve nut
Olive
Barb fitting
Cover bolts
Reservoir cover
Membrane
Reservoir
Master cylinder

Caliper mount
Magura disc-tube (prefit end)
Banjo assembly
Rotor slot
Magura disc-tube ("straight-in" prefit end)
Caliper
Bleed screw
Pad retaining bolt
Pad
Four-prong spring
.2mm shim washer*
Caliper retaining bolt
Pad
*Amount varies to align caliper-mount rotor slot centered to rotor
Caliper-mounting bolt
Frame/fork mount (not part of brake)
Caliper-mounting bolt

37.3 *Magura Gustav M hydraulic disc brake caliper and lever.*

PAD REPLACEMENT

The pads have "ears" at the end of the caliper opposite the hose. A shaft goes through the ears, which retains the pads in the caliper. With the brake operated to close the pads firmly to the rotor, measure the distance between the ears. If the measurement is 4.8mm or less, the pads must be replaced. With fresh pads in the caliper, this measurement is about 6.8mm. Remaining pad life can be estimated by calculating the reduction of the current measurement from the original 6.8mm as a percentage of the 2mm total wear life. In other words, if the current measurement is 5.8mm (1mm reduction from 6.8mm), then the pads have 50% of their life remaining (1mm is 50% of 2mm).

1. [ ] Remove wheel, then unthread bolt through ends of pad plates with 2mm Allen wrench.
2. [ ] Remove pads and four-prong spring out rotor slot in inner edge of caliper.
3. [ ] Clean inside caliper at piston with water and detergent on brush. *CAUTION: Don't use automotive brake cleaners, seal damage will occur!*
4. [ ] Assemble replacement pads and four-prong spring so braking-material sides face each other and spring is sandwiched between them, with prongs contacting metal plates (not contacting surface of braking material). When properly assembled, tips of spring prongs point to edge of pads that pad ears angle away from.
5. [ ] Install pad assembly into caliper slot so closed end of spring goes in first and ear-ends of pads are at end of caliper opposite where hydraulic hose attaches.
6. [ ] Treat pad-retaining bolt threads with Loctite 222.
7. [ ] Install pad-retaining bolt through hole in inner face of caliper and through holes in ears of pads, then secure bolt to 9in-lbs.
8. [ ] Face backside of caliper, put your thumbs into access holes on back face of caliper, then press firmly against inner brake shoe. This causes slave pistons to retract fully into caliper, which allows adequate clearance for the rotor.
9. [ ] Install wheel.

HOSE INSTALLATION AND SIZING

If the caliper hose is damaged, too short, or too long, then it is necessary to install a new hose or resize the existing hose. The same procedure suffices for both. A hose is too short if it must bend sharply at any time. A hose is too long only if it interferes with other components or snags on things during use of the bicycle. Performance of the brake system is not affected by hose length.

1. [ ] Slide plastic sleeve on lever-end of hose away from brake lever, then unthread 8mm hose fitting from brake lever. It may be necessary to remove brake lever from handlebar if hose twists with fitting.
2. [ ] Only if replacing hose, unthread bolt through banjo fitting (or hex-fitting built into end of hose) at brake caliper.
3. [ ] Only if replacing hose, install bolt (with new washer) through banjo fitting (or thread in hex fitting built into end of hose) and secure to 35in-lbs. Note: Use only hoses marked "Magura disc-tube."
4. [ ] Route hose to lever and decide on appropriate length. Use Magura hose cutter or sharp razor knife to trim hose to desired length. End should be cut as square as possible.
5. [ ] Place plastic fitting cover (small-end first), sleeve nut (hex-end first), then new Magura olive fitting (black, never brass) onto cut end of hose.
6. [ ] Press hose into slot in red tool (part of service kit) so approximately 20mm of hose extends past tool, then insert new barbed fitting into hose until fitting head contacts hose. If installation is difficult, sandwich red tool and hose in soft jaws of vise and tap barbed fitting in with plastic mallet.
7. [ ] Insert end of hose into hole in brake lever, then hand thread sleeve nut into brake lever.
8. [ ] After installing sleeve nut as far as possible by hand, secure nut to 35in-lbs.
9. [ ] Perform FILLING AND BLEEDING procedure.

FILLING AND BLEEDING

Filling and bleeding are normally done as part of hose replacement or sizing. Magura does not recommend filling and bleeding as routine maintenance.

CAUTION: At all times while working with oil, it is critical to keep oil off rotor surface and brake pads!

1. [ ] Remove wheel from bike.
2. [ ] Remove both brake pads.
3. [ ] Put bike in position so that head of bleed screw (at opposite end of caliper from hose) is at top of caliper.
4. [ ] Remove bleed screw with 5mm Allen wrench.
5. [ ] If necessary, attach hose and 6mm-thread bleed fitting to syringe, then fill syringe with Magura Blood hydraulic oil. With syringe upright, pump until all air bubbles are out of syringe and bleed hose. Other mineral oils such as Finish Line 5wt suspension oils are also suitable.
6. [ ] Thread bleed fitting into caliper where bleed screw was removed and gently secure fitting.

7. [ ] Position bike and/or brake lever so that reservoir cap on face of brake lever is completely horizontal.
8. [ ] Use T7 Torx wrench to remove 4 bolts that retain reservoir cap, then remove cap and rubber membrane.
9. [ ] Slowly pump syringe contents into system, being prepared to catch overflow at lever. Continue pumping until no air bubbles are seen in reservoir.
10. [ ] Place rubber membrane into bottom face of reservoir cap, then insert four bolts into reservoir cap.
11. [ ] Place reservoir-cap assembly on top of lever so that overflow hole in edge of reservoir cap will be at top edge of cap when brake lever is in normal position.
12. [ ] Gradually tighten 4 bolts in crisscross pattern until all are tight to equivalent of 5in-lbs.
13. [ ] Return bike to position that puts caliper in same position as when bleed screw was removed, then unthread bleed fitting from caliper.
14. [ ] Install bleed screw into caliper and secure to 51in-lbs.
15. [ ] Clean caliper of any oil, then install brake pads and wheel.
16. [ ] Operate brake and check for soft or spongy feel and leaks at hose fittings and bleed screw. Repeat bleeding procedure if brake feels soft or spongy.

MAGURA LOUISE & CLARA DISC BRAKES

ABOUT THIS SECTION

This section specifically covers the Magura Louise and Clara disc-brake systems. Service techniques are identical for both systems. The procedures covered in this section include wheel building guidelines, rotor and wheel installation, lever installation, hose installation, filling and bleeding the system, caliper installation, and pad replacement. This section does not cover rebuilding the caliper, which Magura does not support.

TOOLS

No special tools are required for normal installation and adjustment. Hose replacement and bleeding and filling the system requires a syringe, a bleed fitting, hose, and a tool for holding the hose when installing the barbed fitting, all of which are part of the Louise Service Kit.

INSTALLATION

Wheel building guidelines

The recommended cross patterns are limited to 3X and 4X. Deceleration can occur much more rapidly than acceleration, so consequently the torsional loads from deceleration are much higher than those generated during acceleration. The recommended cross patterns are required to transfer the higher torsional loads that hub-mounted brakes can generate during rapid deceleration.

Although Magura makes no recommendation regarding lacing patterns, other manufacturers require that the left-side head-out spokes radiate clockwise from the hub and that the right-side head-in spokes radiate counterclockwise from the hub. These are the same directions that result from following the wheel-lacing instructions in this manual. The vernacular terms for these patterns are that the "pulling" spokes are "head out" and the "pushing" spokes are "head in." An alternate term to "pulling" is "trailing" and an alternate term to "pushing" is "leading."

Rotor and wheel installation

If installing the rotor on a 1999 Magura Gustav hub or Mavic Crossmax or CrossLink wheels, use the 3mm-thick spacer between the rotor and the hub. If using a Magura Louise Pro or Louise Comp hub, no spacer is needed behind the rotor.

NOTE: Build wheel before installing rotor.

1. [ ] Place rotor on hub with rotation arrow facing out from hub.
2. [ ] If rotor-mounting bolts are being reused, treat threads with Loctite 242 (not needed for first-time installation).
3. [ ] Thread in all six rotor bolts until heads just contact rotor.
4. [ ] Use marker to mark each bolt clockwise 1 to 6, then tighten each to 35in-lbs in a sequence of 1, 3, 5, 2, 4, then 6.

It is recommended that the quick-release skewer be installed opposite of normal. This insures that the quick-release lever, when fully closed, cannot interfere with the rotor. Although quick-release security is always of critical importance, wheel security is an even greater issue on a disc-brake hub than a hub with no brake. When securing the skewer, be sure to follow the guidelines in Chapter 18.

5. [ ] Install quick-release skewer into right end of axle (opposite of normal) then install adjusting nut on skewer.
6. [ ] Install wheel in proper alignment and with optimum quick-release security.

Brake lever and hose installation

7. [ ] Install brake lever in normal lateral and rotational position, then secure mounting bolt to 35in-lbs.

8. [ ] Adjust reach with 2mm Allen screw (at lever pivot) to middle of range (approximate two turns from either end of range). *Note: reach adjustment does not affect clearance adjustment or brake operation–this adjustment is only intended to make reach appropriate for average-sized hands.*

Caliper installation and adjustment

NOTE: *For frames or forks with Hayes-type post mounting (bolt holes aligned parallel to bike, rather than perpendicular to bike), an adapter plate must be mounted first. Install adapter and secure bolts to 55–70in-lbs.*

9. [ ] Loosen volume-adjusting bolt on outer face of caliper fully with 5mm Allen wrench.

10. [ ] Remove fixed-shoe adjusting plate from inside face of caliper with 5mm Allen wrench, treat threads with Loctite 242, then install plate until face is just flush with inner face of caliper.

11. [ ] Remove plastic pad spacer (if any) from between brake pads, then slide caliper over rotor and align bolt holes in caliper with mounting holes of fork or frame.

12. [ ] If caliper-mounting bolts are being reused, treat threads with Loctite 242 (not needed for first-time installation).

13. [ ] Install and gently snug caliper-mounting bolts. Check clearance between rotor and inner edge of caliper slot (spin rotor). If there is contact, remount caliper with a .2mm shim washer between caliper and each fork/frame mount and check for rub again.

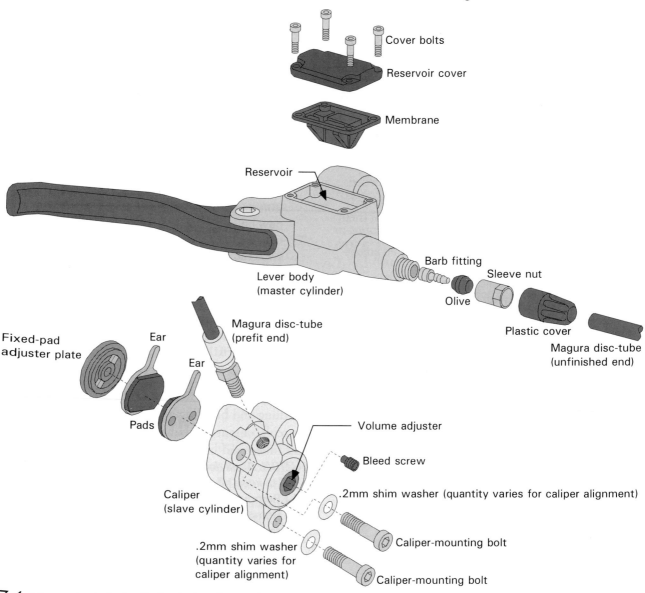

37.4 *Magura Louise hydraulic disc brake caliper and lever.*

TOOL CHOICES

Table 38-1 is a list of all the suspension-specific tools required to perform *all* of procedures in this chapter. If a tool's use is limited to a specific brand or model, it is indicated in the **Fits and considerations** column.

SUSPENSION TOOLS (table 38-1)

Tool	Fits and considerations
RockShox 70100	Kit for servicing many RockShox models, and useful in many applications for non-RockShox suspensions (includes: stanchion-clamping blocks #70101, seal and bushing installer #70103, seal and bushing puller #70113, valve-body tool #70105, and dropout vise blocks #70107)
RockShox 70106	Bushing-removal tool for Quadra 5, 21, and 21R
RockShox 70108	Bushing-installation tool for Quadra 5, 21, and 21R
RockShox 70113	Friction-ring installer for original (1993) Quadra
RockShox 70118	Bushing-removal tool for Judy fork
RockShox 70119	Bushing-installation tool for Judy fork
RockShox 70142	Judy damper-cartridge-service tool kit
RockShox 70165	Kit for servicing Deluxe and Super Deluxe rear shocks
RockShox 59309	Pump required for pressurizing Deluxe and Super Deluxe rear shocks
Risse bullet tool	For installing seal head on Risse Genesis and Elroy rear shocks
12mm Allen wrench	For Marzocchi Zokes fork
United Bicycle Tool RS-109	Needle-type pump with 60psi capacity, bleeder valve, and gauge for pressurizing Rock Shox air/oil systems
United Bicycle Tool RS-300R	Needle-type pump with 300psi capacity, bleeder valve, and gauge for pressurizing Risse air/oil systems without Schrader valve
United Bicycle Tool RS-300S	Schrader-valve pump with 300psi capacity, bleeder valve, and gauge for pressurizing forks with recessed Schrader valve
Amp vise blocks	Split block of aluminum with split holes for clamping to various diameters of Amp damper shafts
Marzocchi 104	For threading onto Schrader valve to pull air cap out of stanchion on various Marzocchi air/oil suspensions
6"section of 3/8" round bar stock	For servicing Amp and Risse shocks, available at hardware store
6"section of 5/16" round bar stock	For servicing Amp and Risse shocks, available at hardware store
Bicycle Research 1–1/8" frame block	Used for holding Risse piston in vise
Sport-ball inflation needle	Use for depressurizing air chambers, must be type that has hole in end, not hole on side of tip (wrong type will damage air seal)
Bulb syringe (automotive battery type)	Useful for adjusting oil level in air/oil forks
United Bicycle Tool CV-521	Reversible snap-ring pliers with assorted tips in a variety of angles and thickness

COMPLICATIONS

Difficult seal removal on air/oil forks

Seals are deliberately a very tight fit. Most forks with seals require some sort of puller, but some manufacturers expect the mechanic to use brute force. These methods are inconsistent, messy, and potentially dangerous.

Air contamination in rear shocks

Certain units are designed to have no air in the chamber where there is oil. The presence of air may be noisy, or it may interfere with the passage of oil through tiny valve holes. Furthermore, air can introduce a spring effect. Special care is required to get the unit assembled without air getting inside, and in some cases it is required to perform the assembly while the whole unit is submerged in the same hydraulic fluid that is going inside the unit.

Frozen bolts in bottom of slider

A number of products put bolts down in the bottom of the slider, where moisture from condensation collects. This can lead to corrosion developing on threads, and very difficult bolt removal. Persistence and penetrating oil are the only solutions.

Stripped threads in fork crowns and sliders

Very soft materials, such as aluminum and magnesium, are used in certain sliders and fork crowns. Female threads in these parts strip easily when bolts are over-tightened. Use Loctite to eliminate the need for higher torques, and *always* use torque wrenches.

Unreplaceable bushings

Some poorly-designed forks rely on bushings that are a permanent part of the slider or the stanchion tube. The only way to replace these bushings is to replace the slider or stanchion, which is usually impractical (due to price or availability).

Wear on impractical-to-replace parts

Some forks are designed so that the bushings slide up and down against the inside surface of an aluminum or magnesium slider. These softer materials wear out easily; replacement is usually impractical (due to price or availability). Stanchion tubes on air/oil forks can fail in two ways: the surface may become nicked or scratched so that seal integrity is lost, or the stanchions may become bent from excessive load.

Clip failure

The snap-rings, c-clips, e-clips, and circlips used in suspensions are delicate; expansion or compression is required to install them, and they are easily damaged.

If they are slightly deformed, they may appear to be secure, but may fail during use. There is sometimes a great deal of load placed on these clips. Most clips have asymmetrical faces; one face has sharp corners on the edges, and the other has more rounded corners on the edges. As a rule, always install these clips so that the sharper-edged side faces away from the direction of the load (or pressure) that is against the item being retained by the clip.

Hydraulic-fluid toxicity

The fluids used in oil-damped systems may be toxic. Minimize your exposure and wear rubber gloves while working with these units.

OIL-VISCOSITY TESTING

Viscosity testing is needed for two reasons. First, there is no way to know what oil is being removed from a suspension without testing. If the original oil is unknown, then there is no way to know what might be suitable as a replacement. Second, manufacturer's ratings of their own oils are often unreliable. By testing, it is possible to know how different oils compare.

Viscosity testing of suspension fluid

The viscosity of shock fork fluid has a large impact on the performance of the fork. The following fluid-viscosity table (page 38-6), and fluid viscosity-test procedure (page 38-6), can help the mechanic estimate the current relative viscosity of a shock fork fluid.

When a shock fork is disassembled, most mechanics simply remove the old fluid and dump it in the recycling barrel. The new fluid selected may be quite different than the old fluid. This will, of course, affect the handling in a way which may or may not be desired by the customer. It is possible to determine the approximate viscosity of the old fluid, then compare it to known viscosities of popular brands. It is likely that the old fluid is dirty. This particulate matter may, in fact, have changed the viscosity of the fluid. However, because the dirty fluid is what the customer was most currently using, it is still appropriate to test the old fluid. Remember that the test rates the "effective viscosity" of the old fluid, not necessarily its original viscosity.

Needed testing equipment

Clear "Bic" pens (the Bic Classic Stic, model #MSP10). These are plastic, and are somewhat fragile, so purchase several. Older and used pens are often warped and deformed, so purchase new pens.

Stop watch accurate to one tenth of a second.

Magnet strong enough to hold a ball bearing through the plastic.

A 3/16" ball bearing.

A vise or other devises that will hold the pen steady and vertical during the testing. Again, the pens are plastic, so take care in how you hold it.

The Bic Classic Stic pen needs some modification.

Use a drop of super-glue to cover the side-hole.

Remove the top cap.

Remove the pen tip and pull the ink tube off of the pen tip. The ink tube is not needed for the test.

Reinstall pen tip.

Put a rubber-coated strap clamp (that fits tubing the size of the pen) around the pen, then secure the clamp with a nut and bolt. Grasping the bolt and nut in the vise will be the way the pen will be held upright.

Mark the "starting line" for the test with a permanent marker or a scribe line. The starting line for the ball bearing is the middle of the U in the phrase, "Made in USA." This is 5mm from the top.

Viscosity-test procedure

1. [ ] **Secure pen vertically in vise.**
2. [ ] **Fill to top with fluid to be tested.**
3. [ ] **Inspect for air bubbles; allow oil to sit if bubbles are present.**
4. [ ] **Place 3/16" ball bearing on a magnet.**
5. [ ] **Place ball in top of pen, then force it off magnet with your finger while holding magnet close to pen top (magnet will hold bearing inside pen, at top).**
6. [ ] **Position center of bearing at middle of U in USA, or at marked line.**
7. [ ] **Pull magnet away and start timer simultaneously.**
8. [ ] **Stop timer when ball stops at bottom.**
9. [ ] **Repeat at least three times, to see if results are consistent. Record time here: _____ secs.**
10. [ ] **See table 38-2 for data for common bicycle-suspension fluids, and compare result in step 9 to determine what fluid might be comparable.**

Upon completing the test, remove the pen tip and drain the fluid. Clean inside the pen with a mineral spirit solvent. Do not use acetone or other solvents that harm plastics. Dry the inside with compressed air, then install the tip.

Hydraulic-fluid viscosity

Table 38-2 can be used to compare the relative viscosity of popular brands of bicycle hydraulic fluids. Viscosity is a nominal measurement of the degree to which a fluid resists flow under applied force. The popular measurement of this property is referred to as a fluid's *weight*. The more a fluid resists flow, the more the assigned *weight*. Manufacturers are not necessarily consistent with one another regarding their assigned weights, but they tend to be consistent within their own product line. For example, one manufacturer's *5 weight* can have a higher viscosity than another manufacturer's *5 weight*.

Table 38-2 (below) is based on the preceding test of fluid viscosity (see preceding procedure). Note that the table is only a measure of a fluid's relative viscosity, and is not intended to be a statement on its quality. The exact viscosity may also differ between different shipments from the same manufacturer.

COMMON BICYCLE-SUSPENSION FLUIDS (table 38-2)

Brand	Weight or Designation	Time at 72° (in seconds)	Time at 45° (in seconds)	% change 72° to 45°
Englund	blue 5w	5	9	80%
Finish Line	2.5w	6	8	33%
RockShox	5w	7	18	128%
Englund	purple (approx. 7w)	7	13	85%
Finish Line	5w	9	17	88%
Englund	red (approx. 10.5 w)	11	21	91%
Finish Line	10w	13	28	115
RockShox	8w	14	36	157%
Pedro's	no designation	15	32	133%
Englund	gold (approx. 12.5 w)	18	39	117%
Finish Line	20w	22	60	172%

CANE CREEK REAR SHOCKS

ABOUT THIS SECTION

This section applies to the following models: AD-4, AD-5, AD-8, and AD-10. Procedurally, there is virtually no difference between the AD-4 and AD-5, and there is also virtually no difference between the AD-8 and AD-10. There are small technique differences between the 4 or 5 and the 8 or 10, but one procedure with notations about the differences follows.

TOOLS

There are no special tools provided by the manufacturer for working on these shocks. The AD-4 and AD-8 have a large ring that is unthreaded by hand that can be difficult to break loose. Wrapping a large rubber band around the ring, such as the rubber band that comes in Aheadset packages, improves grip. A section of inner tube also works, but not quite as well.

FULL SHOCK SERVICE

Services include cleaning and lubrication, replacement of seals when air leaks develop, and changing the valving for tuning purposes (AD-4 and AD-5 only).

Disassembly

1. [ ] Depress valve plunger to deflate shock.
2. [ ] *AD-8 and AD-10 only:* Loosen compression and rebound adjusters to just short of point O-rings are revealed.
3. [ ] Clamp body eyelet carefully into soft jaws in vise (use rag to protect finish).
4. [ ] Wrap wide rubber band around black ring at top of body to improve grip, then turn ring counterclockwise to unthread.
5. [ ] Pull up on shaft to remove shaft/piston assembly from shock body.
6. [ ] Clamp eyelet end of shaft assembly in the soft jaws in vise (protect finish with rag).
7. [ ] Use pin spanner (Park SPA-1) to unthread piston.
8. [ ] *AD-8 and AD-10 only*: Remove compression cylinder and compression washer from inside of shaft assembly, and record compression washer thickness here: _____
9. [ ] *AD-4 and AD-8*: Pull seal head off shaft, then inspect and remove damaged seals and O-rings.
   AD-5 and AD-10: Pull lockring off shaft assembly, then pull seal bushing off shaft assembly. Inspect and remove damaged seals and O-rings from lockring and seal bushing.

10. [ ] *AD-4 and AD-5 only*: Pull up on white plastic plug to remove it from volume adjusting plate. *AD-8 and AD-10 only*: Pull on aluminum adjuster rod to remove it from volume adjusting plate.
11. [ ] Remove shaft from vise, then insert rubber-tipped blow gun into hole in volume adjusting plate and use compressed air to force out plate. *Note: Be prepared for plate and two small plastic adjusting ramps to fly out of shaft!*
12. [ ] *AD-8 and AD-10 only*: Inspect inside shaft for valve adjuster ramps that may have remained in shaft during step 11.
13. [ ] Inspect and remove damaged O-rings from volume adjusting plate.
14. [ ] Remove compression and rebound adjusters fully. O-rings will provide light resistance to removal after threads are disengaged.
15. [ ] Use 8mm socket to remove valve nut from bottom face of piston.
16. [ ] Remove washer, then remove compression valve shim and record thickness here: _____

Cleaning

17. [ ] Clean all parts with mild detergent and dry with compressed air and/or lint-free rag.

Volume adjustment

18. [ ] If it is desired to change volume to change spring rate, carefully remove circlip inside shaft and move to higher groove to increase spring rate, or lower groove to decrease spring rate.

Assembly

19. [ ] Replace all damaged O-rings and seals that were removed, then grease all O-rings.
20. [ ] Install compression shim, small washer, and then valve nut into piston.
21. [ ] *AD-4 and AD-8 only*: Slide seal head onto closed end of shaft, threaded-end first. *AD-5 and AD-10 only*: Install seal bushing (small end first) over closed end of shaft, then install lockring (knurled-end first) over closed end of shaft.
22. [ ] Secure eyelet end of shaft into vise (open-end up).
23. [ ] *AD-8 and AD-10 only*: Inspect ramp housing inside shaft unit. It must be aligned with its center divider parallel to axis of holes for adjuster bolts. Push one adjuster bolt into its hole to see if tip of bolt appears inside ramp housing. If not, try rotating ramp housing 180°.

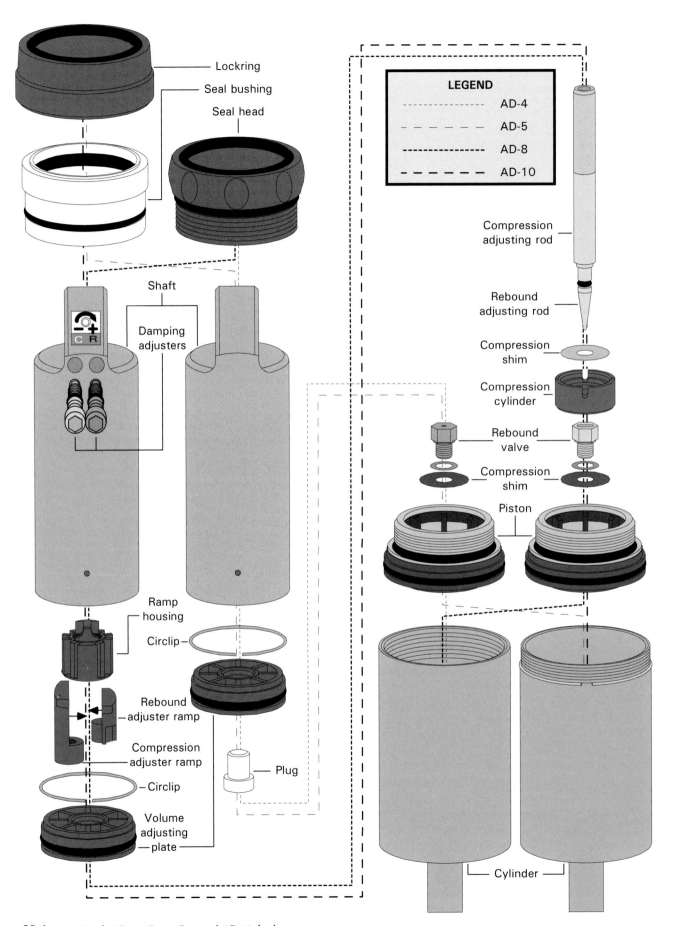

LEGEND
- ———————— AD-4
- — — — — AD-5
- — · — · — AD-8
- — — — — AD-10

Lockring

Seal bushing

Seal head

Compression adjusting rod

Rebound adjusting rod

Compression shim

Compression cylinder

Rebound valve

Compression shim

Piston

Shaft

Damping adjusters

Ramp housing

Circlip

Rebound adjuster ramp

Compression adjuster ramp

Plug

Circlip

Volume adjusting plate

Cylinder

38.1 *Cane Creek AD-4, AD-5, AD-8, and AD-10 shocks.*

In the next step, when the bolts with O-rings are inserted into the holes in the shaft, it is difficult not to damage the O-rings by catching them on the lips of the holes. Use a small chamfering tool to chamfer the holes and it will be no problem.

24. [ ] *AD-8 and AD-10 only:* Thread silver adjusting screw into hole marked "C, " and black adjusting screw into hole marked "R," taking care not to deform or tear O-rings. Thread in bolts just until first calibration mark on smooth bolt shaft reaches the top of hole.

25. [ ] *AD-4 and AD-5 only:* Insert white plug into volume adjusting plate.
AD-8 and AD-10 only: Grease blunt end of adjuster-rod assembly, mate valve adjuster ramps together, then install ramp assembly onto blunt end of adjuster-rod assembly. Insert assembly into ramp housing inside shaft so that slope of ramps face toward holes for valve adjusters.

26. [ ] Insert volume-adjusting plate into shaft, smooth-face up, until it seats fully.

27. [ ] *AD-8 and AD-10 only:* Place compression valve shim on top of valve adjusting rod, then place compression cylinder (notched end first) on top of compression valve shim.

28. [ ] Thread in and secure piston.

29. [ ] Grease inside of shock body with recommended grease, then carefully slide over piston.

30. [ ] Turn shock over and carefully grasp body eyelet in vise.

31. [ ] *AD-4 and AD-8 only:* Thread seal head into shock body as far as it will go (wrap with rubber band to improve grip).
AD-5 and AD-10 only: Slide bushing seal as far as it will go into body, then slide lockring over seal bushing and thread it onto body (until lockring covers half of wire clip at end of body threads).

32. [ ] Inflate shock. Cover with soapy water to check for leaks.

TUNING OPTIONS

Air pressure

A simple formula can be used to determine an appropriate pressure for the shock, depending on the rider's weight: rider's weight (in pounds) plus 10 equals pressure (in psi). If the rider finds the suspension bottoms out too frequently, the pressure should be increased. If the rider finds the suspension is too stiff, pressure should be reduced. Adjustments should be used in five-pound increments.

Air volume

These shocks have a volume adjusting plate in the shaft section of the shock. Changing the volume changes how progressive the spring is. For example, with the plate adjusted to reduce volume, even if the starting pressure is constant, it will take more force to compress the suspension fully. The suspension will be progressively more stiff the more it is compressed and less likely to bottom on big hits. Conversely, if the plate is adjusted to increase volume, even if the starting pressure is constant, it will take less force to compress the suspension fully. The suspension will be less stiff when it is compressed the same amount and the ride will be softer.

Compression and rebound adjusters

The AD-8 and AD-10 have external adjusters for compression and rebound damping. They are clearing marked. The rider should determine the optimal settings by using simple trial and error. The AD-4 and AD-5 have no external adjustment, but rebound damping can be adjusted by means of replacing the valve nut with one with a different size orifice, and compression damping is adjusted by changing a valve shim washer inside the shock.

AD-4 and AD-5 compression shim washers

Cane Creek makes available a tuning kit with an assortment of thickness of compression shim washers. Changing the compression washer is the only way to change the compression damping on the AD-4 and AD-5. The washer(s) should be changed on the AD-8 and AD-10 only if the external adjuster cannot be loosened or tightened enough to achieve the desired amount of damping. All models have a compression washer that is removed in step #16 (of the preceding procedure) from beneath the valve nut. Another compression washer is the washer removed in step #9 (AD-8 and AD-10 only).

Three washers are available with thickness measurements of .10mm, .15mm, and .20mm. These increments are large, so in most cases a change of one step up or down should be the most attempted at first.

AD-4 and AD-5 valve orifice diameter

The tuning kit also includes three sizes of valve nuts, with orifice diameters of .56mm, .61mm, and .66mm. These are used to adjust the rebound damping on the AD-4 and AD-5 only. Smaller orifice size creates greater damping. To identify the size of the installed valve or the replacement valve, look for a number stamped on the side of the valve. The number "6" indicates the smallest size, "7" the middle size, and "8"

moved to different slots to change the pre-load. When the clip is moved further up, the pre-load is increased, and decreased when the clip is moved further down.

Keeper plate

38.6 *To change the pre-load adjustment on the Comp and Pro XC models, move the keeper plate to a different slot.*

Adjusting SX pre-load

The adjuster knobs at the tops of the sliders can be turned to change the effective spring stiffness. Turning the knobs clockwise increases spring stiffness and turning the knobs counterclockwise decreases spring stiffness.

Adjusting damping on Manitou SX left leg

The adjusting knob on the bottom of the left slider primarily adjusts rebound damping but compression damping will be increased slightly whenever rebound damping is increased significantly. Turning the knob counterclockwise decreases rebound damping and turning the knob clockwise increases rebound damping.

See *MANITOU MACH 5 SX OIL DAMPERS* (immediately following this section) for damper service.

Changing oil in damper in SX left leg

Oil weight affects the damping rate. The weight of the oil affects both the compression and rebound damping. Heavier-weight oils increase the damping effect (retarding compression and rebound); lighter-weight oils decrease the damping effect (speeding up compression and rebound).

Oil weight also might be varied to compensate for weather conditions, with very light-weight oils being used for extreme-cold conditions.

See *MANITOU MACH 5 SX OIL DAMPERS* (immediately following this section) for damper service.

MANITOU MACH 5 SX OIL DAMPERS

The oil damper is built into the left stanchion tube on SX models. The damper can be replaced as a whole by replacing the stanchion, or the damper can be serviced by disassembling the stanchion assembly.

DISASSEMBLY

1. [ ] Use DISASSEMBLY steps 1–15 of *MANITOU MACH 5 FORKS* (page 38-10) to access oil damper.
2. [ ] Remove left stanchion assembly from fork crown.
3. [ ] Prepare to catch ball bearing that is trapped under elastomer on end of shaft, then carefully remove elastomer from shaft.
4. [ ] With stanchion held upside down, carefully unthread seal-head with large hex fitting on bottom end of stanchion, then pull seal-head a few millimeters away from stanchion.

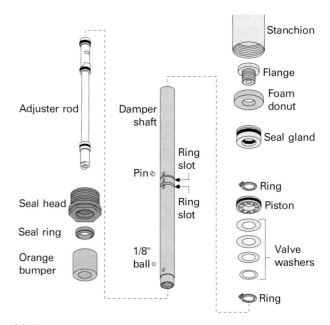

38.7 *Blow-up of EFC and Mach 5 SX oil damper.*

5. [ ] Turn stanchion over so that oil will drain into catch pan.
6. [ ] Carefully pull seal-head off end of shaft.
7. [ ] With end of stanchion still pointing into catch pan, pump shaft fully in and out to pump oil out of stanchion.

NOTE: If changing oil only, go to step 32 now. Do not go to step 8 unless in possession of a rebuild kit.

8. [ ] Insert long rod into top of stanchion tube, then push remaining parts out bottom of stanchion.

9. [ ] Holding shaft securely by bottom 25mm (in fashion that will not mar shaft), use 5mm Allen wrench to unscrew flange from top end of shaft.
10. [ ] Pull foam donut and seal gland off top end of shaft.
11. [ ] Remove O-ring from outside of seal gland, then seal ring from inside of seal gland.

For the remaining steps, it is important to differentiate between the top and bottom of the shaft. The bottom end has a diameter reduction for the last 7mm and also has a hole in the shaft about 12mm from the end.

12. [ ] Being careful not to scratch shaft, remove external snap-ring from topside of piston/ valve assembly at center of shaft.
13. [ ] Remove small metal washer, plastic washer, two large metal washers, and then piston.
14. [ ] Remove O-ring from outside of piston.
15. [ ] Find pin that was covered by piston, then tap shaft on soft surface so that pin will fall out; pushing plastic adjuster rod inside shaft one way or other can relieve load on pin, so that it will fall out.
16. [ ] Pushing from top end of shaft, push adjuster rod out bottom end of shaft.
17. [ ] Remove three O-rings from adjuster rod.
18. [ ] Remove O-ring from outside of threaded stanchion seal-head, then seal ring from inside of seal-head.

CLEANING AND INSPECTION

19. [ ] Clean all parts with mild detergent and water, then dry thoroughly with compressed air. *Avoid leaving solvents or lint from rags on, or in, any part!*
20. [ ] Inspect shaft for scratches or gouges on portions of shaft that move through O-rings in seal gland and seal-head.

ASSEMBLY

21. [ ] Thoroughly grease all O-rings and seal rings.
22. [ ] Install O-ring (outside) and seal ring (inside) of threaded seal-head.
23. [ ] Install 3 O-rings on adjuster rod.
24. [ ] Install O-ring (outside) and seal ring (inside) of seal gland.
25. [ ] Install O-ring on outside of piston.
26. [ ] Slide onto top end of shaft in order: piston, two large metal washers, plastic washer, then small metal washer.
27. [ ] Carefully slide external snap-ring over top end of shaft, then seat in groove above washer(s).
28. [ ] Slide foam donut over top end of shaft.

29. [ ] Find face of seal gland that internal seal ring is closest to, then carefully slide seal gland (with that face first) over top end of shaft.
30. [ ] Holding shaft securely by bottom 25mm (in fashion that will not mar shaft), use 5mm Allen wrench to secure flange into top end of shaft.
31. [ ] Taking care to not damage seal-gland O-ring on threads in end of stanchion, insert shaft/ piston assembly into end of stanchion (flanged-end first), then bottom shaft fully into stanchion.
32. [ ] Holding stanchion tube upside down, carefully fill stanchion with 2.5w, high-quality, suspension oil.
33. [ ] Without moving shaft to its limit in either direction, slowly pump shaft up and down, several times to pump air out of system.
34. [ ] When bubbles have dissipated from top of oil, add more oil until level is 2–3mm below end of stanchion.
35. [ ] Look at bottom face of seal-head to find location of bleed hole.
36. [ ] Keeping track of location of bleed hole, carefully slide stanchion seal-head over end of shaft until threads of seal-head contact threads in end of stanchion.
37. [ ] Wrap rag around stanchion, then thread stanchion onto seal-head while holding seal-head stationary, until seal-head is engaged a few threads.
38. [ ] Tip stanchion in direction that will keep bleed hole on high side, until stanchion is leaning at about 45°.
39. [ ] Holding seal-head stationary, thread stanchion on to seal-head until O-ring just contacts end of stanchion.

In the following step, great care is needed to prevent the O-ring from becoming trapped between the seal-head flange and the end of the stanchion. As the seal-head is threading in, the oil coming out the bleed hole tends to force the O-ring out of its groove. Backing the seal-head out slightly after threading it in a little encourages the O-ring to settle back down into the groove of the seal-head. *Important! If at any time it appears that the O-ring is being squeezed between the seal-head flange and the end of the stanchion, remove the seal-head and start over again!*

40. [ ] Thread seal-head in tiny amount, back out slightly less, in again, out slightly less again (repeatedly), until flange on seal-head is seated against end of stanchion.
41. [ ] Secure seal-head to 35–50in-lbs.
42. [ ] Turn adjuster rod in end of shaft fully counterclockwise.

43. [ ] **Pull shaft out of stanchion to its limit.**
44. [ ] **Place ball bearing in its socket 12mm from end of shaft, then slip bumper over shaft to retain bearing.**
45. [ ] **Place upper end of stanchion fully into fork crown, then secure bolt in fork crown to 110–130in-lbs.**

TUNING OPTIONS

Adjusting damping on Mach 5 SX left leg

The adjusting knob on the bottom of the left slider primarily adjusts rebound damping but compression damping will be increased slightly whenever rebound damping is increased significantly. Turning the knob counterclockwise decreases rebound damping and turning the knob clockwise increases rebound damping.

Damper oil change in Mach 5 SX left leg

Oil weight affects the damping rate. The weight of the oil affects both the compression and rebound damping. Heavier-weight oils increase the damping effect (retarding compression and rebound); lighter-weight oils decrease the damping effect (speeding up compression and rebound).

Oil weight also might be varied to compensate for weather conditions, with very light-weight oils being used for extreme-cold conditions.

MANITOU '98–'00 SX & XVERT FORKS

ABOUT THIS SECTION

This section covers a wide range of Manitou SX and XVert models from 1998 through 2000 models. This section does not cover the air-sprung 2000 Mars models, which were not available at the time of this writing. This section does not cover the 1999 Spyder or 2000 Magnum models. The covered 2000 models can be distinguished from the covered 1998 and 1999 models by looking for the "preload" adjuster, which is on the right side on the 2000 models. These 2000 models are essentially the same fork to service as the earlier ones, with one significant exception. In 1998 and 1999, all the models had a spring assembly in the right leg and a hydraulic damper in the left leg. For the 2000 models, this is reversed. This section covers full fork service, including bushing replacement.

The bushing removal and installation procedure utilizes the following tools. The removal tool can be easily modified to improve its function. The modifications are described at the point in the procedure where the use of the tool is described. These bushing tools were introduced in 2000, but are similar to the older tools (remover #85-3892 and installer #38-3893).

Answer Products #85-3909 bushing remover
Answer Products #85-3911 bushing installer
Other tools needed are:
Modified 24mm socket ground on end to eliminate internal bevel to improve purchase.
Modified 27mm socket ground on end to eliminate internal bevel to improve purchase.

FULL FORK SERVICE

This section covers a wide range of Manitou models from 1997 through 2000 models, as long as they feature TPC damping. All the covered models should have a decal that indicates it is a TPC model.

Slider-assembly removal

1. [ ] **Pull plastic adjuster knob from bottom of left leg (right leg if 2000 model).**
2. [ ] **Remove bolt that adjuster was removed from with 8mm Allen wrench.**
3. [ ] **Remove second bottom bolt with 4mm Allen wrench, then remove bushing (if any).**
4. [ ] **Pull slider assembly off stanchion tubes, then remove boots from stanchions.**

Spring-stack and plunger-shaft removal

5. [ ] **Count number of turns to turn pre-load adjuster on top of sprung leg fully counterclockwise and record here: _____ turns**
6. [ ] **Unthread cap with pre-load adjuster with fingers (27mm wrench if equipped with flats), then remove spring-stack assembly.**
7. [ ] **Remove elastomer stack from shaft on spring side and note sequence of elastomers and spacers.**
8. [ ] **Push plunger shaft out top end of stanchion where spring was removed. A spoke or similar long, skinny object may be necessary to push shaft fully out.**
9. [ ] **Remove accordion-like top-out bumper from shaft by pulling it off bottom end of shaft.**

Damper removal

Dampers are removed to facilitate cleaning and inspection. Damper-valve disassembly is not necessary, and is not supported by separate parts from the manufacturer.

10. [ ] **With fork upright, unthread top cap and slowly remove damper piston to avoid spilling oil.**

11. [ ] Carefully turn fork over to drain oil from stanchion into waste receptacle.

12. [ ] Be prepared to catch small ball bearing trapped under bumper on rebound-damper shaft, then remove bumper(s) from end of shaft, noting sequence if multiple.

13. [ ] Push rebound-damper shaft almost fully into seal nut on bottom of stanchion.

14. [ ] Use 24mm or 27mm socket to remove seal nut, then pull damper piston out bottom of stanchion.

15. [ ] Pull seal nut off end of rebound-damper shaft.

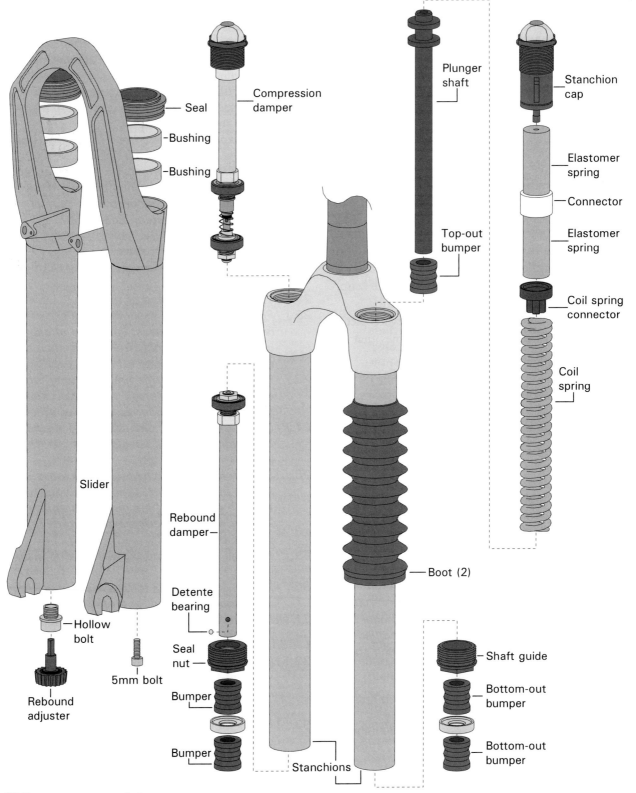

38.8 *Manitou '00 X-Vert fork.*

57. [ ] **Treat bottom bolts with Loctite 242, insert bolts (and bushing, if any) through holes in bottoms of sliders, then thread bolts into shafts.**
58. [ ] **Stabilizing plunger shaft with 6mm bit socket on the extension(s), secure small bolt to 25–30in-lbs.**
59. [ ] **Secure large bottom bolt to 25–30in-lbs with 8mm bit socket.**
60. [ ] **Insert plastic adjuster knob into large bolt.**

Spring and compression-damper installation

61. [ ] **Thoroughly grease spring elastomer and coils, insert spring assembly into side with small bolt at bottom, then secure top caps with wrench flats to 20–30in-lbs (no wrench flats–finger tight).**

Answer Products recommends over ten different oil-level ranges for the forks covered in this section. Many of these recommended ranges overlap, so the following four recommended ranges are all within the manufacturer's recommendations, but may not be as wide a range as the manufacturer's recommendations. Furthermore, the manufacturer cautions strongly against too much or too little oil, and oil level can be difficult to measure, so these more conservative ranges reduce the risk of ending up with an unacceptable oil level.

'00 XVert, '00 XVert DC	80–85mm
'99 XVert TI and all other double-crown XVerts	205-225mm
'98 XVert TI	130-175mm
Other single-crown XVerts except XVert TI, all SX's	95-105mm

59. [ ] **Fill stanchion with 5wt suspension fluid to appropriate level.**
60. [ ] **Carefully insert compression damper, then thread in and secure top caps with wrench flats to 20–30in-lbs (no wrench flats–finger tight).**

TUNING OPTIONS

Compression damping

On some models, compression damping is externally adjustable. There is a clearly-marked adjusting knob on top of the left top cap, if this is the case. It is on the opposite side from the knob marked "preload."

On models that are not externally adjustable, the compression damper may be internally adjustable. The compression damper is the top damper piston. It can be removed without any other fork disassembly. Be careful of overflowing oil that will occur if the damper is removed too quickly. Once removed, locate the small Allen set screw in the side of the top end of the piston assembly. Tightening the screw increases the damping, and loosening the screw reduces the damping. Use one-turn increment adjustments. If there is no set screw, the model has no compression adjustment.

In some cases, it is possible to disassemble the valving on the compression piston, and in other cases the nut has been permanently bonded. In addition to this complication to customizing the valving, there is the fact that the manufacturer has been very poor at supporting customization with individual valve parts. Add to these problems the fact that understanding and evaluating changes in valving is too esoteric for the vast majority of mechanics, and the practicality of customizing the valving is close to none. If the ability to adjust valving by the means provided by the manufacturer was inadequate, this would be a problem, but the built-in adjustability has a very broad range of performance.

Rebound damping

The rebound damper is the lower damper piston in the left leg. It is externally adjustable by turning the adjuster knob on the bottom of the left leg. Turning the knob clockwise increases the rebound damping, and counterclockwise reduces the damping. The knob moves in 1/6 turn clicks so that it is possible to track the amount of adjustment. From fully clockwise to fully counterclockwise is about 40-42 clicks, or up to seven full turns.

Although it is theoretically possible to disassemble the valving on the rebound damper, the same complications that make it impractical to customize the compression damper apply to the rebound damper.

Spring pre-load adjustment

The spring system has adjustable pre-load. When the knob is turned clockwise the spring is stiffened, and when it is turned counterclockwise the spring is softened. The pre-load adjustment is used to set the desired sag. The manufacturer does not provide recommended sag guidelines, but sag is typically set in a range from 10–20% of total travel.

Spring-tuning kits

Spring-tuning kits are available in a range of spring stiffness. If the fork has inadequate sag when the pre-load is fully loose, or the fork never bottoms under any of the conditions the rider experiences, then a softer spring kit is called for. If the fork has too much sag no matter how much the pre-load is tightened, or bottoms frequently when ridden, then a firmer spring kit is called for.

MARZOCCHI '99–'00 FORKS-COIL & OIL-DAMPER TYPES

ABOUT THIS SECTION

Marzocchi made three basic types of forks during this period. The most basic type is a simple coil spring with non-adjustable oil damping, which is covered in this section. This type is identified by the lack of any slotted rods protruding from the top caps and the lack of air valves (on front or back of top end of slider tubes, or hidden under a plastic cap on top of the stanchion cap). Another type has coil springs, but adjustable oil damping. These are covered in *MARZOCCHI '97–'00 FORKS-COIL & ADJUSTABLE OIL TYPES* (page 38-22). The third type has air springs and oil damping. These are covered in *MARZOCCHI '99–'00 FORKS-AIR SPRUNG TYPES* (page 38-26).

The forks covered in this section include many models (listed below), but have a few minor variations (regarding service techniques). One variation is distinguished by external pre-load adjusting knobs. Another variation is distinguished by pre-load adjusters hidden under rubber caps on top of the stanchion top caps. The models and the type of pre-load adjuster used are:

Year and model	Pre-load adjuster
'00 Z3 BAM 80	external
'99 &'00 Z1 Dropoff	external
'00 Z3 QR 20	external
'99 &'00 Jr T & Jr T QR 20	external
'99 Z3 Light, Z3 Long Travel	external
'99 Z4 Alloy	hidden
'00 Z3.5 & Z3 M80	hidden
'00 Z5 QR 20 Spring	hidden

Some of the models, regardless of the pre-load adjuster type, have removable stanchions, and some have stanchions permanently fixed in the fork crown. The presence of two bolts in the crown at the top of each stanchion indicates the stanchions are removable. Some models have one additional difference. Most of the other models have a stanchion top cap that threads into the stanchion, but a few models have a top cap that inserts into the stanchion and is retained by an internal circlip.

All of these variations are covered in the following procedure. It can be difficult to correctly identify the year and model of fork being worked on, but when there are variations and alternate procedures are provided, by reading all the alternate procedures and examining the features on the fork, it should be possible to determine which alternate procedure is appropriate.

TOOLS

Marzocchi makes two tools for servicing this fork, specifically for bushing and seal removal and installation. These are the Slider Protector #536003AB and the Seal Press #R5068. In addition, two sizes of sockets are needed for the top caps. Due to the low profile of the wrench flats on the top caps, it is necessary to custom grind the ends of the sockets to eliminate any internal bevel. The socket sizes are 21mm and 26mm.

RockShox Dropout Vise Blocks #70107 are very useful for securing the sliders in the vise with minimal chance of cosmetic or structural damage. The dropout vise blocks only work on models that fit a standard quick-release hub. An alternative is to put a dummy axle set into the dropouts, clamp the axle set directly into the vise jaws, then attach the fork to the axle set. One more alternative is to use a fork mount such as those used for securing a bike in the bed of a pickup truck.

FULL FORK SERVICE

Top-cap and spring removal

1. [ ] Remove brake calipers and cable system from fork.
2. [ ] *External pre-load models:* Counting number of turns, turn pre-load adjuster knobs fully in "−" direction and record number of turns here: right _____ left _____
   Hidden pre-load models: Remove rubber cap (if any), or unthread cap with 4mm Allen fitting from stanchion cap, then use 4mm Allen to turn pre-load adjuster. Counting number of turns, turn pre-load adjuster fully counterclockwise (until it reaches top of stanchion cap) and record number of turns here: right _____ left _____
3. [ ] *All external pre-load models except '00 Z3 BAM 80:* Remove circlips from grooves in stanchion caps (just above top of fork crown).
4. [ ] *Models with removable stanchions:* Remove crown bolts, then remove stanchions from crown.
5. [ ] *'00 Z5 only:* Depress top cap slightly, then remove internal snap-ring. *Caution–spring may eject top cap suddenly. Do not stand directly over stanchion!*

6. [ ] *If stanchions have been removed and top caps are still in place:* Clamp stanchion tube in bike-stand clamp, then unthread stanchion cap from stanchion.
All others: Unthread stanchion caps.
7. [ ] Remove aluminum sleeves (if any), washers, and springs from inside of stanchions.
8. [ ] Carefully drain old oil into waste receptacles, pumping stanchions to drain out oil.

Slider and plunger removal

9. [ ] Place RockShox dropout vise blocks on dropout, and secure in vise so that access hole on bottom of slider is accessible.
10. [ ] Use 15mm socket on extension to break loose bolt inside access hole in bottom of slider.
11. [ ] While pulling continuously on stanchion, continue to loosen 15mm bolt until stanchion separates from slider.
12. [ ] Remove bolt from bottom of slider.
13. [ ] Repeat previous three steps for other side.
14. [ ] Remove aluminum caps from bottoms of plunger rods (caps may have fallen off inside stanchions).
15. [ ] Remove snap-rings from bottoms of stanchions, then pull out plunger-rod assemblies.
16. [ ] Remove valve sleeves, plastic washers, stop rings, and top-out springs from shafts.
17. [ ] Remove split rings from piston heads on plunger rods.
NOTE: *Do not proceed with further disassembly unless inspection or symptoms have indicated need for seal replacement or bushing replacement. If either item is removed, it must be replaced with a new one.*

Seal and bushing removal

18. [ ] If necessary, re-clamp slider in dropout vise blocks so top end of slider is accessible.
19. [ ] Pry out dust seals, then use screwdriver or seal pick to pry out triple-dip clip that retains seal in slider.
20. [ ] Place slider protector over top of slider, and use large flat screwdriver to pry out seal (be careful not to get screwdriver under washer that is just below seal, pry as though you were trying to lift seal through slot in protector).
21. [ ] Lift large washer out of slider.
22. [ ] Using seal pick with 90° bend, lift bushing out by catching tip of seal pick under lip of bushing at slot in bushing.

Cleaning and inspection

23. [ ] Using mild detergent, thoroughly clean and dry all parts, making sure there is no cleanser or lint left on parts.
24. [ ] Inspect all O-rings for nicks and tears.

Bushing and seal installation

NOTE: *If bushings and seals were not removed, skip to step 32.*
25. [ ] With slider clamped upright in dropout vise blocks, carefully slide thoroughly-oiled bushing into slider so that slot in bushing ends up on side of slider.
26. [ ] Place large steel washer over bushing
27. [ ] Place thoroughly greased seal (lip side up) onto seal installer then tap seal into slider until bottomed.
28. [ ] Place triple-dip clip into slot above seal.
29. [ ] Check carefully that triple-dip clip is fully seated in groove inside slider.
30. [ ] Repeat steps 25–29 for other side.
31. [ ] Place dust seal(s) onto seal installer and install into slider(s).

Plunger and slider installation

32. [ ] Install split rings into grooves in piston heads on top ends of plunger rods.
33. [ ] Install onto plunger rods in order: short top-out springs, metal stop plate (with three tabs on inner perimeter), plastic washer (lip-face first), then valve sleeve (cupped-face first).
34. [ ] Insert plunger assemblies into stanchions, install snap-rings into stanchions (sharp-edged-faces out), then install aluminum caps onto ends of shafts.
35. [ ] Insert 15mm-head bolt in socket, and check whether any portion of bolt more than the wrench flats is inside socket. If too much bolt is in socket, wad some tissue paper to fill socket until no more than wrench flats are in socket.
36. [ ] Clamp slider in dropout vise blocks so that slider is upright and hole on bottom of slider is accessible to 15mm socket on extension.
37. [ ] Use socket on extension to hold bolt in access hole on bottom of slider in place.
38. [ ] Install stanchions into sliders.
39. [ ] Using foot-long 7/8" dowel or similar device, exert downward pressure on plunger unit while turning extension to engage 15mm bolt. Maintaining downward pressure on plunger unit, tighten nut to 80in-lbs.
40. [ ] Repeat steps 36–39 for other side.

Oil, spring, and top-cap installation

41. [ ] Pull stanchions fully up.

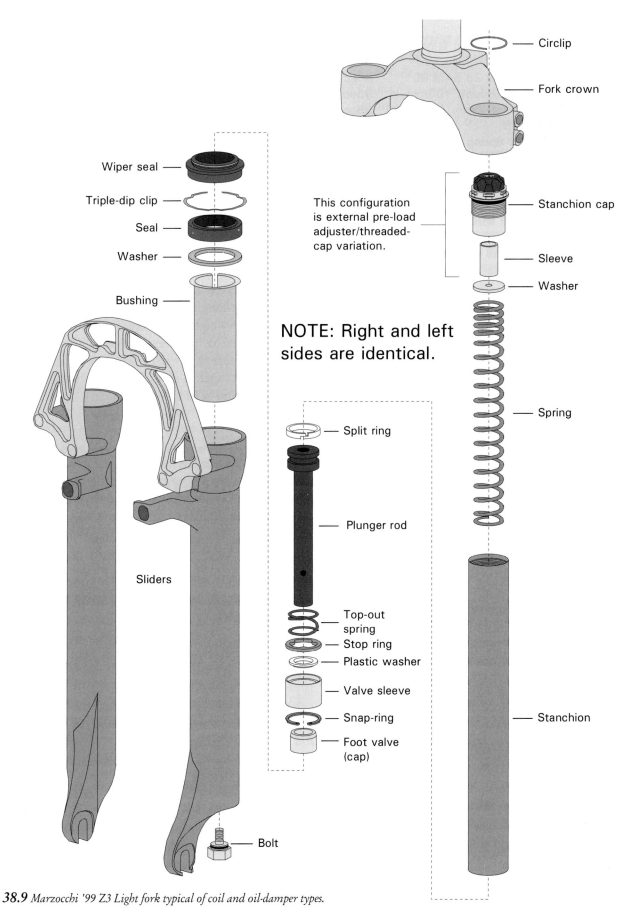

Circlip

Fork crown

Wiper seal

Triple-dip clip

Seal

Washer

This configuration is external pre-load adjuster/threaded-cap variation.

Stanchion cap

Sleeve

Washer

Bushing

NOTE: Right and left sides are identical.

Spring

Sliders

Split ring

Plunger rod

Top-out spring

Stop ring

Plastic washer

Valve sleeve

Snap-ring

Foot valve (cap)

Stanchion

Bolt

38.9 *Marzocchi '99 Z3 Light fork typical of coil and oil-damper types.*

Seal and bushing removal

NOTE: *Do not proceed with further disassembly unless inspection or symptoms have indicated need for seal replacement or bushing replacement. If either item is removed, it must be replaced with a new one.*

17. [ ] If necessary, re-clamp slider in dropout vise blocks so top end of slider is accessible.
18. [ ] Pry out dust seals, then use screwdriver or seal pick to pry out triple-dip clip that retains seal in slider.
19. [ ] Place slider protector over top of slider, and use large flat screwdriver to pry out seal (be careful not to get screwdriver under washer that is just below seal, pry as though you were trying to lift seal through slot in protector).
20. [ ] Lift large washer out of slider.
21. [ ] Using seal pick with 90° bend, lift bushing out by catching tip of seal pick under lip of bushing at slot in bushing.

Cleaning and inspection

22. [ ] Using mild detergent, thoroughly clean and dry all parts, making sure there is no cleanser or lint left on parts.
23. [ ] Inspect all O-rings for nicks and tears.

Bushing and seal installation

NOTE: *If bushing and seal were not removed, skip to step 30.*

24. [ ] With slider clamped upright in dropout vise blocks, carefully slide thoroughly-oiled bushing into slider so that slot in bushing ends up on side of slider.
25. [ ] Place large steel washer over bushing.
26. [ ] Place thoroughly greased seal (lip-side up) onto seal installer and tap seal into slider until bottomed.
27. [ ] Place triple-dip clip into slot above seal.
28. [ ] Check carefully that triple-dip clip is fully seated in groove inside slider.
29. [ ] Repeat steps 24–28 for other side.
30. [ ] Place dust seal(s) onto seal installer and install into slider(s).

Plunger and slider installation

31. [ ] Install stanchions (threaded-ends up) into sliders.
32. [ ] Install short top-out springs into stanchions.
33. [ ] Clamp slider in dropout vise blocks so that slider is upright and hole on bottom of slider is accessible to 15mm socket on extension.

34. [ ] Use socket on extension to hold nut in access hole on bottom of slider in place, then drop plunger (left side of single-damped models) or damper unit (all others) into stanchion so coarse-threaded stud (of either) is pointing down. *Note: Double-cartridge '00 models have different left and right cartridges. Cartridge with multiple holes at bottom end of cylinder is left-hand cartridge.*
35. [ ] *Side without adjustable damper:* Using foot-long 7/8" dowel or similar device, exert downward pressure on plunger unit while turning extension to engage 15mm nut. Maintaining downward pressure on plunger unit, tighten nut to 105in-lbs.
    Side(s) with adjustable damper: Maintaining downward pressure on adjuster rod, tighten nut to 105in-lbs.
36. [ ] Repeat steps 33–35 for other side.

Oil, spring, and top-cap installation

37. [ ] Pull stanchions up fully, then fill each stanchion with appropriate amount of 7.5wt oil:

Model	Volume Lt./Rt.
'97-'98 Z2	85/75cc
'99 Z2 Atom Bomb & Z2 Alloy	85/75cc
'99 Z2 BAM & '00 Atom 80	100/900cc
'97-'98 Z1 & Mr. T	90/90cc
'99 Z1 Alloy	96/96cc
'99 Z1 BAM & Z1 Dual Slalom	100/100cc
'99-'00 Z1 QR 20	100/100cc
'99 Mr. T	160/160cc
'00 Mr. T QR 20	170/170cc
'99-'00 Monster T	380/380cc

38. [ ] Push stanchions down, then carefully pump damper-unit rod(s) up and down repeatedly to pump air out, and oil into, damper.
39. [ ] Place long compression springs into stanchions, then place plastic washers (cavity-face up) on top of springs.

NOTE: *In the next four steps, the right-side version of each step is done at the fork assembly, but the left-side version is done with parts that are not yet part of the fork assembly. The left-side versions only apply to single-adjustable damper models. Double adjustable models use right-side versions on both sides.*

40. [ ] Thread pre-load adjuster cylinder (round-end first) onto stud that goes through stanchion cap, until four threads are exposed beyond hex-end of cylinder.
41. [ ] Slide stanchion cap(s) onto pre-load adjuster cylinders until caps snap into place and expose e-clip slot on stud (above top of cap).
42. [ ] Put e-clips into slots in studs.

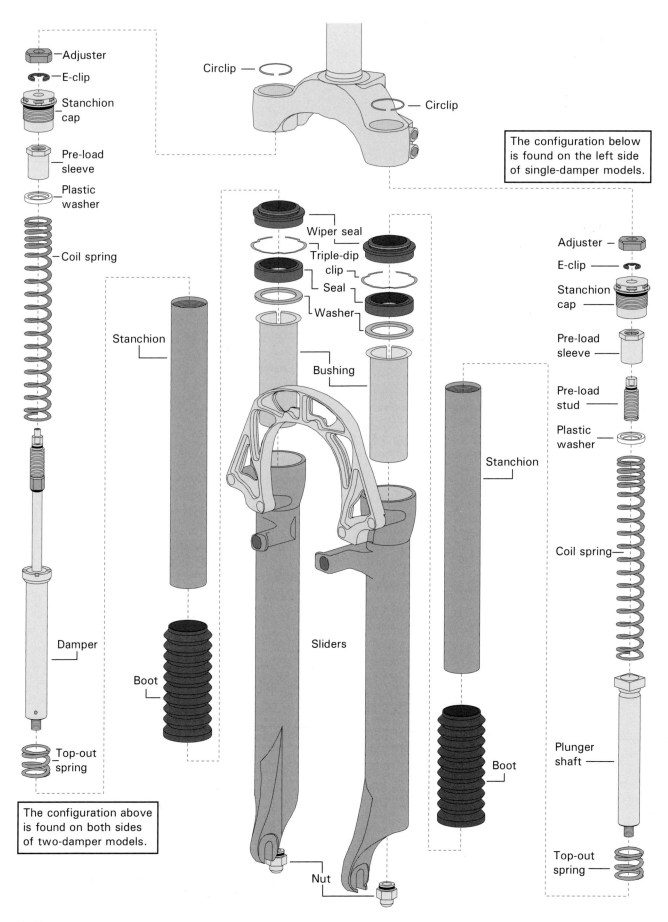

Adjuster
E-clip
Stanchion cap
Pre-load sleeve
Plastic washer
Coil spring
Damper
Top-out spring

The configuration above is found on both sides of two-damper models.

Circlip
Circlip

The configuration below is found on the left side of single-damper models.

Wiper seal
Triple-dip clip
Seal
Washer
Bushing
Stanchion
Boot
Sliders
Nut

Adjuster
E-clip
Stanchion cap
Pre-load sleeve
Pre-load stud
Plastic washer
Coil spring
Stanchion
Boot
Plunger shaft
Top-out spring

38.10 *Marzocchi '99 Z2 fork typical of coil and adjustable-oil types.*

43. [ ] Place pre-load adjuster rings on flats of stud, then secure setscrews with 1.5mm Allen.

44. [ ] Pull stanchions up, then hand thread stanchion caps fully into stanchions until cap lips contact tops of stanchions.

45. [ ] *All except '00 Z2 Atom 80:* Secure each stanchion into bike-stand clamp, and secure each stanchion cap to 105in-lbs.
    Only '00 Z2 Atom 80: Secure each stanchion cap to 105in-lbs.

46. [ ] Slide boots (if any) over stanchions and engage boots to lips on dust seals.

Stanchion installation and final setup

NOTE: When tightening a pair of clamp bolts, always go back and forth between bolts until both are stationary at the recommended torque!

47. [ ] *All except '00 Z2 Atom 80:* Insert stanchions into fork crown fully, then secure stanchion clamp bolts to 70in-lbs.

48. [ ] *All except '00 Z2 Atom 80:* Engage circlips in grooves in stanchion caps.

49. [ ] Re-attach brake system and install wheel.

50. [ ] Turn pre-load adjuster rings fully counterclockwise, then clockwise number of turns indicated in step 2.

51. [ ] Turn rebound damper adjuster fully counterclockwise, then clockwise number of turns indicated in step 3.

52. [ ] Check torque on crown bolts at base of fork column. Recommended torque is 70in-lbs.

TUNING OPTIONS

Spring pre-load adjustment

The pre-load on the springs is adjustable. Pre-load should be adjusted to achieve the desired amount of sag. Pre-load in both legs should be adjusted equally. The manufacturer does not provide sag guidelines, but when the rider sits stationary on the bike, the fork should compress about 10–20% of its total travel. More sag improves comfort, and less sag suits high-performance or competitive riding.

On the models with external pre-load adjusting knobs, the knobs are turned fully in the "–" direction to maximize sag, and fully the opposite way to minimize sag. On the models with hidden pre-load adjusters, a rubber cap must be pried out, or an aluminum cap threaded out, then the adjuster is turned with a 4mm Allen wrench. The direction of adjustment is the same on the external and hidden adjusters.

Damping adjustments

Depending on the model year, these forks have different degrees of adjustable damping.

With 1997 and 1998 models, single and dual adjustable cartridge models are both adjustable for rebound damping by turning the adjuster rod(s). Clockwise increases rebound damping. The only way to change compression damping is by changing oil weight. The stock oil is 7.5wt non-foaming oil. Changing the oil weight also changes the potential amount of rebound damping.

With 1999 models, single and dual adjustable cartridge models are adjustable for compression and rebound by turning the adjusting rod(s). Clockwise adjustments increase rebound and compression damping simultaneously.

With 2000 models, single adjustable cartridge models are adjustable for rebound only. Compression damping can only be changed by changing oil weight, which also affects the potential amount of rebound damping. For this model year only, dual adjustable cartridge models have compression damping adjustment in the left cartridge and rebound damping adjustment in the right cartridge. Turning either adjuster clockwise increases the damping.

MARZOCCHI '99–'00 FORKS-AIR-SPRUNG TYPES

Marzocchi made three basic types of forks during this period. The most basic type is a simple coil spring with non-adjustable oil damping, which is covered in *MARZOCCHI '99–'00 FORKS-COIL & OIL-DAMPER TYPES* (page 38-19). Another type has coil springs but adjustable oil damping. One or two slotted rods protruding out the top caps identifies a fork as belonging to this type. These are covered in *MARZOCCHI '97–'00 FORKS-COIL & ADJUSTABLE OIL TYPES* (page 38-22). The third type, covered in this section, has air springs and oil damping. For identification purposes, look for a standard air valve in one of three locations: on the front of the slider adjacent to the brake-pivot stud, on the back of the fork directly behind the brake-pivot stud, or under a three-pronged cap in the top cap on each stanchion.

The forks covered in this section include many models (listed below), but have a few minor variations (regarding service techniques). One variety has adjustable oil dampers. These have the air valve on the front or back of the sliders. The other variety has non-adjustable oil dampers. This variety has the air valves inside the top caps.

Year and model	Adjustable dampers
'99 Z5 Alloy	no
'99 Z2 Superfly	yes
'00 Z5 QR 20	no
'00 Z5 Flylight Air	no
'00 Z5 Flylight 100	no
'00 Z4 Flylight Air	no
'00 Z2 X Fly QR 20	yes
'00 Z2 X Fly	yes
'00 Z1 X Fly	yes

Several of these models, have removable stanchions. The presence of two bolts in the crown at the top of each stanchion indicates the stanchions are removable. Other models have stanchions that are an integral part of the fork crown. These differences in stanchion configuration occur with no correlation to other differences. Additionally, some of the models have stanchion caps that thread in, and others are threadless and retained by a snap-ring. When alternate procedures exist for all these variations, the following terms will be used:

Adjustable and *non-adjustable* dampers
Integral and *non-integral* stanchions
Threaded and *unthreaded* stanchion caps
Front, *back*, and *top* air valves

All varieties are covered in the following procedure. It can be difficult to correctly identify the year and model of fork being worked on, but when there are variations and alternate procedures are provided, by reading all the alternate procedures and examining the features on the fork, it should be possible to determine which alternate procedure is appropriate.

TOOLS

Marzocchi makes five tools for servicing these forks, two of which are specifically for bushing and seal removal and installation. These are the Slider Protector #536003AB and the Seal Press #R5068. The third Marzocchi tool is a Seal Guide #R5082CD, which is used in servicing the adjustable-damper models. The fourth tool, pump #R4002, is essential for inflating models with front or top air valves. The fifth tool, Stanchion Cap Puller #R5008BZ, is used to remove unthreaded stanchion caps.

In addition, two sizes of sockets are needed for the top caps. Due to the low profile of the wrench flats on the top caps, it is necessary to custom grind the ends of the sockets to eliminate any internal bevel. The socket sizes are 21mm and 26mm.

RockShox Dropout Vise Blocks #70107 are very useful for securing the sliders in the vise with minimal chance of cosmetic or structural damage. The dropout vise blocks only work on models that fit a standard quick-release hub. An alternative is to put a dummy axle set into the dropouts, clamp the axle set directly into the vise jaws, then attach the fork to the axle set. One more alternative is to use a fork mount such as those used for securing a bike in the bed of a pickup truck.

FULL FORK SERVICE

Top-cap and oil removal

1. [ ] Remove brake calipers and cable system from fork.

2. [ ] Find and uncap air valves. Deflate fork completely.

3. [ ] *Removable stanchion models with threaded stanchion caps:* Remove circlips from stanchion caps, unthread crown bolts, remove stanchions from crown, then clamp each stanchion in bike-stand clamp to hold while unthreading stanchion caps with custom 26mm socket.
   Removable stanchion models with unthreaded stanchion caps: Depress stanchion caps several millimeters, pry out circlips from stanchions, thread cap puller onto valve threads, then pull on tool to remove cap(s).
   Integral stanchion models: Use custom 21mm socket to unthread stanchion caps from stanchions.

4. [ ] Carefully drain old oil into waste receptacles, pumping stanchions to drain out oil.

Slider and damper removal

5. [ ] *Adjustable-damper models:* Find 2.5mm Allen fitting inside 10mm nut in bottom end of sliders, then turn fully counterclockwise, counting turns:
   _____ turns counterclockwise on right
   _____ turns counterclockwise on left

6. [ ] *'99 Z5 Alloy only:* Use 17mm socket on extension to break loose bolts inside access hole in bottom of slider.
   Adjustable-damper models: Use 10mm socket on extension to break loose nuts inside access hole in bottom of slider.
   Non-adjustable-damper models: Use 15mm socket on extension to break loose nuts inside access hole in bottom of slider.

7. [ ] While pulling continuously on slider, continue to loosen nuts or bolts until sliders separate from stanchions.

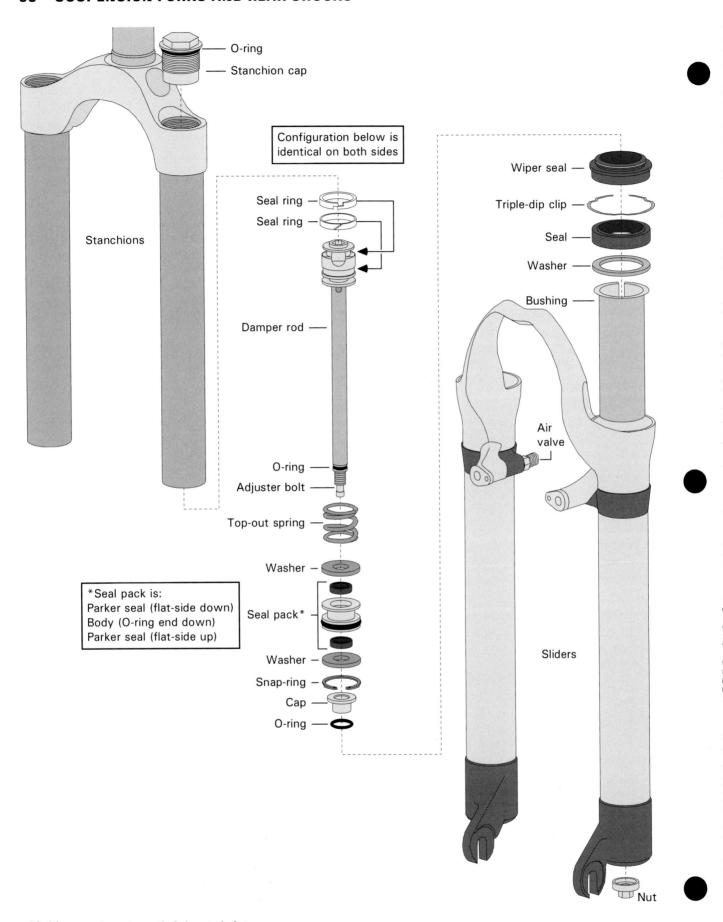

O-ring

Stanchion cap

Stanchions

Configuration below is identical on both sides

Seal ring

Seal ring

Damper rod

O-ring

Adjuster bolt

Top-out spring

Washer

*Seal pack is:
Parker seal (flat-side down)
Body (O-ring end down)
Parker seal (flat-side up)

Seal pack*

Washer

Snap-ring

Cap

O-ring

Wiper seal

Triple-dip clip

Seal

Washer

Bushing

Air valve

Sliders

Nut

38.11 Marzocchi '00 Z2 X-Fly fork typical of air-sprung types.

8. [ ] *Adjustable-damper models:* Remove caps from ends of plunger rods. If caps are not on rods, push rods from below out tops of sliders.
Non-adjustable-damper models: Remove foot valves from ends of plunger rods.

9. [ ] *Adjustable-damper models only:* Inspect caps for external O-rings. If O-rings are missing, inspect inside sliders and remove O-rings.

10. [ ] *Adjustable-damper models:* Remove snap-rings from bottoms of stanchions, then carefully pull out plunger-rod assemblies.
Non-adjustable-damper models: Remove damper assemblies from tops of stanchions.

11. [ ] *Adjustable-damper models:* Remove washer, seal pack, washer, then top-out springs from shafts.
Non-adjustable-damper models: Remove top-out springs from bottoms of shafts.

12. [ ] Remove split rings from piston heads on plunger shafts.

Seal and bushing removal

NOTE: *Do not proceed with further disassembly unless inspection or symptoms have indicated need for seal replacement or bushing replacement. If either item is removed, it must be replaced with a new one.*

13. [ ] Clamp slider in RockShox dropout vise blocks so top end of slider is accessible.

14. [ ] Pry out dust seals, then use screwdriver or seal pick to pry out triple-dip clip that retains seal in slider.

15. [ ] Place slider protector over top of slider, and use large flat screwdriver to pry out seal (be careful not to get screwdriver under washer that is just below seal, pry as though you were trying to lift seal through slot in protector).

16. [ ] Lift large washer out of slider.

17. [ ] Using seal pick with 90° bend, lift bushing out by catching tip of seal pick under lip of bushing at slot in bushing.

Cleaning and inspection

18. [ ] Using mild detergent, thoroughly clean and dry all parts, making sure there is no cleanser or lint left on parts.

19. [ ] Inspect all O-rings and seals for nicks and tears.

20. [ ] If air pressure has been leaking, remove and replace seals in seal pack and O-rings on top caps and air valves.

Bushing and seal installation

NOTE: *If bushings and seals were not removed, skip to step 29.*

21. [ ] Grease all O-rings, seals, and plastic split rings.

22. [ ] With slider clamped upright in dropout vise blocks, carefully slide thoroughly-oiled bushing into slider so that slot in bushing ends up on side of slider.

23. [ ] Place large steel washer over bushing.

24. [ ] Place thoroughly greased seal (lip side up) onto seal installer then tap seal into slider until bottomed.

25. [ ] Place triple-dip clip into slot above seal.

26. [ ] Check carefully that triple-dip clip is fully seated in groove inside slider.

27. [ ] Repeat steps 22–26 for other side.

28. [ ] Place dust seal(s) onto seal installer and install into slider(s).

Damper assembly and installation

29. [ ] *Adjustable-damper models only:* With 3mm Allen wrench engaged to head of adjuster rod (through top of piston), use 2.5mm Allen wrench to check that bolt on bottom end of adjuster rod is secure. If not, remove bolt and reinstall with Loctite 242.

30. [ ] Install split rings into grooves in piston heads on top ends of plunger rods. *Note: On adjustable-damper models, stepped-split ring goes in top groove and diagonal-split ring goes in next groove.*

31. [ ] *Adjustable-damper models:* Install onto plunger rods in order: short top-out springs, washer, seal-guide tool #R5028CD, seal pack (O-ring-end last), then second washer. Remove seal-guide tool.
Non-adjustable-damper models: Install top-out springs onto bottoms of shafts.

32. [ ] *Adjustable-damper models:* Insert plunger assemblies into stanchions, then install snap-rings into stanchions (sharp-edged-face out).
Non-adjustable-damper models: Install damper shafts through tops of stanchions, then install foot valves on ends of shafts.

33. [ ] *Adjustable-damper models only:* Install caps onto shafts, then install O-rings onto caps.

Slider installation

34. [ ] Install boots (if any) onto stanchions, then carefully push slider assembly onto stanchions only 2-3".

35. [ ] *Adjustable-damper models:* Turn fork upside down, then inject 7cc of 7.5wt oil into each hole in bottoms of sliders, then push slider assembly further onto stanchions until shafts protrude from holes.
Non-adjustable damper models: Turn fork upside down, then push sliders on until ends of shaft assemblies contact ends of sliders.

22. [ ] Watching carefully for the spring/bearing détente mechanism that is under the R or C end of the assembly, lift the assembly off the shock cylinder.
23. [ ] Remove détente springs from holes in cylinder, remove O-rings from oval grooves in cylinder, remove 3/32" détente bearing from bottom face of R and C ends of damper units, pull both ends of damper units off adjustment shafts, then remove O-rings from both end pieces of damper units. Remove 3/16" ball bearing and spring from inside the blocks with the engraved arrow.

O-ring and seal removal

24. [ ] Remove O-ring from inside and outside of seal-head.
25. [ ] Remove wiper seal from end of seal-head.
26 [ ] Remove O-ring from shaft eyelet.
27. [ ] Remove O-rings from floating piston.

Cleaning and inspection

28. [ ] Clean all parts with mild detergent and water, then dry thoroughly with compressed air. *Avoid leaving solvents or lint from rags on, or in, any part!*
29. [ ] Inspect valve shims (thin washers) for chipping or cracks
30. [ ] Inspect O-rings and seals for tears, nicks, and cracks.

O-ring installation and floating-piston assembly

31. [ ] Grease all O-rings and wiper seal.
32. [ ] Install wiper seal (conical-lip out) in end of seal-head.
33. [ ] Install O-rings on floating piston, and inside and outside of seal-head.

Shaft assembly

34. [ ] Put Shaft Clamp around piston-end of shaft, then clamp tool into vise with piston end pointing up.
35. [ ] Install shim stack that was below piston onto end of shaft in reverse order of removal.
36. [ ] Install piston. Side with smaller-diameter valve holes in flat surface faces up.
37. [ ] Install shim stack that was above piston onto end of shaft.
38. [ ] Apply Loctite #242 to threads of nut, then thread nut onto stud (slightly snug).
39. [ ] Torque nut to 70–80in-lbs (12–13lbs@6").
40. [ ] Turn shaft/ Shaft-Clamp assembly over in vise, then clamp securely.
41. [ ] Insert air piston, spring-end first, fully into piston shaft.
42. [ ] Install 1–1/2" Bullet Tool in end of shaft.

43. [ ] Install remaining O-ring over tool and onto shaft.
44. [ ] Install seal-head (threaded-end first) over tool and onto shaft, then remove tool.
45. [ ] Apply Loctite 242 on threads of shaft eyelet, then secure shaft eyelet to 100in-lbs (17lbs@6").

Damper-adjuster assembly

During normal disassembly, there is no reason to remove or loosen the adjusting rings on the adjusting rods. If the rings have been loosened, then it is possible the numbers on the rings are not in correspondence with the correct-size orifices. When the adjuster ring is correctly positioned and you are seeing the "1," you should simultaneously be seeing the smallest orifice through the next-to-largest orifice.

46. [ ] Install O-rings into adjuster-rod damper blocks, and O-rings into oval grooves in shock cylinder.
47. [ ] Insert orifice-end of adjuster rods into R and C blocks, insert spring and 3/16" ball bearing into each "arrow" block, then insert remaining end of each adjuster rod into each arrow block.
48. [ ] Insert détente bearings and springs into small holes in back faces of R and C blocks.

The Terminator shock has a rebound damper and a compression damper. Either can be installed facing either way, but only one way allows the dampers to function in the correct way. When correctly installed, the arrow on the rebound damper points toward the body eyelet and the arrow on the compression damper points away from the body eyelet. Simply put, the arrows point the way the body moves during rebound and compression strokes.

49. [ ] Holding damper unit with bottom face facing up, position shock body over damper unit with eyelet end of body pointing the same way as arrow end of "R" damper unit, then mate together so détente spring inserts into spring hole (smaller hole) in mounting surface for damper unit.
50. [ ] Insert and tighten eight bolts that hold damper to shock cylinder.
51. [ ] Repeat previous two steps for compression damper unit, but install so arrow end points away from eyelet end of body.

Oil filling and assembly

52. [ ] Attach pump to air valve, then pressurize to pressure recorded in step 1.
53. [ ] Remove shaft assembly from vise (if appropriate).
54. [ ] Push O-rings and seal-head to piston-end of shaft assembly.

55. [ ] Place shock body upright in vise, and fill with 5wt oil.
56. [ ] Manually thread seal-head as far as possible into shock body.
57. [ ] Check that O-ring under seal-head flange has disappeared inside shock body.
58. [ ] Use Combo Bearing Wrench to secure seal-head into to end of shock body to torque of 240in-lbs (24lbs@10").
59. [ ] Install shock into bike.
60. [ ] Test shock by sitting in saddle and bouncing. Rear suspension should have damping. No sound of air in valving should be present. Listen for unusual noises, such as "gurgling" or "sucking" noise, which would indicate presence of air.

TUNING OPTIONS

Air pressure

Typical pressure is from 150–200psi. Increasing air pressure increases spring stiffness, which reduces rate of compression and increases rate of rebound while decreasing air pressure decreases spring stiffness, which increases rate of compression and decreases rate of rebound. Air pressure should be adjusted to create the desired amount of static sag. With the rider on the bike, the shock should compress 5%–20% of its total compression for cross-country riding, or 30%–40% for downhill riding.

Damping adjustment

Turning each numbered damper-adjusting ring adjusts the damper unit through five progressive orifice settings, corresponding to the numbers on the rings. The rebound and compression damping are completely independent.

ROCKSHOX '97–'99 INDY & JETT FORKS

ABOUT THIS SECTION

This section covers RockShox Indy model forks from 1997 and 1998, including the S, C, SL, and XC models. In addition, the 1999 RockShox Jett C, 1999 Jett T2, and 2000 Jett XC can be serviced using these instructions. These are all similar to each other and are described with one procedure, with notes regarding the minor differences.

TOOL CHOICES

See table 38–3 for tool requirements. All the tools in the table are required for the job.

INDY & JETT FORK TOOLS
(table 38-3)

Tool	Fits and considerations
6mm Allen bit socket	minimum 4" bit length
Ratchet extension	6" may be adequate, longer is recommended
RockShox 70096	Judy/Quadra/Indy bushing remover
RockShox 70098	Quadra/Indy/Jett bushing installer
UBT AL-11912B	22mm socket custom ground for optimal purchase

FULL SERVICE

Spring-stack removal

1. [ ] Leave fork in bike, but release front brake cable from brake lever.
2. [ ] Count number of turns require to loosen spring pre-load knobs fully counterclockwise and record here: left_____ right_____
3. [ ] Use 22mm socket to unthread plastic caps in tops of stanchions, then remove cap/spring-stack assemblies. ('99 Indy C and '00 Jett XC have spring stack only in right side.)

Slider removal

4. [ ] Compress fork completely.
5. [ ] Use ratchet drive, extension, and 6mm bit socket to unthread plunger bolts down in bottom of stanchions.
6. [ ] Remove wheel from fork.
7. [ ] Slide slider assembly off bottom of stanchion tubes.
8. [ ] Poor oil from sliders into waste receptacle.
9. [ ] Attach small O-rings or rubber bands to plunger bolts exposed below bottoms of plungers, so that bolts cannot escape into plungers.

Friction-damper removal (SL model only)

10. [ ] Use snap-ring pliers to remove internal snap rings at bottoms of stanchions.
11. [ ] Use extension with bit socket to push or tap plunger assemblies out bottoms of stanchions.
12. [ ] Remove friction dampers from ends of plungers.
13. [ ] Remove O-rings from friction dampers.

Seal and bushing removal

14. [ ] Remove boots and wiper seals from tops of slider tubes (insert screwdriver through seal and pry up on inside bottom edge of seal).

NOTE: *Before removing lower bushings, it is recommended to measure depth from top of slider to top edge of lower bushing.*

15. [ ] Place upright on top of slightly open vise jaws RockShox Seal Separator (large-end up), and place sleeve from RockShox Bushing Remover (small-end up) on top of Seal Separator.

16. [ ] Holding slider upside down, insert RockShox Bushing Remover with 28mm-long extractor plate up into one side of slider and engage plate against back of first bushing.

17. [ ] With tool still engaged to bushing, drop end of tool through sleeve, Seal Separator, and vise jaws until slider seats on sleeve, then firmly secure vise on Bushing Remover handle.

18. [ ] Hold one cylinder of Seal Separator stationary and rotate other cylinder to pull bushing out.

19. [ ] Repeat previous three previous steps for other bushing, then repeat for both bushings in other side.

20. [ ] Using a spoke or seal pick, fish bottom-out bumpers out of sliders.

Cleaning and inspection

21. [ ] Clean all parts with mild detergent and thoroughly dry with compressed air and/or lint-free rag.

22. [ ] Inspect wiper seals for nicks or tears.

23. [ ] Inspect and replace all elastomer and coil springs that do not meet RockShox specifications.

Seal and bushing installation

24. [ ] Install bottom-out bumpers in sliders so conical ends face down.

25. [ ] Thoroughly grease all replacement bushings with Judy Butter or equivalent non-lithium grease.

26. [ ] Place in order on Bushing Installer: 25mm sleeve, 85mm sleeve #110-02265-00 marked "98 Indy," and lower (smaller O.D.) bushing. Note: '97 Indy uses 78mm sleeve #70196 instead of 85mm sleeve.

27. [ ] Insert assembly into fork and tap with plastic mallet until assembly is fully bottomed, then remove tools.

28. [ ] Place in order on Bushing Installer: 25mm sleeve and upper bushing.

29. [ ] Insert assembly into fork and tap with plastic mallet until assembly is fully bottomed, then remove tools.

30. [ ] Repeat steps 26–29 for other side.

31. [ ] Grease wiper seals, then place wiper seals in top ends of sliders and tap into place with plastic mallet.

Friction-damper installation (SL model only)

32. [ ] Grease and install O-rings into friction dampers.

33. [ ] Slide top-out bumpers half-way down plunger shafts if bumpers have been forced over flange-ends of plungers.

34. [ ] Install friction dampers onto ends of plungers so that end of damper with groove in outer perimeter goes on first.

35. [ ] Wiggle and push plungers into stanchions.

36. [ ] Use 15mm socket or 7/8" PVC pipe to seat friction dampers just beyond snap-ring grooves.

37. [ ] Use snap-ring pliers to install internal snap-rings (sharp-edged-face out) into bottoms of stanchions.

Slider assembly

38. [ ] Remove rubber bands or O-rings from plunger bolts, then prep plunger-bolt threads with Loctite 242.

39. [ ] Check alignment of conical bottom-out bumpers in bottoms of sliders, then use spoke to align flat as necessary (conical-side down).

40. [ ] Put 5wt oil in each slider (15cc in XC, or 10cc in S, C, SL, and Jett T2).

41. [ ] Grease bushings, and fill pockets in wiper seals with Judy Butter or similar grease.

42. [ ] Use fingers to check if wiper seals are deformed at bottom edge, and pull wiper seals out just enough to eliminate deformity (if found).

43. [ ] Place slider assembly onto stanchions and compress fully.

44. [ ] Use extension and bit socket to engage plunger bolts into sliders.

45. [ ] Use torque wrench to tighten plunger bolts to 80in-lbs.

46. [ ] Pull sliders down fully, then engage bottoms of dust boots to wiper seals.

Spring-stack installation

47. [ ] Grease elastomer and/or coil springs.
48. [ ] Insert cap/spring-stacks into stanchions, and secure caps to 30in-lbs. ('99 Indy C and '00 Jett XC have spring stack only in right side.)
49. [ ] Restore pre-load settings.
50. [ ] Install wheel in fork.
51. [ ] Connect brake cable.

Crown-bolt security

52. [ ] Check crown bolt torque (if any). RockShox recommended torque is 60in-lbs.

TUNING OPTIONS

Sag and pre-load adjustment

RockShox recommends 7–10mm of sag for 72mm-travel models, 5–8mm of sag for 60mm-travel models, 3–5mm for 48mm-travel models. Adjust the pre-load adjusters (up to 5 full turns from loosest to tightest) to achieve sag in the recommended range. Check sag by measuring the change in distance from the top of the slider tube to the bottom of the crown after the rider gets on the bike. If it is not possible to achieve the recommended sag with the existing springs, then consider changing springs.

Spring-rate adjustment

Spring rate can be changed two ways. The spring-rate adjusters can be changed, and the coil springs can be changed. The spring-rate adjuster is the plastic stud that inserts into the coil spring. When the length of the stud is changed, the point at which the coil spring is fully compressed is changed. This, in turn, changes the point of fork compression when only the elastomer part of the spring set continues to compress. The spring-rate adjuster kit (#59136) contains different-length adjusters. A shorter length of stud makes the spring system softer, and a longer length of stud makes the spring stiffer.

Coil springs are available in four degrees of firmness. These are soft (red, #110-000591-00), medium (yellow, #110-000592-00), firm (green, #59141), and extra firm (purple, #59139).

Travel adjustment

Travel kit #59123 converts '97–'98 Indy XC/SL and '98 Indy C to 75mm of travel.

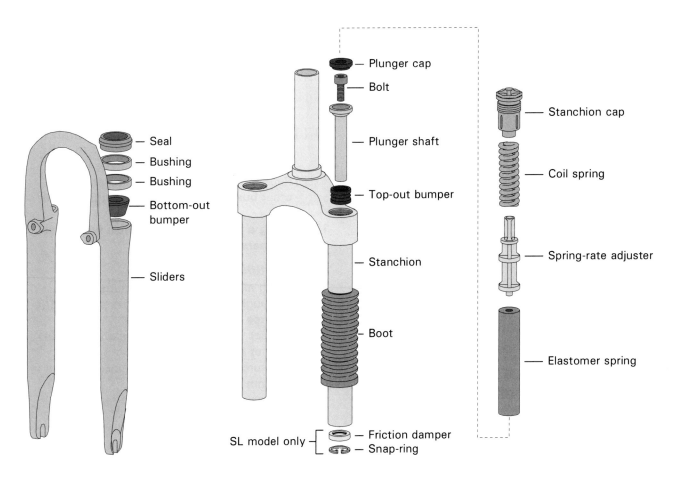

38.14 RockShox '98 Indy.

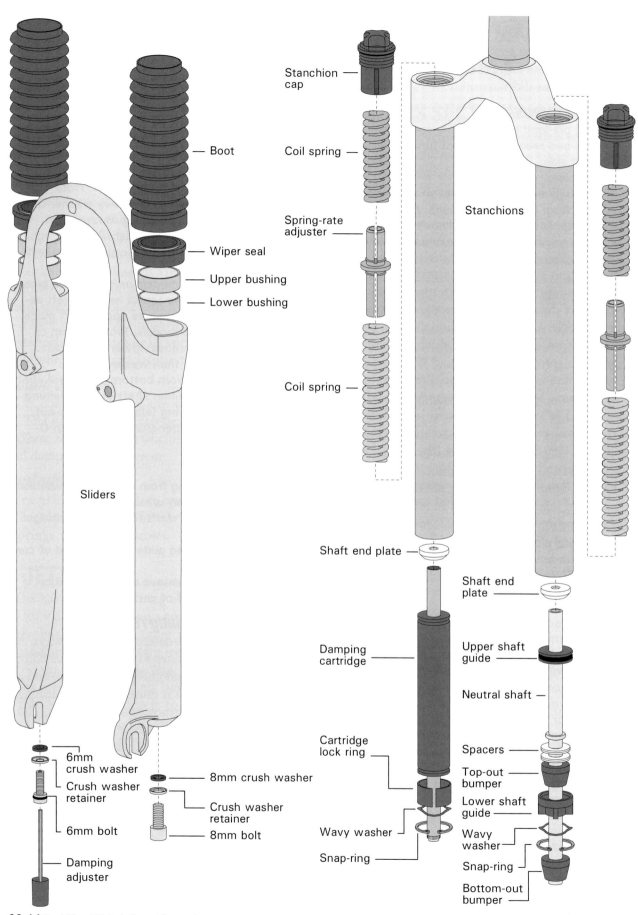

Boot

Wiper seal

Upper bushing

Lower bushing

Sliders

6mm crush washer

Crush washer retainer

6mm bolt

Damping adjuster

Stanchion cap

Coil spring

Spring-rate adjuster

Coil spring

Stanchions

Shaft end plate

Damping cartridge

Cartridge lock ring

Wavy washer

Snap-ring

8mm crush washer

Crush washer retainer

8mm bolt

Shaft end plate

Upper shaft guide

Neutral shaft

Spacers

Top-out bumper

Lower shaft guide

Wavy washer

Snap-ring

Bottom-out bumper

38.16 RockShox '98 Judy (cartridge type).

21. [ ] Install 30mm-long extractor plate onto extractor tool, push slider onto end of extractor tool until upper bushing clears extractor plate, then pull out on slider until extractor plate catches on edge of upper bushing.
22. [ ] Guide handle of extractor down through Seal Separator and vise jaws until top of slider tube rests on Seal Separator, then firmly secure extractor handle in vise. *Note: Vise may need to be repositioned to enable end of tool to clear bench.*
23. [ ] Hold large cylinder of Seal Separator stationary and rotate other cylinder to pull bushing out.
24. [ ] Remove slider, then pull extractor tool out of Seal Separator and retrieve bushing.
25. [ ] Repeat procedure for upper bushing in other slider tube.

Lower bushing removal
26. [ ] On top of slightly open vise jaws, place RockShox Seal Separator (large-end up), and place sleeve from RockShox Bushing Remover (small-end up) on top of Seal Separator.
27. [ ] Holding slider upside down, insert RockShox Bushing Remover with 30mm-long remover plate up into one side of slider and engage plate against back of first bushing.
28. [ ] With tool still engaged to bushing, drop end of tool through sleeve, Seal Separator, and vise jaws until slider seats on sleeve, then firmly secure vise on Bushing Remover handle.
29. [ ] Hold one cylinder of Seal Separator stationary and rotate other cylinder to pull bushing out.
30. [ ] Repeat previous three previous steps for other lower bushing.
31. [ ] Using a spoke or seal pick, fish bottom-out bumpers out of sliders.

Cartridge overhaul or replacement
Only the 1997 forks came with a cartridge that can be overhauled. It is possible that a 1997 fork has already had the cartridge replaced with a newer model that cannot be overhauled. Look at both ends of the cartridge body for an internal snap-ring, which indicates it is a 1997 cartridge.

With all 1998 and 1999 cartridges, replacement is the only option. It may also be more economical to replace the 1997 cartridge instead of overhauling it. Check with RockShox technical support for upgrade options to newer improved cartridges.
32. [ ] Push cartridge shaft to limit both ways and inspect both ends of shaft for wear marks that indicated need of replacement.

33. [ ] While pushing and pulling cartridge shaft, listen for gurgling sounds that indicate air in cartridge, which is reason for replacement or overhaul.
34. [ ] Thoroughly clean outside of cartridge, then pump shaft repeatedly. Look for oil seepage at both ends of cartridge, indicating need of replacement or overhaul.

Cartridge-service procedure
NOTE: Skip this procedure if cartridge is being replaced or there are no problems indicated in steps 32-34.
35. [ ] Firmly grasping shaft with fingers, use Allen key (3mm, occasionally 2mm) to turn adjuster rod (if any) in lower end of shaft fully clockwise (counting turns), and record number of turns here: _____.
36. [ ] Unthread adjuster rod (if any) from shaft.
37. [ ] If adjuster rod has been removed, point lower end of shaft into waste-oil receptacle and pump damper unit repeatedly until oil has been pumped out.
38. [ ] Place Cartridge-Body Fixture on bench (small-I.D.-end up) then place lower end of cartridge body centered on end of fixture.
39. [ ] Gently tap on shaft with plastic mallet to ease seal out end of cartridge body. Increase effort gradually if light tapping is insufficient.
40. [ ] Remove cartridge body from top of Cartridge-Body Fixture, then carefully drain remaining oil into receptacle while withdrawing shaft assembly from cartridge body.
41. [ ] Remove seal, aluminum washer, and top-out O-ring from lower end of shaft.
42. [ ] Remove internal snap-ring from end of cartridge body.
43. [ ] Place cartridge body into large-I.D. end of Cartridge-Body Fixture, then support other end of fixture on bench.
44. [ ] Insert Upper-Seal Installer tool into cartridge body, then tap vigorously on tool to drive out plastic shaft guide and upper seal.
45. [ ] Inspect shaft for nicks and scratches (replace if any).
46. [ ] Inspect glide ring on piston for nicks and scratches (replace if any). Inspect that glide ring floats freely.
47. [ ] Clean all parts with a lint-free rag.
48. [ ] Install internal snap-ring in groove in upper end of cartridge body, making sure face of snap-ring with sharp edges faces out of cartridge body.
49. [ ] Coat new upper seal with Judy Butter (or non-lithium Teflon grease) inside and out.
50. [ ] Place seal (cavity-side first) onto shaft of Upper-Seal Installer tool.

Travel adjustment

All-Travel models only (2000): As described in the procedure in this section, these models can be set up as 63mm, 80mm, or 100mm travel, depending on the location of the All-Travel spacers. There are two spacers in each leg, which can be switched between being on the shafts below the top-out springs, or being positioned below the main springs. The correct spacer locations are:

63mm travel   two below each top-out spring
80mm travel   one below each spring
100mm travel   two below each main spring

All other models (1999): Travel kits are available to convert from 63mm to 80mm, and from 80mm to 100mm. The XLC is the only model that can be set up with 100mm travel. The travel kit includes plunger and damper shafts, springs, and spring spacers.

ROCKSHOX '98 SID FORKS

ABOUT THIS SECTION

This section covers RockShox 1998 SID fork service, including bushing removal and replacement. The 1998 SID forks can be distinguished by looking at the RockShox decals. If the decals have a black background, the fork is a 1998 model. If the decals are missing, inspect the bolt heads at the bottom of the slider tubes. If the bolt heads are titanium and have six 2mm diameter holes drilled in each head, the fork is a 1998 SID. If neither the decals or bolt heads confirm the SID fork is a 1998 model, then the fork is a later model, in which case see **ROCKSHOX '99–'00 SID FORKS** (page 38-56).

TOOL CHOICES

This fork requires several tools that are used to service other RockShox forks, but no tools that are unique to servicing only the SID fork. For bushing replacement, the same tools are required that are used with Judy forks. This includes the Universal Bushing Removal Tool #70096, the Judy Bushing Installer #70119, and the RockShox Seal Separator #70113.

FULL FORK SERVICE

Top-cap and slider-assembly removal

1. [ ] **Remove front wheel, and disconnect brake cable from brake lever.**

2. [ ] **Remove Phillips screws in stanchion caps (note small O-rings under screw heads).**
3. [ ] **Grease RockShox inflation needle, and insert into stanchion caps to release air pressure from both sides of fork.**
4. [ ] **Use 22mm socket or adjustable wrench to unthread stanchion caps (note O-rings under cap flanges).**
5. [ ] **Turn fork over to drain oil out tops of stanchions.**
NOTE: Observe Allen fittings accessible inside each stanchion tube. The 8mm Allen fitting adjusts spring rate. 2mm Allen fitting inside the 8mm Allen fitting adjusts damping.
6. [ ] **Use 8mm Allen to unthread titanium bolts at bottoms of sliders 4 full turns.**
7. [ ] **Gently tap on bolt heads until heads are seated against sliders again, then finish removing bolts.**
8. [ ] **Turn fork over and drain oil out bottoms of sliders.**
9. [ ] **Pull sliders off stanchion tubes, then remove boots from stanchion tubes.**

Cartridge and neutral-shaft removal

10. [ ] **Remove internal snap-rings from bottom ends of stanchions, then remove wavy washers.**
11. [ ] **Thread bolts back into damper shaft and neutral shaft.**
NOTE: Remove neutral shaft for cleaning and lubrication, negative-spring adjustment, replacement of piston rings if air pressure is being lost, or to change top-out bumper spacers.
NOTE: Remove damper cartridge for cleaning and lubrication of piston rings, replacement of piston rings, adjustment of negative spring, or replacement of damper cartridge.
12. [ ] **Insert spoke through holes in bolt heads, and pull on spoke to remove damper cartridge and/or neutral shaft assembly from stanchion tubes.**
13. [ ] **If adjusting negative spring, move e-clip on damper shaft down to increase negative-spring force, or up to reduce. (Negative spring can be removed entirely by unthreading piston, then removing e-clip and spring.)**
14. [ ] **With 8mm Allen, remove pistons from tops of shafts. Remove shaft guide, bumper, and washers from bottom of neutral shaft.**
NOTE: If not servicing bushings, go to step 27.

Seal and upper-bushing removal

Bushing wear can be determined in two ways. After removing the seals in step #15, insert the stanchions into the sliders again and check for any fore-and-aft play. Obvious looseness is caused by worn bushings. Alternatively, before removing the bushings, clean

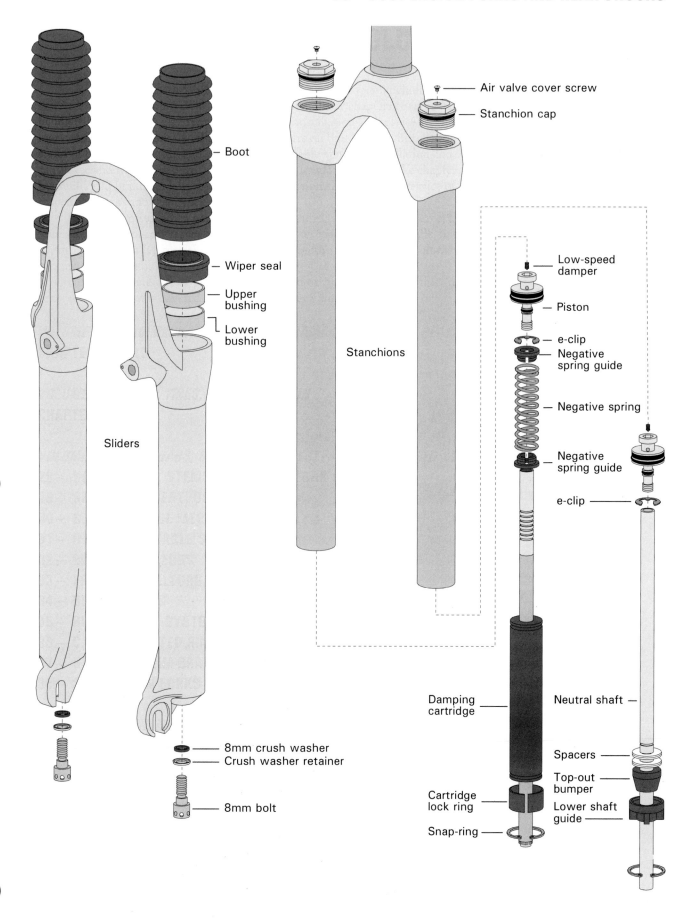

Boot

Wiper seal

Upper bushing

Lower bushing

Sliders

8mm crush washer

Crush washer retainer

8mm bolt

Air valve cover screw

Stanchion cap

Stanchions

Low-speed damper

Piston

e-clip

Negative spring guide

Negative spring

Negative spring guide

e-clip

Damping cartridge

Neutral shaft

Spacers

Cartridge lock ring

Top-out bumper

Lower shaft guide

Snap-ring

38.18 RockShox '98 SID.

them thoroughly and inspect their condition with the aid of a flashlight. Good bushings have a gray coating. Worn bushings are metallic gold or bronze in appearance where the coating has worn away.

15. [ ] **Insert screwdriver into seal on top of slider, then pry seal out.**
16. [ ] **Place Seal Separator upright on slightly open vise jaws with large-diameter end up.**
17. [ ] **Install 30mm-long extractor plate onto extractor tool, push slider onto end of extractor tool until upper bushing clears extractor plate, then pull out on slider until extractor plate catches on edge of upper bushing.**
18. [ ] **Guide handle of extractor down through Seal Separator and vise jaws until top of slider tube rests on Seal Separator, then firmly secure extractor handle in vise. *Note: Vise may need to be repositioned to enable end of tool to clear bench.***
19. [ ] **Hold large cylinder of Seal Separator stationary and rotate other cylinder to pull bushing.**
20. [ ] **Remove slider, then pull extractor tool out of Seal Separator and retrieve bushing.**
21. [ ] **Repeat procedure for upper bushing in other slider tube.**

Lower-bushing removal

22. [ ] **Place RockShox Seal Separator (large-end up) on top of slightly open vise jaws then place sleeve from RockShox Bushing Remover (small-end up) on top of Seal Separator.**
23. [ ] **Holding slider upside down, insert RockShox Bushing Remover with 30mm-long remover plate up into one side of slider and engage plate against back of first bushing.**
24. [ ] **With tool still engaged to bushing, drop end of tool through sleeve, Seal Separator, and vise jaws until slider seats on sleeve, then firmly secure vise on Bushing Remover handle.**
25. [ ] **Hold one cylinder of Seal Separator stationary and rotate other cylinder to pull bushing.**
26. [ ] **Repeat previous three previous steps for other lower bushing out.**

Cleaning and inspection

1998 damper cartridges cannot be overhauled. Replacement is the only option.

27. [ ] **Use mild detergent to thoroughly clean all parts. Dry with lint-free rag and/or compressed air. Avoid solvents, which may damage seals and other non-metallic parts.**
28. [ ] **Inspect all rubber O-rings and glide rings for nicks and tears, and replace as necessary.**
29. [ ] **Replace crush washer on each shaft bolt.**

30. [ ] **Push cartridge shaft to limit both ways and inspect both ends of shaft for wear marks that indicated need of replacement.**
31. [ ] **While pushing and pulling cartridge shaft, listen for gurgling sounds that indicate air in cartridge, which is reason for replacement.**
32. [ ] **Thoroughly clean outside of cartridge, then pump shaft repeatedly. Look for oil seepage at both ends of cartridge, indicating need of replacement.**
33. [ ] **Inspect stanchion tubes for bends, scratches, or heavy wear.**
34. [ ] **Inspect fork crown for cracks.**

Bushing and seal installation

35. [ ] **Secure Judy Bushing Installer base upright in vise, with vertical post positioned out past end of vise jaws.**

The Judy Bushing Installer tool comes with four long sleeves of various lengths. Originally, these sleeves were intended for setting the correct lower-bushing height for different models. Because travel can be changed on any model, RockShox now recommends using the red (128mm) sleeve only, which sets the lower bushing at the correct height regardless of model or travel configuration.

36. [ ] **Place red (128mm) sleeve on tool shaft, then place smaller-diameter bushing (O.D. 30.5mm) on tool shaft.**
37. [ ] **Place one slider tube over tool shaft, insert small end of driving tool into hole in end of slider, then tap on driving tool until bushing is fully seated.**
38. [ ] **Remove slider and repeat previous two steps for other slider tube.**
39. [ ] **Remove red sleeve and place short (10mm) sleeve on tool shaft, then place larger-diameter bushing (O.D. 31.0mm) on tool shaft.**
40. [ ] **Place one slider tube over tool shaft, insert small end of driving tool into hole in end of slider, then tap on driving tool until top edge of bushing is even with second shoulder from top of slider. *Note: It is possible to insert bushing too far, with top edge below second shoulder. During installation, stop and inspect depth repeatedly!***
41. [ ] **Remove slider and repeat previous two steps for other slider tube.**
42. [ ] **Insert bottom-out bumpers into slider tubes and push both down until they are below lower bushings.**
43. [ ] **Insert seals into top end of each slider tube, then tap with mallet until each is fully seated and level.**
44. [ ] **Thoroughly grease all bushings and pockets inside seals with Judy Butter grease.**

Cartridge and neutral-shaft installation

45. [ ] Replace worn or damaged O-rings, glide rings (on pistons), or seals.
46. [ ] Thread pistons fully into tops of shafts, but do not secure.
47. [ ] Install in order onto bottom of neutral shaft: plastic washers, conical bumper (large-diameter-end first), then shaft guide (cupped-face first).
48. [ ] Grease shaft and piston of damper cartridge assembly, then slide piston-end first into right-side stanchion.
49. [ ] Use 7/8" O.D. PVC pipe or similar cylinder to gently seat cartridge body just beyond snapring groove, then install snap-ring.
50. [ ] Pull damper shaft out as far as negative spring will allow.
51. [ ] Grease neutral shaft piston rings and top-out bumper.
52. [ ] Slide neutral shaft into left leg, engage snapring, then pull shaft out until even with damper shaft.

Slider assembly and top-cap installation

53. [ ] Install boots on stanchions.
54. [ ] Use Judy Butter or equivalent grease to grease stanchion tubes, bushings in sliders, and pockets in inner perimeters of wiper seals.
55. [ ] With bike/fork upright, put 5cc of oil in each stanchion tube, then install top caps to 35–40in-lbs each.
56. [ ] Put 5cc of oil in each slider tube and swirl around to coat inside of tubes.
57. [ ] Place sliders onto stanchions until just short of point shafts will be compressed.
58. [ ] Invert fork/bike, then pour 15cc of oil into bolt hole at bottom of each slider.
59. [ ] Treat both bottom bolts with Loctite 242.
60. [ ] Press sliders on fully, then engage bolts through holes in bottoms of sliders into neutral shaft and damper shaft and torque to 50in-lbs.
61. [ ] Use pump with RockShox inflation needle to pressurize both stanchions to desired pressure.
62. [ ] Install Phillips screws in stanchion caps.
63. [ ] Install wheel and reattach brake cable.

TUNING OPTIONS

Air-spring pressure

The fork should sag when the rider's weight is on it. Sag helps keep the tire in contact with the ground on rough terrain, when rolling over dips or holes. The air pressure should be adjusted to create the correct amount of sag, when the rider sits on the bike. The recommended sag for this fork is between 3mm and 8mm. The air pressure should be adjusted to create this amount of sag. RockShox recommends the following depending on rider weight:

< 130lbs	40psi
120–150lbs	50psi
140–170lbs	60psi
160–190lbs	70psi
> 180lbs	80psi

The rider's style affects the necessary pressure, as well. This is why the weight ranges in the list overlap somewhat. For example, a less aggressive 165lb rider might do best with the 60psi recommendation, but a more aggressive 165lb rider might do best with the 70psi recommendation. If air pressure cannot be maintained, seals may need replacement, or there may be a problem with the low-speed damping adjusters. See the following section *Low-speed-damping adjustment*.

Changing air-spring volume

The air springs get more progressive if the volume is reduced. A more progressive spring gets more resistant to compression at a given point in the travel than a less progressive spring. To adjust the volume, the springs must be depressurized and the top caps removed. A long 8mm Allen wrench can be used to adjust the piston height at the bottom of the air chamber. First, turn the wrench clockwise, counting the number of turns until it stops, to determine the current position. From the fully bottomed position, the pistons can be turned up to five full turns counterclockwise. It is critical to start by finding the bottom, because there is no stop to prevent loosening the pistons more than five full turns, which will cause the air chamber to not maintain pressure.

The pistons do not have to be adjusted equally, so maximum volume is with both turned fully clockwise. A medium adjustment is with both up 2.5 turns, or with one fully down and the other up five full turns. A minimum volume is with both turned five full turns up (counterclockwise).

Cartridge damping-rate adjustment

The damping cartridge is not adjustable, but three damping cartridges are available: soft (#20882-001), medium (#20882-002), and firm (#20882-003). RockShox recommends switching to the firm cartridge if 70psi or more is the best air pressure for the rider, but the fork acts to quick (too lightly damped) at this pressure. Conversely, the soft cartridge is recommended if the correct pressure for the rider is 50psi or less, but at that pressure the fork seems too heavily damped (sluggish).

Low-speed-damping adjustment

RockShox no longer feels the low-speed damping adjustment is effective, and may be a source of air-pressure leaks. RockShox recommends installing the low-speed damping screws with Loctite 242 and tightening each fully. If pressure loss continues, remove the piston heads from the neutral and damper shafts and seal the holes in the threaded studs on the bottom ends of the pistons. Alternatively, put rubber plugs under the low-speed damping adjuster screws.

Negative-spring adjustments

There are two possible adjustments to the negative spring. The negative-spring pre-load can be adjusted, and there are two strengths of springs available.

The negative spring serves to counteract the inherently high main-spring pre-load that exists with air-sprung forks. With the fork pre-load too high, the fork tends to not react to small bumps. Increasing negative-spring pre-load decreases the fork pre-load.

The negative-spring is on the damper shaft. When the damper is removed, the e-clip on top of the negative spring can be moved into one of several grooves. The fork has the most pre-load when the spring is removed, and the least pre-load when the e-clip is in the lowest groove. Each groove changes the spring rate by 4 lb-in.

The stock spring is the light spring. Light riders (under 130lbs) may need the heavy spring (#510-00689-00).

ROCKSHOX '99–'00 SID CARTRIDGE FORKS

ABOUT THIS SECTION

This section is specific to RockShox SID forks made in 1999 and 2000. For the 2000 models, this section only applies to the Race, SL, and XL models. The 2000 SID XC and 100 are a different design and are not available at the time of this writing. The 1999 and 2000 models this section does apply to are distinguished by the C3 cartridge adjuster knob on the bottom of the left leg. This 23mm-long aluminum knob can be pulled down another few millimeters to change between compression and rebound damping adjustment. Decals that say "C3 Dual Adjust" further identify the models this section applies to. See *ROCKSHOX '98 SID FORK* (page 38-52) for the 1998 model, which is signifi-

cantly different. The lack of the adjuster knob and the large RockShox decals with a black background distinguish 1998 models.

TOOLS

Servicing this fork requires one specialized tool that is unique to this model, the RockShox Cartridge Sleeve Retainer Tool #140-001905-00. For sake of brevity, the following procedure will refer to this tool simply as the "cartridge driver." This fork needs one other tool common to several RockShox forks for removing the caps at the tops of the legs, the United Bicycle Tool AL-11912B (custom-ground 22mm socket for fitting low-profile wrench flats). The standard RockShox pump is adequate for inflation, with the addition of a 1999 Sid valve adapter.

For bushing replacement, the same tools are required that are used with Judy forks. This includes the Universal Bushing Removal Tool #70096, the Judy Bushing Installer #70119, and the RockShox Seal Separator #70113.

FULL FORK SERVICE

Slider removal

1. [ ] Remove plastic valve caps from top and bottom of left leg and top of right leg.
2. [ ] Push in adjuster knob on bottom of right leg, unscrew Phillips screw, then remove adjuster knob.
3. [ ] Depressurize air valve in bottom of left leg.
4. [ ] Unthread 8mm nut on bottom of right leg just until hex-shaped adjuster rod no longer protrudes.
5. [ ] Unthread 10mm nut on bottom of left leg about 5mm.
6. [ ] Depressurize both air valves at tops of legs.
7. [ ] Use 22mm socket to remove both air cap assemblies from tops of legs.
8. [ ] Tap on nuts at bottoms of legs with plastic mallet until nuts are against sliders, then unthread both nuts completely. *Note: Be prepared for oil to drain out holes at bottoms of sliders!*
9. [ ] Pull slider assembly of bottoms of stanchions, then remove boots. Drain remaining oil from sliders.

Cartridge and negative spring disassembly

There are two cartridges in the stanchions of the fork. The left cartridge is a negative air spring and the right cartridge is a hydraulic damper. The damper car-

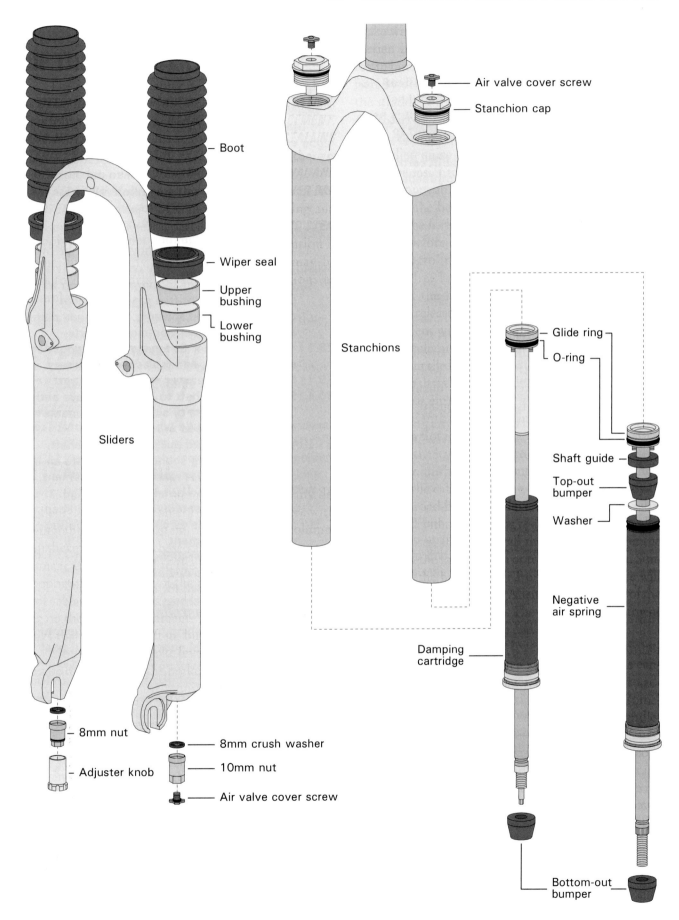

— Boot

— Air valve cover screw

— Stanchion cap

— Wiper seal

— Upper bushing

— Lower bushing

Stanchions

— Glide ring

— O-ring

Shaft guide —

Top-out bumper

Washer

Sliders

Negative air spring

Damping cartridge

— 8mm nut

— 8mm crush washer

— Adjuster knob

— 10mm nut

— Air valve cover screw

Bottom-out bumper

38.19 RockShox '99 SID.

Sag adjustment

RockShox recommends setting sag at 20% of total travel for cross-country riding (recreational) or 10% of total travel for racing. Sag is adjusted by balancing the main spring and negative-spring pressures. If the sag is correct, but the fork bottoms too easily on bumps, increase all pressures proportionally. If the sag is correct but the fork never bottoms on severe bumps, decrease all pressures proportionally. Changing negative-spring pressure independently of main-spring pressure will also affect responsiveness to small bumps. More negative-spring pressure increases responsiveness to small bumps.

Travel adjustment

On the 1999 models, travel can be adjusted only by replacing the cartridge. The 2000 models come with an All Spacer Kit, which are spacers that can be repositioned to change the travel.

Adjusting main-spring progressiveness

Changing the volume of the main-spring air chambers varies the progressiveness of the spring. Less volume creates more progressiveness. A more progressive spring gets more resistant to compression at the same amount of travel. RockShox has spacers available that are added to the bottoms of the top caps that reduce the volume of the main-spring air chamber.

ROCKSHOX DELUXE REAR SHOCK

This shock is a air/oil shock with an external coil spring. It is available in several lengths of travel and with several different spring ratings. Some versions have a floating piston that separates the air and oil in the shock body, but others have no piston for this purpose. The service of all these variations is so similar that the following procedure is adequate for all of them.

There is another model, called the Super Deluxe, that is significantly different. Instead of a uniform-diameter shock body, the Super Deluxe body gets substantially fatter at the end that is not inside the spring. There is a section called *ROCKSHOX SUPER DELUXE REAR SHOCK* (page 38-64) that should be used for servicing this type.

This procedure requires several tools that are included in the RockShox 70106 tool kit. The tool kit is designed for other models as well, so some tools in the kit will not be used in this procedure. In some cases, there may be two tools that are very similar,

except for slight differences in dimension. The individual tools are unmarked, so make sure that the tool you select seems dimensionally appropriate for the procedure being performed.

SHOCK AND SPRING REMOVAL

Shock removal

The compressed spring length needs to be measured, so that the customer's pre-load setting can be restored.
1. [ ] **Measure length of spring between red adjuster ring and silver stop plate: _____mm**
2. [ ] **Turn red adjuster ring fully away from spring, until spring moves easily between plates.**

The shock unit may mount to the frame in a variety of ways, depending on the design of the frame. Usually, there will be a bolt and nut through the shock eyelets, or their will be a stud with retaining clips on each end.
3. [ ] **Remove shafts that go through both shock eyes, then remove shock from bike.**

Spring removal
1. [ ] **Thread red spring-adjuster ring off end of shock.**
2. [ ] **Slide spring off shock unit.**

OIL CHANGE/SHOCK DISASSEMBLY

NOTE: Perform complete SHOCK AND SPRING REMOVAL *procedures before proceeding further.*

Body-eyelet-bushing removal

There is an air valve hidden by the bushing located inside the eyelet on the end of the shock body. The bushing must be removed to depressurize the shock.
1. [ ] **Place flat face of body eyelet on top of vise, with vise jaws open enough to permit eyelet bushing to clear.**

The bushing tool used in the next step is a cylinder with different diameter reductions at each end.
2. [ ] **Place large-diameter end of bushing tool against bushing, then tap on bushing tool with plastic mallet to drive out bushing.**

Depressurization
1. [ ] **Remove needle from pump, by unscrewing first brass fitting at base of needle.**

The pump needle needs to be removed from the pump for depressurization. The needle has a sharp tip that punctures the air valve (the puncture self seals when the needle is removed). Goggles are needed because hydraulic fluid can spray out the end of the needle at high speed.

2. [ ] Wearing safety goggles to prevent getting hydraulic fluid in your eyes, insert needle through small hole in end of body eyelet, then into air valve that was covered by eyelet bushing.

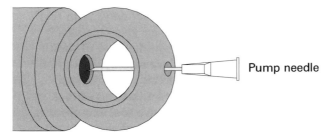

38.20 *Depressurizing the shock.*

3. [ ] Remove needle.

Shaft-assembly removal, and oil draining

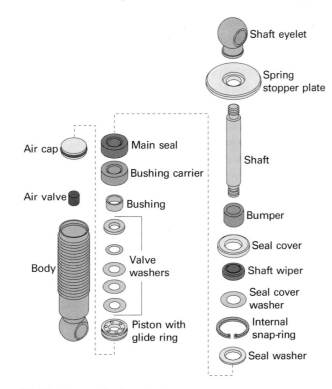

38.21 *Blow-up of Deluxe shock.*

4. [ ] Clamp faces of body eyelet in vise soft jaws.
5. [ ] Hold drift or screwdriver against bottom edge of seal cover (on top end of body), then tap on tool with hammer to remove seal cover from body.
6. [ ] Place shaft-clamping blocks around shaft, then firmly secure shaft-clamping blocks in vise.

7. [ ] Place rag over flats of shaft eyelet to protect finish.
8. [ ] Grasp flats of eyelet securely in large adjustable-wrench jaws.
9. [ ] Turn wrench counterclockwise to unthread eyelet from shaft.
10. [ ] Remove spring-stopper plate and bumper.
11. [ ] Remove shaft from shaft-clamping blocks.
12. [ ] Remove seal cover, shaft wiper, and seal-cover washer from end of shock.
13. [ ] Use snap-ring pliers to remove internal snap-ring from inside shock body.
14. [ ] Clamp body-eyelet flats in soft jaws in vise.
15. [ ] Thread shaft eyelet back onto shaft.
16. [ ] Wearing safety goggles, insert round bar through shaft eyelet; using rocking/pulling motion to pull shaft assembly out of shock body (oil will spill).
17. [ ] Remove shock body from vise, then carefully drain oil into waste receptacle for later recycling.

NOTE: If performing oil change only, go to step 40.

18. [ ] Inset 2mm spoke through small hole in end of body eyelet, then push air valve and floating piston (piston not in all models) out open end of body.
19. [ ] Remove seal washer and seal from shaft.
20. [ ] Remove bushing carrier and bushing from shaft.

NOTE: Remaining parts on piston assembly are unnecessary to remove, except to change, add, or subtract washers.

CLEANING AND INSPECTION

21. [ ] Clean all parts with mild detergent and water, then dry thoroughly with compressed air. *Avoid leaving solvents or lint from rags on, or in, any part!*
22. [ ] Inspect shaft for scratches or nicks that will compromise oil seal.
23. [ ] Inspect inside of threaded tube for nicks or scratches that will compromise oil seal.
24. [ ] Inspect glide ring on piston for nicks or scratches, and remove now if damaged.
25. [ ] Inspect bushing in bushing carrier for wear, and check for loose fit between bushing and shaft (use large end of bushing tool to drive bushing out of carrier if bushing is worn).

23. [ ] *If can stayed on threaded tube:* Pull reservoir can carefully off threaded tube, being careful not do damage O-rings as they pull past threads on end of tube.
24. [ ] Pull the floating piston out the large-diameter end of the reservoir can.
25. [ ] Remove O-rings from inside and outside edges of floating piston.
26. [ ] Remove O-ring from edge of eyelet cap.
27. [ ] Remove O-ring from threaded tube.

Piston/valve disassembly

The disassembly procedure from this point forward assumes you have access to all seals, O-rings, and a replacement seal-head. It is not recommended to go further without the necessary parts on hand. It is also recommended to replace the seal-head, all the seals, and all the O-rings, each time a service is performed.

28. [ ] Slide seal head up against piston. Put shaft-clamping blocks around shaft, and secure clamping blocks in vise with high force; *it is critical that the shaft not spin in the clamping blocks in the next step!*
29. [ ] Use 10mm box wrench (or socket), to unthread nut on end of shaft.

In the next steps, a series of different washers (that were sandwiched between the just-removed bolt and the piston) need to be removed. The number and dimensions of the washers will vary, because these factors are what enable customization of the damping rate. There are several washers that are nearly identical. Critical variations might be as slight as .05mm. If unable to measure dimensions this precise (or if no valving changes will be made), carefully transfer the washers to a bundling tie, maintaining the order and orientation of the washers as they are removed. Keep them bundled together from the time of removal until the time of installation. There is a similar bundle of washers on the other side of the piston. It is critical to not confuse the two sets of washers.

30. [ ] Remove washers one at a time from above piston, measuring O.D. (outside diameter), thickness, and I.D. (inside diameter) of each washer as it comes off:

O.D. _____ Thickness _____ I.D. _____
O.D. _____ Thickness _____ I.D. _____
O.D. _____ Thickness _____ I.D. _____
O.D. _____ Thickness _____ I.D. _____
O.D. _____ Thickness _____ I.D. _____
O.D. _____ Thickness _____ I.D. _____
O.D. _____ Thickness _____ I.D. _____

31. [ ] Remove piston only, noting which side faces up (if not symmetrical).

In the next steps, a different series of washers (below the piston location) need to be removed. The number and dimensions of the washers will vary, because these factors are what enable customization of the damping rate. There are several washers that are nearly identical. Critical variations might be as slight as .05mm. If unable to measure dimensions this precise (or if no valving changes will be made), carefully transfer the washers to a bundling tie, maintaining the order and orientation of the washers as they are removed. Keep them bundled together from the time of removal until the time of installation.

32. [ ] Remove washers and shims one at a time from below piston, measuring O.D., thickness, and I.D. of each washer as it comes off:

O.D. _____ Thickness _____ I.D. _____
O.D. _____ Thickness _____ I.D. _____
O.D. _____ Thickness _____ I.D. _____
O.D. _____ Thickness _____ I.D. _____
O.D. _____ Thickness _____ I.D. _____
O.D. _____ Thickness _____ I.D. _____
O.D. _____ Thickness _____ I.D. _____
O.D. _____ Thickness _____ I.D. _____
O.D. _____ Thickness _____ I.D. _____

33. [ ] Remove aluminum base-plate washer, noting which side faces up (if not symmetrical).
34. [ ] Inspect glide ring for nicks or scratches, and if damaged, remove glide-ring from outer perimeter of piston.

Damping-adjuster-rod removal

35. [ ] Push adjuster rod out end of shaft where eyelet was removed.
36. [ ] Remove O-ring from adjuster rod.

Seal-head removal and disassembly

Some early versions of RockShox service literature described disassembling the seal head. This is likely to damage the seal head, and is no longer recommended. If the bumper plate and washer (below the bumper plate) come out accidentally, it is not a problem. Removing the seal from the open end of the seal-head is when damage will occur.

37. [ ] Pull seal-head off end of shaft.
38. [ ] Note orientation of bumper plate, so that it can be reinstalled if it accidentally falls out.
NOTE: If oil has been leaking from seal between seal head and shaft, RockShox requires replacing seal-head as a unit. Do not attempt further disassembly of seal-head.

CLEANING AND INSPECTION

39. [ ] Clean all parts with mild detergent and water, then dry thoroughly with compressed air. *Avoid leaving solvents or lint from rags on, or in, any part!*

40. [ ] Inspect shaft for scratches or nicks that will compromise oil seal.

41. [ ] Inspect inside and outside of threaded tube for nicks or scratches that will compromise oil or gas seal.

42. [ ] Inspect inside of reservoir can for nicks or scratches that will compromise gas seal.

43. [ ] If no gas hissed out of needle during depressurization step, air seal is bad; pry air seal out of can, grease new air seal, then push air seal back into can (until flush).

ASSEMBLY

Damping-adjuster-rod assembly

44. [ ] Grease small O-ring, then install O-ring on adjuster rod.

45. [ ] Push adjuster rod into end of shaft where eyelet was removed.

46. [ ] Grasp shaft in shaft-clamping blocks in vise *very* securely (full-diameter end up).

47. [ ] Make sure red adjusting rod is threaded fully counterclockwise, then thread eyelet onto shaft.

48. [ ] Protect eyelet flats with rag.

49. [ ] Grasp eyelet flats snugly with adjustable wrench, then secure eyelet to shaft to 100in-lbs (17lbs@6").

Seal-head assembly

NOTE: *Steps 51–52 are only required if bumper and bumper washer have accidentally come out of seal-head*

50. [ ] Place seal-head assembly (flange-side down) on flat surface.

51. [ ] Install bumper washer into seal-head.

52. [ ] Install bumper (flat-face first) into seal-head.

Shaft-unit assembly

53. [ ] Place conical bumper on shaft (large-diameter end first) and fit onto eyelet, then clamp flats of shaft eyelet securely in soft jaws in vise (shaft pointing up).

In the next step, a tool called a bullet is used. The bullet is called a bullet because it looks just like a bullet. It enables the seal to slide onto the shaft without the soft inner lip of the seal catching on the sharp edge at the top of the shaft. The tool kit includes a bullet for this shock, and a different version for the Deluxe model. The correct bullet will closely match the diameter of the shaft.

54. [ ] Place shaft bullet on top of small-diameter end of shaft, then coat bullet & shaft with grease.

55. [ ] Place seal-head (flange-end first) over top of bullet.

56. [ ] Push seal-head assembly fully onto shaft.

57. [ ] Remove bullet from shaft.

58. [ ] Clean grease from outside and inside of shaft.

59. [ ] Install aluminum base-plate washer (conical-face, if any, up) on shaft.

60. [ ] Install washers listed in step 32 on shaft, in reverse order of list.

61. [ ] Install piston, 3-leg-protrusion face up.

62. [ ] Install washers listed in step 30 on shaft, in reverse order of list.

63. [ ] Treat shaft-bolt threads with one small drop of Loctite 242.

64. [ ] Thread shaft bolt into end of shaft, taking care to align shim washers so that shaft bolt inserts through all washers above piston.

65. [ ] Secure shaft bolt with 10mm box-end wrench or socket to 60in-lbs (20lbs@3").

NOTE: *If glide ring was not removed, go to step 88.*

Glide-ring installation

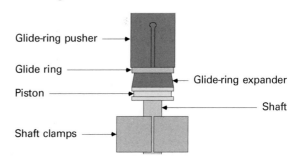

38.28 Installling the glide ring.

66. [ ] Place glide-ring expander on top of piston.

67. [ ] Install new glide ring onto tapered end of glide-ring expander.

68. [ ] Place large-I.D. end of glide-ring pusher over glide ring, then push glide ring down until glide ring snaps into groove in piston.

69. [ ] Remove glide-ring expander & glide-ring pusher.

70. [ ] Slide seal-head fully away from piston.

71. [ ] Pack top-out-bumper-end of seal head with light-weight grease to eliminate air pockets.

NOTE: *If performing oil-change only, go to step 87.*

In the next step, a tool called a glide-ring sizer is installed over the glide ring, then left in place for at least one minute. The glide-ring sizer is a cylinder that slips over the glide ring and compresses it. The material the glide ring is made of has "short-term memory." This memory allows the material to remain shrunk for a short while, once the glide-ring sizer is removed. This enables the glide ring to fit more easily into the shock body. Once there, the glide-ring expands to fit closely along the inside of the shock.

The tool kit includes a glide-ring sizer for this shock, and a different one for the Deluxe model. The correct glide-ring sizer will fit somewhat snugly over the glide ring.

72. [ ] Place large-I.D. end of glide-ring sizer over glide ring fully, then leave in place until ready to install shaft into shock body.
73. [ ] Remove shaft assembly from vise.

Reservoir/body assembly

74. [ ] Grease all O-rings with light-weight, high-quality grease, then grease all seal-mounting points.
75. [ ] Carefully slide O-ring over end of threaded tube, then seat seal in groove.
76. [ ] Install O-rings in inside and outside edges of floating piston that fits inside reservoir can.
77. [ ] Install O-ring in outer perimeter of eyelet cap cap.
78. [ ] Clamp flat tab of threaded-tube clamping tool in end of vise, so that short-threaded end of tube points up.
79. [ ] Slide small-I.D. end of reservoir can over end of threaded tube, until can is seated against shoulder on threaded tube.
80. [ ] Slide floating piston (cavity-side first, conical-face up) carefully over end of threaded tube, just until it clears threads on threaded tube.
81. [ ] Clean grease off tube threads.
82. [ ] Apply drop of Loctite 271 to tube threads.
83. [ ] Thread body-eyelet cap onto tube.
84. [ ] Place rag over body-eyelet-cap flats to protect finish.
85. [ ] Grasp flats securely with large adjustable wrench, then secure to 100–120in-lbs (17–20lbs@6").
86. [ ] Loosen bolts and remove body from threaded-tube clamp. Remove clamp from vise.

Oil filling and final assembly

87. [ ] Grasp flats of body eyelet in soft saws in vise.
88. [ ] Insert pump needle into air valve, then pressurize to 50psi (floating piston may seat with a "pop").
89. [ ] Thread red adjusting ring (flatter-face first) onto threaded tube.
90. [ ] Pour 5wt oil into threaded tube until oil level reaches bottom of threads inside threaded tube.
91. [ ] Let bubbles rise and dissipate from oil for at least 5 minutes.

92. [ ] Using thin slotted screwdriver, turn damping adjuster rod fully counterclockwise.
93. [ ] Remove glide-ring sizer from shaft assembly, then immediately insert piston-end of shaft assembly slowly into threaded tube, until top of piston is at least 1/2" below top of threaded tube (oil will spill). Stop before seal head reaches threaded tube.
94. [ ] Let bubbles rise and dissipate from oil for at least 5 minutes.
95. [ ] Holding piston/shaft assembly stationary, push seal-head down shaft and engage seal-head in threads of threaded tube (oil will spill).
96. [ ] Thread seal-head fully into threaded tube (oil will spill), then secure to 100–120in-lbs (17–20lbs@6").
97. [ ] Clean assembly of all excess oil.
98. [ ] Thread red adjuster ring off of threaded tube.
99. [ ] Insert needle in air valve and pressurize to 225psi (nitrogen preferred, air is acceptable).
100. [ ] Inspect for leaks at all seams and seals.

SPRING AND SHOCK INSTALLATION

1. [ ] Thread red adjusting ring back onto threaded tube, then thread fully-down.
2. [ ] Turn red damper-adjusting shaft fully clockwise with thin slotted screwdriver.
3. [ ] Slide spring over shaft-end of shock.
4. [ ] Compress spring (if necessary) with spring-compression tool, then install silver spring keeper plate (recessed side facing towards eyelet) onto shaft.
5. [ ] Apply Loctite 222 to Allen bolt that retains damper-adjusting knob.
6. [ ] Attach damper-adjusting knob to damper-adjusting shaft, and secure by threading in adjusting-knob retaining bolt.
7. [ ] Turn damper-adjusting knob fully counter-clockwise.
8. [ ] Turn damper-adjusting knob in, number of returns recorded in SHOCK AND SPRING REMOVAL (step 4).
9. [ ] Install shock on bike.
10. [ ] Turn red spring adjusting ring out to restore measurement recorded in SHOCK AND SPRING REMOVAL (step 1), unless this requires more than 8 full turns.

EYELET-BUSHING REPLACEMENT

1. [ ] Place flat face of body eyelet or shaft eyelet on top of vise, with vise jaws open enough to permit shaft eyelet bushing to clear.
2. [ ] Use large-diameter end of bushing tool to drive bushing out of eyelet.

3. [ ] Place new bushing on small-diameter end of bushing tool.
4. [ ] Supporting eyelet face on flat surface, place bushing-tool/bushing on top face of eyelet, then use plastic mallet to tap bushing into eyelet.

TUNING OPTIONS

Spring pre-load

RockShox recommends compressing spring length by no more than 8 full turns of the spring-adjuster ring. Compressing the spring increases the resistance to compression and increases the speed of rebounding. If the 8-full-turn adjustment does not stiffen the spring adequately, or if the spring is too stiff at the lowest pre-load setting, consider using a different spring.

Different springs

RockShox makes springs rated from 500 to 800 lbs. Higher ratings mean the spring is stiffer. Stiffer springs resist compression more, and rebound more quickly.

Gas pressure and type of gas

The recommended gas pressure is 225psi. Nitrogen is recommended, but regular air can be used with only a small performance loss.

Changing damper setting

The damper adjustment affects compression and rebound damping. Turning the damper-adjusting knob clockwise increases damping while turning the adjuster knob counterclockwise reduces damping. Increased damping slows the rate of compression or rebound.

Changing oil weight

RockShox recommends 5w oil, but anything from 2.5w to 8w may be used. The heavier-weight the oil, the more damping will occur.

Changing valving

The shim washers on either side of the piston controls the rate of damping. The washers between the shaft nut and piston control the rebound damping rate; the washers between the piston and the conical washer control the compression damping. Increasing a stack of washers will increase damping rate and reducing the stack will reduce damping rate.

RST '98 MOZO FORKS

ABOUT THIS SECTION

This supplement covers full service of 1998 RST Mozo XL, Mozo Pro, and Mozo Comp forks, including bushing replacement.

TOOL CHOICES

RST provides a bushing remover and installer (Hot Karl tool) for remove bushings from the models that have pressed-in bushings.

FULL FORK SERVICE

Disassembly

1. [ ] Remove front wheel and front brake.
2. [ ] Remove slider brace from both sliders.
3. [ ] Turn pre-load adjusters on stanchion caps fully counterclockwise, noting number of turns: _____
4. [ ] Loosen stanchion clamp bolts slightly.
5. [ ] With fingers, unthread stanchion-cap/spring-assemblies from stanchion tubes.
6. [ ] Compress sliders completely.
NOTE: Only the Mozo XL and Pro have air dampers in the stanchions. In all the following steps, models with no air-damper have a simple plunger shaft instead of a damper shaft with an air valve. For these models, substitute the word "plunger" for "damper," and ignore all references to the air valve.
7. [ ] Insert 8mm Allen bit socket on 6" extension into 8mm fitting in top of damper shaft (inside stanchion).
8. [ ] Holding extension stationary with ratchet wrench, use 4mm Allen wrench to unthread bolt at bottom of each slider.
9. [ ] Pull sliders off bottom of stanchions.
10. [ ] Pull bottom-out bumpers from damper shafts that extend from bottoms of stanchions.
11. [ ] Remove internal snap-rings from bottom of stanchions.
12. [ ] Pull firmly on damper shafts to remove from stanchions.
13. [ ] Pull damper-shaft guides, then top-out bumpers from damper shafts.
14. [ ] Insert 8mm Allen in fitting in head of damper shaft(s) to hold shaft while unthreading air-valve nut.
15. [ ] Remove air valves from damper shafts.
16. [ ] Inspect all O-rings for nicks and tears, and replace if damaged.

NOTE: The remaining disassembly steps should only be performed if replacing the bushings. If not replacing bushings, skip to step 29.

17. [ ] Carefully pry dust wipers from top of sliders.

NOTE: On the Mozo XL model, the bushings retained by a circlip) are not a press fit, and can be pulled out with a hooked seal pick or bent spoke, and inserted by hand. Use this hand technique for removal and installation, then skip to step 29.

18. [ ] Unthread double-flatted plate from shaft of Hot Karl bushing remover, and drop plate into slider. It should pass through bushings and rest flat on top of spool spacer.

19. [ ] Unthread nut from tool shaft, then insert non-flatted end of shaft into slider and engage into threads of double-flatted plate. Make sure shaft is engaged with plate with threads to spare.

20. [ ] Slide large washer over tool shaft, then thread nut on until double-flatted plate snugs up against bottom of lower bushing.

21. [ ] Hold flats of tool shaft in soft jaws of vise. Tighten nut against washer while holding slider from rotating. After one inch of tightening against resistance, lower bushing will become loose, then several more inches of effortless tightening will be needed before tool begins to pull upper bushing out.

22. [ ] Remove tool, remove bushings from tool, then remove spool spacer from bottom of slider.

NOTE: Repeat steps 18–22 for other slider.

Assembly

23. [ ] Put spool spacers (cavity-end up) into bottom of each slider.

24. [ ] Place smaller-diameter bushing on fat end of Hot Karl bushing installer, and insert tool and bushing into slider.

25. [ ] Tap on tool with plastic mallet until line in middle of sticker on tool is even with top of slider. Repeat for other slider.

26. [ ] Place larger-diameter bushing over small-diameter end of Hot Karl bushing installer until it seats against fattest part of tool, then insert tool into slider until tool passes through lower bushing.

27. [ ] Tap on tool with plastic mallet until top of bushing is even with shoulder that is approximately 10mm down from top of slider. Repeat for other slider.

28. [ ] Press dust wipers into tops of stanchions.

29. [ ] Clean and dry all parts, making sure they end up lint and solvent free.

30. [ ] Grease threads on damper-shaft heads.

31. [ ] Grease O-rings on air valves, then slide air valves onto damper shafts so that face with large slots faces away from shaft-head. (Reversing orientation of valve will decrease rebound damping and increase compression damping).

32. [ ] Hold damper shaft with 8mm Allen, then secure valve nut on shaft. Repeat for other side.

33. [ ] Grease top-out bumpers (shorter ones), and slide onto damper shafts flat-face first.

34. [ ] Grease shaft guides and slide onto damper shafts cavity-face first.

35. [ ] Insert air-damper assemblies into stanchions head-ends first.

36. [ ] Install internal snap-rings into bottom ends of stanchions.

37. [ ] Grease and install bottom-out bumper onto damper shafts, round-ends first.

38. [ ] Place sliders onto thoroughly-greased stanchions, and engage boots to dust wipers. Compress sliders fully.

39. [ ] Treat slider-securing bolts with Loctite 242.

40. [ ] Use 8mm Allen bit socket on ratchet with extension to hold damper shaft(s) from turning, then install slider-securing bolt(s) in bottom of slider(s) to 40in-lbs.

41. [ ] Grease spring assemblies (steel coil and elastomer stacks) that are attached to stanchion caps.

42. [ ] Install stanchion-cap/spring-assemblies fully into stanchions, then secure with fingers.

43. [ ] Pull down on stanchions until stanchion-cap flanges are against fork crown.

44. [ ] Secure stanchion-clamp bolts to 80in-lbs.

45. [ ] Check that fork-column-clamp bolts are secured to 80in-lbs.

46. [ ] Treat slider-brace-bolt threads and brake-pivot-stud threads with Loctite 242.

47. [ ] Install slider brace, then secure slider-brace bolts to 90in-lbs and brake pivot studs to 115in-lbs.

48. [ ] Install front wheel and attach front brake.

WHITE BROTHERS FORKS

ABOUT THIS SECTION

This section specifically covers the '97–'99 White Brothers SC70, SC90, DC90, DC110 and DC118 models, but can be used as a general guideline for servicing other models.

TOOLS

White Brothers sells a tool kit (#97-713) for bushing replacement and cartridge overhaul. The tools are also available separately. The kit includes:

Cartridge Drift	97-707
Cartridge Bleed Tool	97-708
Cartridge Holder	97-700
Cartridge Bush & Seal Driver	97-709
Cartridge Upper Seal R&R Tool	97-710
Fork Bushing Install Tool	97-711
Fork Bushing Removal Tool	97-712

In the following procedure, the Cartridge Drift is called the "small drift," the Cartridge Bush & Seal Driver is called the "medium drift," and the Cartridge Upper Seal R&R Tool is called the "large drift." Each of these tools is a cylinder with several steps in diameter. They also vary in length. The small drift is the short, skinny cylinder. The medium drift is the short, fat cylinder. The large drift is the long cylinder.

The Fork Bushing Removal Tool has a ring that is free to slide up and down the shaft of the tool (when a setscrew in its side is loosened). This ring is called the "depth ring" in the following procedure.

FULL FORK SERVICE

Slider removal

1. [ ] Remove brakes and front wheel.
2. [ ] Loosen bolts at bottoms of stanchions two full turns.
3. [ ] Tap on loosened bolts with plastic mallet until heads contact bottoms of sliders, then complete bolt removal.
4. [ ] Remove slider assembly.
5. [ ] Remove bolts from both ends of slider brace.

Top-cap and spring removal

6. [ ] Turn pre-load adjusters fully counterclockwise, counting number of turns and record here: right: _____ left: _____
7. [ ] Unthread top caps.
8. [ ] *SC70 only:* Remove plastic spacers and spring caps from tops of springs.

9. [ ] Remove springs from tops of stanchions.

Neutral-shaft and cartridge removal

10. [ ] Remove conical bumpers from shafts.
11. [ ] Unthread cartridge from bottom of left stanchion.
12. [ ] Turn stanchions upside down and remove neutral shaft.
13. [ ] Remove top caps from damper shaft and neutral shaft.
14. [ ] Remove top-out bumper from bottom end of neutral shaft.

Seal and bushing removal

15. [ ] Remove circular coil spring from lips of seals.
16. [ ] Insert screwdriver into each seal, catching tip under bottom edge of seal, then pry out seal.
17. [ ] Remove foam ring(s).
18. [ ] Turn right stanchion over and shake out bottom-out spacer (large plastic spool).

Bushings should be cleaned and inspected before removal. The appearance of brass flecks or solid-metallic areas on the surfaces of the bushings indicates need for bushing replacement. Do not remove bushings unless intending to replace them.

19. [ ] Assemble Bushing Removal Tool parts in following sequence onto threaded shaft:
    Flat washer (conical-face first)
    Rectangular plate (flat-face first)
    Expander mechanism (large-end first)
20. [ ] Secure 1/3 of rectangular plate in vise so it sticks out end of vise and rest of tool hangs down past edge of bench.
21. [ ] Push slider onto bottom of tool until expander is heard or felt to snap clear of first bushing.
22. [ ] While holding onto slider, tighten tool shaft continuously until slider is free.
23. [ ] Remove expander and bushing from bottom of tool shaft and repeat bushing removal for lower bushing, then both in other slider.

Cartridge overhaul

24. [ ] Place Cartridge Holder in vise, then place cartridge in Holder so end of shaft with flats points up, but do not secure vise.
25. [ ] Remove circlip (older models) or snap-ring (newer models) from top end of cartridge body, then turn cartridge body over in Cartridge Holder.
26. [ ] Position Cartridge Holder so split end of tool is half way into vise jaws.
27. [ ] Position cartridge in Holder so bottom of body is flush with bottom of Holder, then secure vise.
28. [ ] Place receptacle for waste oil below cartridge.

29. [ ] Place small end of Cartridge Drift (small drift) in top of shaft, then slowly tap on tool to drive parts out bottom of cartridge. Be prepared to catch cartridge shaft.

30. [ ] Place small end of Cartridge Upper Seal R&R Tool (large drift) on top of cartridge, then carefully tap parts out bottom end of cartridge. Be prepared to catch parts.

31. [ ] Use 2mm Allen wrench to unthread adjuster rod off end of cartridge shaft, then remove O-ring from needle end of adjuster rod.

32. [ ] Remove plastic washers and seal from cartridge shaft.

33. [ ] Remove split ring from shaft piston.

Cleaning and inspection

34. [ ] Clean all parts with mild detergent and dry with lint-free rag and/or compressed air.

35. [ ] Inspect stanchion tubes for heavy wear marks or scratches.

36. [ ] Inspect lips of slider-tube seals for tears.

37. [ ] Inspect cartridge shaft for heavy wear marks or scratches.

38. [ ] Inspect inside cartridge body for heavy wear marks or scratches.

39. [ ] Inspect cartridge-seal lips for nicks or tears.

Cartridge assembly

40. [ ] With Cartridge Holder loosely supported in vise, install cartridge body in vise so end with circlip/snap-ring is down.

41. [ ] Place Delrin conical-face washer into cartridge body (conical-face first), then drive it to bottom of cartridge body with large end of large drift.

42. [ ] Grease cartridge seal and install (cupped-face up) into cartridge body, then seat fully with large end of large drift.

43. [ ] Place 2mm flat Delrin washer into cartridge body, then seat fully with large end of large drift.

44. [ ] Remove cartridge body from Holder, insert small end of small drift into seal until large end of drift is flush with conical washer, then put cartridge body (closed-end down) back into Holder.

45. [ ] Put split ring into groove in piston, then place shaft (round-end down) carefully on top of drift.

46. [ ] Fill cartridge body with 2.5wt oil to 1/2" from top of body.

47. [ ] Carefully push shaft down fully into cartridge body, making sure split ring does not catch on top edge of cartridge body. Small drift will fall to floor.

48. [ ] Thread Bleed Tool into top end of shaft, then pump shaft 1/2" up and down repeatedly.

49. [ ] Remove Bleed Tool, then fill cartridge body to top with additional oil. Let sit five minutes or until bubbles are gone.

50. [ ] Fill pocket in seal with light grease and grease outer perimeter of seal.

51. [ ] Place 8mm Delrin washer onto shaft, then use long end of Cartridge Bush & Seal Driver (medium drift) to seat washer to 12mm depth.

52. [ ] Place seal (cupped-side first) onto shaft and use short end of medium drift to seat seal to 5mm depth.

53. [ ] Place conical washer (flat-face first) into cartridge body, then install circlip/snap-ring.

54. [ ] Insert shaft end of bleed tool fully into cartridge shaft to purge shaft of excess oil.

55. [ ] Install new O-ring over pointed end of adjuster rod.

56. [ ] Thread adjuster rod into cartridge shaft until it bottoms. Stock settings from this point are: SC70   2 turns out
    SC90 & DC90   3 turns out
    DC110 & DC118   4 turns out

57. [ ] Wipe excess oil off cartridge.

Bushing installation

58. [ ] Secure dropout of slider into vise with RockShox dropout vise blocks, or other method that will not mar dropout.

59. [ ] Loosen set screw on depth ring of Bushing Install tool, then position and secure ring with setscrew in upper dimple in tool shaft.

60. [ ] Place bushing on bottom end of tool and insert tool into slider, then tap on top of tool until depth ring contacts top of slider.

61. [ ] Remove tool and repeat for other slider.

62. [ ] Remove tool and set depth ring with setscrew in lower dimple on tool shaft, then repeat procedure for both upper bushings.

Cartridge and neutral-shaft installation

63. [ ] Place plastic conical caps on top ends of cartridge shaft and neutral shaft.

64. [ ] Thread cartridge body into bottom end of left stanchion and secure.

65. [ ] Slide smallest conical bumper (conical-end first) onto bottom end of neutral shaft, then insert neutral shaft into top end of right stanchion.

66. [ ] Pull damper and neutral shafts fully down, then place larger conical bumpers (conical-ends first) onto shafts.

Spring and top-cap installation

67. [ ] Grease springs and install into stanchions.

68. [ ] *SC70 only:* Insert discs into stanchions, then insert plastic sleeves.

69. [ ] Thread in top caps fully, then turn pre-load adjusters fully clockwise.

Slider installation

70. [ ] Drop bottom-out spacer (large plastic spool) into right slider.

71. [ ] Place round coil springs over lips of seals.

72. [ ] Grease seals thoroughly (use non-lithium grease) and place onto stanchions (lip-face first), making sure lips do not fold in.

73. [ ] Grease foam rings and place onto stanchions.

74. [ ] Thoroughly grease bushings (non-lithium grease).

75. [ ] Carefully guide right slider onto right stanchion, then carefully guide left slider onto left stanchion.

76. [ ] Attach slider brace to sliders.

77. [ ] Prep slider-brace bolts (anti-seize if bolts are titanium), then secure bolts to 50in-lbs.

78. [ ] Treat bottom bolts with Loctite 242, then insert into holes in bottoms of sliders (hollow bolt, if any, in left) and thread into bottoms of shafts. *Note, it may be necessary to use small hooked tool such as head of spoke to align shafts with holes!*

79. [ ] Compress fork fully, then secure bolts to 60in-lbs. *Note: If bolts will not secure, remove top cap and spring on side not being secured, compress again and secure side with spring.*

80. [ ] Slide foam rings down into tops of sliders.

81. [ ] Slide seals down into tops of sliders and seat seals fully.

82. [ ] Install adjuster knob, if any, in bottom of right-side slider.

83. [ ] Turn pre-load adjusters fully counterclockwise, then clockwise number of turns recorded in step 6.

TUNING DATA REPORT

The following information should be recorded whenever servicing a suspension unit for a customer. All of the information does not apply in every case. The information is recorded during performance of service procedures, but does not occur at uniform points in each procedure, so no step numbers are provided for where the information can be found.

Original damper setting: _____ #/turns

Current damper setting: _____ #/turns

Original air pressure: _____ psi

Current air pressure: _____ psi

Original oil level: _____ mm

Current oil level: _____ mm

Approximate weight of original suspension oil:
    2.5w, 5w, 7.5w, 10w, 15w, 20w,

    other: _____

Brand and weight of current suspension oil:

_____

Valving changes:
    Spring pre-load YES NO Amt: _____mm

    Compression reed-valve washers:
        added/subtracted number? ____

            thickness change? ____
    Rebound reed-valve washers:

        added/subtracted number? ____

            thickness change? ____
    Travel added YES NO Amount: _____mm

Original spring pre-load setting: _____ #/turns

Current spring pre-load setting: _____ #/turns

Original elastomers and/or coil-spring rate:

_____

_____

_____

Current elastomers and/or coil-spring rate:

_____

_____

_____